In Quest
of the
Ashes

By D. R.

JARDINE

In Quest

of the

Ashes

With 31 Illustrations

PUBLISHED BY METHUEN 2005

10 9 8 7 6 5 4 3 2 1

FIRST PUBLISHED IN 1933 BY HUTCHINSON & CO. (PUBLISHERS) LTD.

THIS REVISED AND UPDATED EDITION FIRST PUBLISHED
IN GREAT BRITAIN IN 2005 BY
METHUEN PUBLISHING LTD,
11–12 BUCKINGHAM GATE, LONDON SW1E 6LB

COPYRIGHT © 2005 THE EXECUTORS OF D R JARDINE
COPYRIGHT © 2005 IN THE FOREWORD BY J MICHAEL BREARLEY
COPYRIGHT © 2005 IN THE MEMOIR OF D R JARDINE BY FIANACH LAWRY
COPYRIGHT © 2005 IN THE FOOTNOTES BY B YARDE-BULLER

METHUEN PUBLISHING LTD REG. NO. 3543167

A CIP CATALOGUE RECORD FOR THIS BOOK
IS AVAILABLE FROM THE BRITISH LIBRARY

ISBN 0-413-77455-4

TYPESET BY SX COMPOSING DTP, RAYLEIGH, ESSEX
PRINTED AND BOUND IN GREAT BRITAIN BY
ST. EDMUNDSBURY PRESS, BURY ST. EDMUNDS, SUFFOLK

DEDICATION

For reasons too numerous to set out at length, this book is proudly and gratefully dedicated to the members of the Marylebone Cricket Club Australia Team, 1932–33

G. O. ALLEN
L. E. G. AMES
W. BOWES
F. R. BROWN
G. DUCKWORTH
W. R. HAMMOND
H. LARWOOD
M. LEYLAND
T. B. MITCHELL
THE NAWAB OF PATAUDI
E. PAYNTER
H. SUTCLIFFE
M. W. TATE
H. VERITY
W. VOCE
R. E. S. WYATT

Because of what they are.
Because of what they proved themselves to be.
Because of what they bore and forbore.

CONTENTS

FOREWORD TO THE NEW EDITION

BY MIKE BREARLEY

In a touching Foreword to this strangely appealing book, R.C.N. Palairet, Joint Manager to the M.C.C. Team on the 1932/3 tour, praises Jardine warmly for his leadership. This, he writes, 'contributed more than anything else to the team's success. Your determination, your imperturbability, your calmness when things were going wrong, and your magnanimity when things were going right excited the warmest admiration of all but the most violent partisans.' But violent partisans there were in plenty, who dubbed this the 'Bodyline' series, and famously accused Jardine and his team of unsportsmanlike behaviour.

After this, Jardine plunges straight into the controversy with an interview with a South African magistrate (a Mr Hotson of Cape Town) whose opinions on the series are quoted at length. The reader wonders why this apparently random item is included, especially in so prominent a place. Who is Mr Hotson? How much credit should we give his opinion, favourable to Jardine, especially when, having conceded that 'Larwood occasionally did bump,' he continues, 'But Bradman especially, and even Woodfull, quite often 'ducked' to balls that barely rose above the wicket. In some cases this was done obviously for the benefit of the gallery.' (p.xxvi) Could anyone imagine deliberately ducking 90 mph deliveries barely rising above the height of the wicket, simply for the benefit of the gallery? Quite apart from the physical risk, there is the obvious danger of getting out. As the vice-captain Bob Wyatt argued in *Fighting Cricket*, many of the problems caused by short, leg-theory bowling were due to the variable bounce of the wickets. Not impressive testimony from Mr Hotson, and one feels Jardine should have known better.

However, the blunt fact is that *In Quest of the Ashes* is Jardine's defence – his 'apologia pro vita sua' – and one imagines that, like Socrates, if he were found guilty and invited to propose a penalty, he might well suggest being fed at the city's expense for the rest of his days.

In the first chapter, Jardine maintains that Test cricket is 'at the crossroads'. He lays the blame for this unhappy state of affairs on the behaviour of crowds, the Press, and the Australian Cricket Board. It is their 'invasion' of the arena 'hitherto sacred to eleven players on either side' that 'well may prove the death knell of cricket for those happy ones who still regard it as a survival from the days of chivalry, and a modern substitute for the tourney of Knights, that was played on the same green turf.' Jardine develops at some length his notion of the ideal cricket match, in which there are 'Great deeds done in so knightly fashion that there is no arrogance in triumph, no chagrin in defeat, but only calm of mind, all passion spent.' The spectators have no real place in this knightly encounter: 'The great deeds, the lack of arrogance, and the ability to take defeat philosophically... may safely be left to the players.'

Jardine's case against crowds is amplified by reference to the Australian tendency to consider that 'when England play Australia the whole of their national prestige to be at stake'. This is confirmed by an unnamed Australian acquaintance, who opines that 'If it were only a game of tiddleywinks and there were 50,000 people watching, the whole atmosphere in Australia would become changed; public competition charges the air with partisan electricity.' The atmosphere was also intensified by telegraph, telephone, newspapers and wireless. Add the intensity of crowd mentality generally, and the fact of the Australians being 'persistent, courageous but inveterate gamblers', and you were left with 'no game . . . [but] . . . warfare'.

The argument suggests that the shift from game to warfare, from chivalry to cut-throat competition, had nothing whatever to do with the tactics employed by Jardine and his team, nothing to do with the employment of leg-theory, and the relentless bowling of fast and often short-pitched bowling at the body, with six or seven fielders on the leg-side, but was entirely the outcome of the vociferous partisan barracking of the crowd. If the crowd had been demure, chivalry would never have been in question. It looks rather as if the highwayman blames the darkness of the roads, or the reactions of the public, for hold-ups. Perhaps part of Jardine's extreme loathing of the Australian public was down to their forcing him to examine (and doubt) the truth of his own supposed 'chivalry'.

As to the question of whether a chivalrous approach is fundamentally compatible with keen competition, I believe that it is, although the lines are hard to draw and depend to some extent on the particular customs and standards of the day, in cricket as in other areas of life. Players can drive a coach and horses through those customs and standards, and Jardine did just that, however strongly he felt himself to be behaving within the spirit of cricket, and however much he was able to avoid mentally falling prey to those 'twin impostors' victory and defeat.

Jardine is at pains to establish the respectability of 'leg-theory' (he rejects the term 'Bodyline'). This he does partly by reference to its longevity. He dates it back at least twenty-five years, to George Hirst (of Yorkshire and England), the fast left-arm in-swing bowler, and W. W. Armstrong, the Australian leg-spinner, pointing out that, however irritating such tactics might have been, no one accused the perpetrators of being unfair. Bowling has two aims, he notes, to get the batsman out or to restrict his scoring, and no sane captain would dream of using his fast bowlers for the latter purpose, especially in the heat of Australia. The charge that any of the English bowlers had another aim – that of causing physical harm to the batsman – he ridicules as patently untrue and stupid.

In my view this is disingenuous. Fast bowlers in my experience rarely have the physical injury of the batsman as their prime goal, though they have not always been above adopting it in the heat of battle, or when particularly riled. But Jardine knew perfectly well that the realistic threat of physical harm is part of the fast bowler's armoury. The purpose of persistent short-pitched bowling aimed at the batsman's body is not – usually – to hit or hurt, but to soften up, to shake up, to interfere with the batsman's technique. This is what explains the fact that 18 of Larwood's 33 wickets in the series were either lbw or bowled (a fact which Jardine uses as evidence that he generally bowled at the wicket: another claim which seems to me disingenuous). The ordinary word for such bowling is intimidation, and it is part and parcel of the game.

Another aspect of Jardine's case for leg-theory is that Australian conditions and changes in batting technique had tended to make off-theory both boring as a spectacle and unproductive as a tactic. The ball lost its shine rapidly and thus was far less prone to swing in Australia. Batsmen consequently tended to let more and more balls go, and to move further across in front of the stumps. (The then current lbw law stipulated that the batsman could not be given out lbw if the ball had pitched outside the off stump.) Leg-theory, on the other hand, did not limit the batsman's stroke-play, and in fact Jardine maintains that he would not have deployed it on a rain-affected pitch, for fear of giving away too many runs. If leg-theory did make for uninteresting cricket, it was (according to Jardine) because the Australian batsmen were incapable of responding to his speed trio or quartet. In support of his contention that it did not, he quotes from Jack Ryder and Arthur Mailey, both former Australian Test players, and both of whom attest to the legitimacy of leg-theory, the latter celebrating the electric thrill of anticipation that heralded each ball bowled by Larwood. Jardine also cites the view of the 24-year-old prodigy Archie Jackson, expressed not long before his poignant death from tuberculosis at Brisbane during the Fourth Test then being played in that city. Jackson commented that, if Ponsford and Fingleton had been battered about the body, 'that [was] mostly their own fault', and urged that, 'for the sake of Australia's sporting traditions, it may be left to the players themselves to furnish the only answer to the legitimate tactics employed by the Englishmen.'

As to the origins of the tactic as it was used in 1932/3, Jardine denies that it was devised solely to limit Bradman. It was true that he had heard on all sides of Bradman's being 'far from convincing on the leg stump whilst there was any life in the wicket' during the Oval Test of 1930, and indeed he remarks that this was 'in very marked contrast to Jackson, who was batting at the other end'. But he felt it to be a reasonable assumption that 'a weakness in one of Australia's premier batsmen might find more than a replica in a good many of his contemporaries.' Elsewhere in the book he mentions, along with those who were troubled by leg-theory – Ponsford, Kippax and Bradman – others who thrived on it or were more bothered by an off-stump line – Fingleton, McCabe and Richardson, for instance. He also claims that, having witnessed Larwood trying a few overs of leg-theory in 1928–9, he had not been inclined to 'rate [its] possibilities very highly' at the start of the tour. Indeed, he had 'never imagined that it would stand such a test as would prove its effectiveness throughout a whole tour, but . . . did hope that it might occasionally provide a profitable variation when two batsmen were set.'

In *Fighting Cricket,* Wyatt gives a somewhat different account of the early use of leg-theory on the tour. He suggests that it was first used in the match he captained at Melbourne, against an Australian XI, as a means of countering the Australian technique of moving right across their stumps and playing straight balls through the leg-side. It was, Wyatt wrote, a very quick pitch, on which good length balls were still rising as they reached the keeper. Bradman was dismissed twice by Larwood relatively cheaply. While this little drama occurred, Jardine was 200 miles away fishing in the Bogong Valley. Jardine also avoids any treatment of his alleged meeting, well before the tour began, with A.W. Carr, Larwood's and Voce's captain at Nottinghamshire, at which leg-theory was apparently discussed. According to Allen, the theory was first mooted after the early tour match at Perth against a Combined Australian XI when, on a drying pitch, Bradman was made to look very uncomfortable by Allen and dismissed by him for 10 (without leg-theory). Jardine, however, is generally keen throughout his book to underplay the significance of Bradman in his policy decisions; my reading is that he wants very much to reduce him to the dimensions of the ordinary mortal.

The chief causes of trouble for the Australians in 1932–3 were, Jardine maintains, the speed and accuracy of Larwood and Voce. He does not deny that, in certain conditions – for instance, on a bumpy park pitch with a big 18-year-old bowling fast leg-theory to a younger batsman – such tactics might be 'rather strong meat'. But strong meat, in his view, is what Test cricket is about. If batsmen couldn't deal with bouncers by avoidance or with the bat, then they should 'consider the desirability of giving way to younger talent'. To the objection that the ball often lifted from a good length, he replies that in that case credit should be given to the bowler, and that the batsman needed courage. No one would seriously contend that cricket should not be played on drying pitches. Otherwise we might as well, Jardine suggests, give up the idea of playing with a hard ball.

What then are we to make of the controversy? I have no doubt that Jardine is right in much of what he says. If England had used Bodyline to less effect, there would have been very little opposition. If Australia had won, the offence would have been minimal. If it had been used as an occasional variation, no one would have made a fuss. Does this exonerate him? Not entirely. For there is something about the sheer relentlessness and indeed bloody-mindedness of Jardine, that sets him apart – for instance, in his use of the method after so few overs had been bowled, or in his alleged refusal of one extra fielder on the leg-side for Bowes, yet his willingness to place four extra men there instead. This relentlessness entailed the belief that the end justified the means. It entailed following through his course of action (and his argument) to their logical conclusions. Compunction, concern, self-doubt – the glimmerings of conscience – would in Jardine's system of values appear as signs of weakness, both to others and perhaps also to himself (no doubt he was his own severest critic). He was positively bloody-minded in his timing. Immediately after Woodfull was hit on the chest at Adelaide, Jardine switched over to leg-theory field placing. As for his claim that, had he 'realized the misrepresentation to which we [he and Larwood] were to be subjected, neither of us would have set that particular field for that particular over', this seems to me *faux-naif*. I think Jardine knew full well the significance of the move. If he found the Australian crowds provocative in their barracking, they had reason to find him provocative both in his timing, and in his attitude. In fact this is exactly Wyatt's view. He felt that the use of persistent short pitched leg-theory was against the spirit of the game, and not good for cricket. I agree.

A feature of Jardine's conception of chivalrous cricket was, it will be remembered, the lack of arrogance in the winners, and he may have achieved this, at least according to his lights. One thing, however, that he shows no sign of appreciating is how he came across to Australians (and some others) as superior, unbending, and perhaps also arrogant. His book shows, I think, something of the hatred and contempt he had for the common Australian, at least for the latter's incarnation within a Test cricket crowd. Jardine's stiff manner, his Harlequin cap, his standoffishness before the spectators, notoriously aroused the ire of the Australians. I offer two examples. One was conveyed to Doug Insole by Wyatt in conversation, the other I was told personally by Harold Larwood. The first occurred when, while fielding at in Larwood's leg trap, Jardine was hit on the shin by a full-blooded hook by McCabe. A ball or two later, blood could be seen seeping out over his boots. Wyatt suggested the skipper should go off for treatment. The response was: 'What? And let 90,000 convicts know I'm hurt?' The second came before the last Test, with the Ashes secure. There was a question as to whether Larwood was fit to play. Jardine would not even consider leaving him out: 'We've got them down. Now we tread on them,' he told his fast bowler.

I too was accused of arrogance by some Australians. The ex-Prime Minister of Australia, Labour Party leader Bob Hawke, gave me some friendly advice one day in Melbourne, after I had been loudly booed by large sections of the crowd. 'They're not bad fellows – many of them voted for me,' he said, before counselling, 'They want a response. Give them a wave, laugh a bit, relax. They see your stiffness as colonialist arrogance.' There was a contrast between my rather taut attitude and the more genial, confraternal, sometimes crude gesturing of my predecessor, Tony Greig, which may have been paralleled by the similar contrast between Chapman (who had a bet with a Perth docker within a few minutes of landing in the country) and Jardine. But – and I may of course be biased – I have the impression that Jardine placed himself a good few degrees to the colder end of the scale than I did. In G.O. Allen's words in a letter to his parents: 'Douglas Jardine is loathed and, between you and me, rightly, more than any German who fought in any war. I am fed up with anything to do with cricket . . . He seems too damn stupid and he whines away if he doesn't have everything he wants . . . Some days I feel I should like to kill him and today is one of those days.' However, I have some sympathy for Jardine's cool, defiant way of reacting to the provocations of media and public in Australia. His message was: 'Nothing you can say or do will affect me one jot.'

One more thing about Jardine's account of leg-theory. He leaves a lot out. He fails to mention, for example, that Allen, his fellow-amateur and one of his main fast bowlers, refused to bowl more bouncers, or that the Nawab of Pataudi, another amateur, refused to field in the leg-trap, and was dropped two Tests after scoring a century. One of the book's polemical aims is to imply that the Australian players were on the whole unmoved by the idea that the tactic was unsporting. Hence he also refrains from including any mention of Bradman's proposal that a complaint be made against it after Australia had levelled the series by winning the Second Test at Melbourne. Similarly, he nowhere alludes to the famous remark made by Woodfull, the Australian captain, to P.F. Warner, the England manager, at Adelaide, to the effect that 'there are two teams out there, and only one is playing cricket'.

The book is not only about Bodyline, of course. There are chapters on each Test, as well as others of a more reflective nature. The style is dry: at times preparatory for a 'Hear, hear' from the reader, at times rather circumlocutorily humorous. Too often for a modern reader he leaves out detail that one craves, but perhaps this was a feature of a time when people were less eager to know the inside story or the specifics of human relations or tactics. To give one or two examples of my frustration at random: I wanted to know how many balls an over Larwood and Voce bowled that bounced to rib-height; I wanted to know what sort of a shot led Bradman to offer 'an easy chance off Larwood to Allen, who was standing close in at forward square leg'. Was it a bouncer? And how did he play it, when so often his response to leg-theory was to get to the leg side of the ball and hit through the vacant off side?

But Jardine is a much better writer than this implies. I enjoyed his obliquely telling account of captaining his main spin bowler: 'Verity is one of the most interesting bowlers whom I have had the privilege of observing at close quarters, for I would frequently stand at mid-off when he was bowling, offering him encouragement and advice. I believe that Verity prefers to bowl without advice, but he certainly accepted it with very good grace. Once or twice we registered a doubly satisfying success, though in all probability he would have done as well, if not better, had I been fielding in the deep!'

On tactics, I was interested in how flexible Jardine's batting order was. I rather admire this, as I found a great reluctance in batsmen to be moved around from the position they grew to feel was their own. Perhaps Jardine's autocracy over-weighed any such scruples. I was also impressed by how much he claims to have consulted on tactics, especially with Sutcliffe and Hammond. I admired too his clarity about the roles of different bowlers, his recognition of the role played by the less dramatic bowling of, say, Verity in keeping an end tied up, so that his fast bowlers stayed fresh for short spells downwind. Towards the end of the series the side had clearly allocated roles for batsmen too, Hammond and Leyland being deputed to get on top of O'Reilly and Ironmonger.

But there is no getting away from it. 1932–3 will always be remembered as the Bodyline series. As his cricket master at Winchester, Rockley Wilson, who had toured Australia with M.C.C. in 1920–21, so presciently put it on hearing of his selection: 'Oh, Jardine will probably win us back the Ashes, but he may also lose us a Dominion!' He was right on the first count, and nearly right on the second.

In Quest of the Ashes

REGRETTABLE as were the circumstances which make this book a necessity, there can hardly be two opinions upon the wisdom which prompts Mr. Jardine to disclose finally and with a full sense of responsibility the whole truth about the fight for the Ashes during the recent M.C.C. tour of Australia.

MR. JARDINE confesses that few things have given him more anxious thought than how best to set out the position, and, in giving a fair and accurate picture, to avoid the aggravation of any bitterness. He believes that total silence is neither the best remedy for the present situation nor in the best interests of cricket.

ENGLAND'S captain upholds the leg-theory which the Australian Board of Control resented so strongly and speaks candidly about the Australian barrackers. He reveals much that has hitherto remained undisclosed concerning the tour and the crisis which it brought.

AS a record of events off the field and of the actual fight for the Ashes and the strategy behind it, Mr. Jardine's book is unequalled.

LIST OF ILLUSTRATIONS

Fourth Test Match – Woodfull bowled by Mitchell, who twice had his wicket in this match.

Fourth Test Match – Richardson finely stumped by Ames off Hammond for 83.

Fourth Test Match – Bromley, the young left-hander, caught by Verity off Larwood.

Fourth Test Match – Woodfull ducks to a ball from Larwood which keeps low enough to strike him in the ribs. Here is a full leg field.

Fourth Test Match – McCabe caught by Jardine (arm outstretched) off Allen for 20.

Fifth Test Match – Jardine caught at slip by Richardson off Ironmonger.

Fifth Test Match – Larwood just misses his century: caught by Ironmonger off Lee for 98.

Fifth Test Match – Hammond: a study in forceful grace.

Fifth Test Match – Hammond: a study in expression after a ball from O'Reilly had passed him.

Fifth Test Match – Ames run out for 4. A very much debated verdict.

Fifth Test Match – Hammond and Wyatt coming in at the end of the match.

Cricketers at "Champagne Pool", Wairakei Hot Springs, New Zealand.

FOREWORD

By R. C. N. PALAIRET
(Joint manager of the M.C.C. team, in a letter to
Mr. Jardine)

KNOWLE CROFT,
BUDLEIGH SALTERTON.
6th JUNE, 1933.

My Dear Douglas,

In inviting me to write a foreword to your book on the M.C.C. tour in Australia in 1932–3, I consider that you have done me a great honour, and I accept your invitation with pleasure for many reasons, two of which, being in my opinion the most important, I will set out.

Firstly, I consider that the people of this and other countries should have put before them a full and accurate account of the events of the tour, the troubles that beset us, and the conditions under which the game of cricket, and particularly Test cricket, was played in Australia in 1932–3.

Secondly, I am sure that with your natural modesty you will give to the team all the credit for the success of the tour, and although no praise can be too high for the manner in which the team backed you up, your leadership contributed more than anything else to that success. Your determination, your imperturbability, your calmness when things were going wrong, and your magnanimity when things were going right excited the warmest admiration of all but the most violent partisans, and I am more than glad to have the opportunity of paying you this tribute.

I feel sure that your book will be a great success, and I hope that every lover of our national game will read it.

Yours very sincerely,

R. C. N. PALAIRET

PREFACE

THERE can be little doubt that the man on the field sees most of the game, though he may often miss points which the intelligent observer can take in at a glance from his bird's-eye view.

To give a fair account of the M.C.C. Tour in Australia, 1932–33, is, with the best will in the world, far from easy. Needless to say, I make no claim to infallibility; I shall, however, endeavour to be strictly impartial.

The reader may, however, take the view that no player or writer, be he English or Australian, can, in the circumstances, be a reliable guide. For such a reader I venture to quote, as a preface to this book, an extract from the impressions of a South African magistrate, Mr. J. H. Hotson, of Capetown, who saw the whole series of Test Matches and gave an account to the Cape Times on his return to South Africa. The interviewer writes:

Besides being a keen judge and a great lover of cricket, Mr. Hotson's work for many years has made him especially well equipped to weigh the pros and cons in any matter under dispute, and to remain calm and level-headed when others very often may be carried away momentarily by over-zealous partisanship.

There is no doubt, Mr. Hotson told me, that Bradman, in this last series of Tests, was never happy against Larwood, and played only one really great innings – his 103 not out at Melbourne in the second Test.

Apart from that, he always gave the impression that he knew that he could not remain in for very long, and so hit out, often recklessly, to score as many runs as possible before being sent back.

Woodfull always did his best to keep Bradman away from Larwood, so obviously uncomfortable was the Australian "wonder" against the Notts. fast bowler.

On the vexed question of body-line bowling, Mr. Hotson told me that he never saw anything done throughout the series that was contrary to the spirit of the game. Larwood, with the new ball, swings away to the off. Therefore, he always began by bowling to an off-side field. After a few overs, that swing was lost, and so he switched over to leg-theory.

Being a fast bowler, unable naturally to carry on for very long stretches at a time, it was no use for Larwood to bowl wide of the wicket – as Armstrong used to do. He had to concentrate on trying to bowl out the batsman as quickly as possible. Very often he succeeded.

But if some of Larwood's deliveries were just wide of the stumps, and occasionally hit the batsman, that was only natural with such a fast bowler, and there was never anything deliberate about these occasional hard knocks.

When Woodfull was hurt at Adelaide, said Mr. Hotson, he had himself largely to blame – and his two-eyed stance – for what was purely an accident.

Larwood occasionally did bump. But Bradman especially, and even Woodfull, quite often "ducked" to balls that barely rose above the wicket. In some cases this was done obviously for the benefit of the gallery.

The popular Press, in Mr. Hotson's opinion, was mainly responsible for keeping alive and infusing bitterness into the body-line bowling controversy. After Australia had lost the Ashes, the outcry and the bitterness died down, largely because the Press to a great extent dropped the matter.

Mr. Hotson did not think that the Australian batsmen would find it easy to develop a satisfactory counter to leg-theory bowling like Larwood's, because there were no good, really fast bowlers in Australia at the moment – not even Wall.

Larwood and Jardine were subjected to an incredible amount of barracking. But they stood it amazingly well; and Larwood, of course, was not in a position to defend himself, or to answer those who attacked him so bitterly.

But in the last Test, the "Hillites"[1] swung round and made quite a hero of him, when he scored his brilliant 98. He was given a tremendous ovation at the close of his innings.

As may be imagined, there is no lack of material for a book of this sort: really the difficulty is to cut it down to a reasonable length, concentrating on what is most important and least ephemeral. For this reason, therefore, the amount of space that I have assigned to the five Test Matches has inevitably led to the exclusion of State and up-country games.

The need of such concentration, however, does not make me any the less conscious of the many happy memories of our travels and debts of gratitude which the members of the M.C.C. team owe to the quite unnecessary and frequently embarrassing kindness bestowed upon them by the Orient Line, and particularly Commander O'Sullivan, of R.M.S. Orontes; also by the Canadian Pacific Railway Company and Canadian Pacific Steamships, Ltd.

Colombo, Suva, and Honolulu – the last-named one of the very few places of the tour which did not fly the British flag – vied with each other in welcoming and entertaining us.

Of the Government and private hospitality extended to us in Australia, I would only say that, though as a people the Australians may claim to be a young race, many of them, where hospitality is concerned, must surely have inherited the spirit of the ancient Greeks, for whom the entertainment of guests was a religious observance. Some of the happiest days of the tour we owe to New Zealand, which we dubbed our "home from home". Messrs. Donnelly, Lusk, and Wankelyn were three princes of hospitality to us in the loveliest of our Dominions which it has been my fortune to visit.

Finally, let me pay a very humble tribute to the premier club. The Marylebone Cricket Club sent us round the world

---

[1] The often vociferous spectators occupying The Hill at Sydney Cricket Ground.

and gave us an experience which none of those who shared it is likely to forget.

Not only for this reason are we under an obligation to them which cannot be repaid, but we must, I fear, have been a source of anxiety to them on more than one occasion. They showed their faith in us : I hope that now much of the "tumult and shouting" has died down, they are satisfied that that faith was not misplaced.

I have to thank Mr. Christopher Ogle for his unlimited kindness in revising the proofs of this book. I am, moreover, indebted to him for many helpful suggestions and much sound advice.

To Mr. R. C. N. Palairet my sincerest thanks are due, not only for the charming, though much too flattering, foreword which he has been good enough to contribute to this book, but also for the untiring energy and ability which he and his co-manager, Mr. P. F. Warner, contributed throughout the tour. Few who have not themselves made the Australian tour can realize what a vital part in the enjoyment and success of such a venture is contributed by the managers and the officer commanding the baggage, Mr. W. Ferguson. To Mr. Ferguson, the world's best scorer and baggage master, I am further indebted for the analytical statistics to be found in this book.

D.R.J.

1
Cricket at the Crossroads

Cricket is a game for eleven a side. During the recent tour of the M.C.C. in Australia this short, simple and self-evident fact seems to have been largely forgotten or ignored.

The behaviour or misbehaviour of crowds and the Press reactions thereto the world over lead inevitably to the main question:

Are Test Matches between England and Australia to continue, and, if so, are they really worth while?

Much must depend upon the answer which the responsible authorities in Australia give to the supplementary questions:

(1) Are they in full sympathy and accord with the behaviour of their crowds?

(2) Or are they reduced to pleading inability to control such "masters"?

The arena, hitherto sacred to eleven players on either side, has been invaded by newspapers, broadcasters, and spectators. Well may this prove to be the death knell of cricket for those happy ones who still regard it as a survival from the days of chivalry, and a modern substitute for the tourney of Knights, that was played on the same green turf. A fit setting for "Great deeds done in so knightly fashion that there is no arrogance in triumph, no chagrin in defeat, but only calm of mind, all passion spent." The great deeds, the lack of arrogance, and the ability to take defeat philosophically and in a calm state of mind, may safely be left to the players.

Call them flannelled fools if you will – O *si sic omnes*. Would that all were such!

Yet, in spite of the tragic story of post-War diplomacy, there was a genuine fear at one time that some politicians would try to take a hand in the government of cricket, while an Australian judge saw fit to unburden himself of weighty decisions on hypothetical cases!

M. André Maurois, in his book on England, had some hard things to say about the undue importance we attribute to sport and games. His criticism of England in this respect applies with even greater force to Australia.

However great may have been the interest taken in the Test Matches at home, it cannot compare with the interest and partisanship which were displayed in Australia. Just as wireless has popularized the gramophone, so have newspapers and wireless intensified the popularity of cricket.

In the town in which a Test match is being played, there is but one subject of conversation, and business, if any there be, is incessantly interrupted by the delivery of slips of paper, and telephone calls announcing the latest scores. Whether or no such keenness is wholly admirable is not for me to say, but it is at least unfortunate that, on the day upon which England plays Australia at cricket or football, so many Australians consider the whole of their national prestige to be at stake. England has been for so long the whipping-boy of the world at all sports[1], that such an outlook is, perhaps, hard for us to appreciate.

As to the future, there are three courses open: the first, to play Test Matches as frequently as before; the second, to allow a longer period than usual to elapse before the renewal of these encounters ; and lastly, to let them lapse altogether.

English teams in the past, as now, have been very reticent upon many happenings in Australia. Silence, as we know, is golden. Motives for silence, too, were of the best, for it was hoped that things would improve. Nearly everyone who loves cricket will echo this

[1] Perhaps an exaggeration: the Twenties were a mediocre, but not a dreadful decade for English sport. If the Americans dominated golf and tennis, England still had the best rugby team, winning the Five Nations Championship five times. Along with almost all other European nations, England did not participate in the first football World Cup, held in Uruguay in 1930.

hope. The difficulty, and it is a very real one, is where to draw the line. Of one thing I feel certain, and it is that total silence is neither the best remedy, nor in the best interests of cricket.

Some questions must now be looked fairly and squarely in the face, and the public placed in possession of many essential facts. Few things have given me more anxious thought than how best to set out the position, and, in giving a fair and accurate picture, to avoid the aggravation of any bitterness and ill-feeling.

Perhaps the title of this chapter – "Cricket at the Crossroads" – is misleading. It is not cricket, but Test Match cricket, which is at the crossroads. For it is all too common and too easy to attach to Test matches an importance which is out of all proportion to their true worth. Club and village cricket, which are infinitely more vital to the true interests of the game, are, as far as I am aware, at no crossroads, for which let us be duly thankful.

In Australia there must be more talk of "good sports" and "sportsmanship" than in any other country in the world. Let me pay a tribute to the individual Australian on the golf course, in a squash racket court, at a card-table, or on a racecourse. As a general rule, no nicer or keener individual exists. In his own words, he is always ready to "take chances". Nor does he wince if he picks a "wrong 'un".

There is a certain reticence to be observed about private remarks made confidentially, but, as a member of the other side used to say, "If it were only a game of tiddlywinks and there were 50,000 people watching, the whole atmosphere in Australia would become changed; public competition charges the air with partisan electricity."

Australians, moreover, are persistent, courageous, but inveterate gamblers, as might be expected in a country where horse-racing, with its various ramifications, is reckoned to be the second or third largest industry.

This readiness to bet on anything, even on the athletic prowess of the common fly[2], has unfortunately spread to cricket. Many Australians, I know, find it hard to believe that there is practically no

[2] The aperçu still has currency: a recent publication by the Australian Institute of Criminology on 'Internet Gambling' opens with the sentence 'It has been said that Australians would bet on two flies crawling up a wall.'

betting on our summer game in England. Really large sums of money, and in our eyes an incredible number of bets, were won and lost upon the performances of individual players, and the results of the Test Matches in Australia.

After we lost the dramatic Second Test at Melbourne, following as it did upon our recent easy victory at Sydney, my mailbag was a revelation. A stranger reading it might have been pardoned for thinking that we were a team of dishonest trainers, who had run crooked in order to disguise form, and thereby pick up a packet on the remaining Test Matches!

It was frequently said and written that various members of the team, including myself, had betted heavily on the results of the Tests. Such an accusation, of course, would never bear a moment's impartial investigation, and I am, I think, being more than fair to the retailers of such tittle-tattle, when I say that only their own extraordinary passion for betting made such an accusation possible, since they can never have appreciated the enormity of the charge they were making. It does, however, give me an opportunity of recalling the only two bets which I have ever made on cricket, and it may even supply some Australian papers with a poster, "Jardine's Bets."

The first was in 1919, when, watching a club match, I was rather reluctantly inveigled into venturing half-a-crown on a sweepstake on individual performances. I was fortunate to draw Mr. C. A. E. Greene as my "horse". He had already made 150, and went on to make 200 runs, thereby enriching me by some thirty shillings.

We all like recounting our winning ventures, but my second bet I should have lost with pleasure. After listening to an inspired and highly ingenious sermon on batsmanship by Tommy Mitchell, I laid him 60 to 1 in pennies that he would not make 50 runs in any one innings in Australia. Even the dignity of opening the innings for England on one occasion, in an up-country match, failed to inspire our humorist and leg-spinner to rise to the requisite heights.

On that occasion both Mitchell and his opening partner had made nought in the first innings. A dire struggle to avoid the dreaded "pair" ensued. If Mitchell did not make the 50 he desired, he had, on this occasion at least, the satisfaction of showing up his partner, who is generally reckoned a greatly superior performer with the bat. Both of them gave the rest of us a good laugh. Tommy's hard-earned penny reposes in my waistcoat-pocket as I write.

I shall have something further to say about the psychology of Australian crowds and the desirability of continuing the Test matches. For the moment, my own views can wait, but that it is at least a debatable question an extract from an Australian book called "Down Under", by R. W. Thompson, will prove.

I make no apology for quoting this extensive extract, nor for disguising the names of players under letters of the alphabet. The key is given later, but the reader is asked to read the extract before consulting the key:

"A far more serious series of events now commenced. I refer to the cricket Test matches between England and Australia. The papers and the people relegated all other business and thoughts to the background. I had not realized that cricket could be taken so seriously. The attitude of the general public and of the crowds at the matches was amazing. This was no game. It was warfare. One would have thought that the destiny of a nation hung on the result.

"There was little sporting spirit except in the cases of a few isolated individuals such as A and my doctor friend.

"The merits of England's players were belittled and scoffed at; and, if they were too great to be scoffed at, dismissed as luck.

"In the face of such astonishing feeling it was necessary to remind oneself continually that the cause of it all was a few games of cricket. I am conscious of writing the wrong word every time I write 'games', but since the Romans referred to the throwing of Christians to lions as games, I suppose the term is comparatively in order.

"Argument was now unavoidable. I thanked God for X and his double centuries, and Y and his Z-baffling bowling. These two were unanswerable. Nevertheless, the Australians called X a one-stroke player, and Y, they said, was not as fast as B.

'I replied that, if X could make 200 using only one stroke, it was fortunate for them that he was not a two-stroke player, since he would probably make 400. As for B, he was certainly a great player and a wonderful slip field, but his bowling didn't seem to have the same effect on Z as did Y's; therefore, I thought Y was faster.

"Thus the war waged even more fiercely off the field than on.

"The knowledge of cricket possessed by the average Australian was far in advance of that of the average Englishman. . . . Unfortunately, they were also often unfair, unsporting, and stupid. If two batsmen were engaged in a big stand the shout would come from the hill: 'Call the fire brigade and put 'em out.' Dropped catches were greeted with cries of 'Get a bag.'

"Some players found it hard to give of their best in the face of barracking. . . .

"The D ground is far superior in accommodation to Lord's or the Oval, and is, I believe, a better ground from the cricketer's point of view. The score-board is a work of art, enabling every spectator to know at a glance not only how the game stands, but also the scores of the preceding batsmen, how they were out, and the names of the fieldsmen. As the ball is fielded a red light shines against the fielder's name on the score-board. This is a great help to the spectator. The score-boards at Lord's or the Oval are very poor and inadequate affairs in comparison.

"There were no signs of somnolence amongst the spectators. Fights on the hill were frequent, and the running fire of comment, the shouts of appreciation, or the boos of disgust, kept one well awake even if the game was slow.

"Office work suffers in D during the tests. The facilities for following the matches provided for those who are unable to be present are far ahead of those in England. The big newspaper offices have large score-boards displayed in front of their buildings with, in some cases, a small pitch and electrically controlled ball. It is almost as exciting to watch one of these score-boards as to watch the actual game.

"Once or twice during the tests I was travelling north by train. As the train crossed Hawkesbury River bridge or passed slowly through a small station, the workmen and station officials would shout: 'What's the score?' Cricket occupies the leading position in everybody's mind. Every man, woman, and child in Australia is test match mad. I would not have liked to experience their 'skite' had they won. . . .

"The C Test was a triumph for England; a triumph slightly marred by the accident to B and the illness of J. . . . There was nothing much in this match to provide scope for the journalists, but the D Test atoned.

"It is difficult for the ordinary Englishman to imagine the intense feeling which exists in an Australian city during these matches. If a foreigner were present, he would have good cause to think that the British race are mad. Surely this cannot be a game!

"The D Test provided the newspapers with copy for several weeks, and the general public with material for heated and scathing debate. . . .

"P was barracked unmercifully for many days afterwards, but he behaved like a Stoic and maintained his brilliance in spite of everything. The E incident was discussed unsportingly on every hand.

"I became very keen on cricket, and backed England for all I was worth. I found it very hard to get an acknowledgement of England's worth from anyone, even though we were winning. There was one man, however, whom they found it increasingly difficult to belittle, and that was X. . . .

"The whole of this series of tests was marred by 'incidents': even K was dragged in. They said that he threw down his cap in disgust when the umpire L failed to give M out, when he was run out a yard by N. These incidents were most unpleasant, and it was absolutely impossible to avoid argument. Big business men would greet me with the words: 'What do you think of K now?' and damn silly, childish remarks like that. Of course, I defended my side, and thus brought myself down to their level.

"If these games cannot be played as games, it would be better for them not to be played at all. It is said that test matches help to keep alive the spirit of friendship between the Mother Country and the Dominions. The people who say this cannot have been to Australia."

The passage has reference to the tour of Mr. A. P. F. Chapman's side in 1928–9. The key is as follows:

A – T.P.	J – Kelleway.	P – Duckworth.
B – Gregory.	K – Jack Hobbs.	X – Hammond.
C – Brisbane.	L – Jones	Y – Larwood.
D – Sydney.	M – Ryder.	Z – Ponsford.
E – Kippax.	N – Leyland.	

So much, then, for Mr. R. W. Thompson's views in a book quite unconnected with cricket.

2
Choosing our Team

There is a pleasant story about an Australian which will appeal to every cricketer. When first he visited Lord's he reverently looked about him. Then, removing his hat, he stood to attention, uncovered. He had "come home".

I have good reason for believing this tale about hallowed ground, though Australians themselves would readily admit that they are sometimes inclined to be critical and impatient of respect for age and tradition. I like this story the more because no one who has seen the cricket grounds of Australia would seriously suggest that, judged purely from the standpoint of utility or convenience, any English ground is their equal or superior.

Just as Lord's was the Mecca of this Australian, so Australia has been the Mecca of our cricket pilgrimages abroad. Let it not be thought that I am underestimating the merits of South Africa, New Zealand, the West Indies or India, all of which countries have made great strides forward in recent years. One by one they have gained promotion and the prize which goes with elevation to Test match rank; nor will anyone who has seen their cricketers in action grudge them the honours they have earned so deservedly.

In the past, however, the sides sent to these countries have been experimental to some extent, for personnel and finance have sometimes been uncertain quantities.

The Marylebone Cricket Club has been prepared to bear a loss upon such tours, and, indeed, has frequently done so gladly, in order to encourage cricket throughout the Empire. This is well-known and appreciated abroad; at home it is too little realized.

The Marylebone Cricket Club has played the part of a benevolent government. In its executive capacity it has given encouragement and financial support, while in the exercise of its administrative functions it has provided a Privy Council or Supreme Court of Judicature, resulting in a uniform code of rules and procedure.

It will not be long, I hope, before England and Australia will have to look to their laurels in earnest, in facing challenges from new and hitherto unexpected quarters of the world, while the ranks of cricket may be enriched by new exponents and artists more than worthy of their forerunners.

The gallery of cricketing giants is already adorned with Australian names – in a measure that is out of all proportion to the share which might be expected of a land which has today a population of barely seven millions, and is remotest among the continents. The cricketers of Australia have so often proved themselves foemen more than worthy of our steel, that English cricketers in the past have always been ready and willing to make special sacrifices to go on *the Tour*.

Counties have readily granted leave and licence for their chosen players to participate, when honoured with an invitation.

All this, and more, was no doubt present in the minds of the M.C.C. Committee when in 1931 they appointed a Selection Committee of three, to act for two years instead of the customary one. Of all the thankless jobs which this world can offer, I think the Selectors' task is about the least enviable, fascinating though it may be. Plenty of kicks and parlous few ha'pence are their daily portion. The evil they do is almost invariably remembered and quoted against them, while the good is often forgotten or interred amid the Ashes.

Let me, then, hasten to pay an overdue tribute to Messrs. P. F. Warner (Middlesex), P. A. Perrin (Essex), and T. A. Higson (Lancashire).

As everyone knows, England lost the Ashes in the final Test match at the Oval in 1930. This result surprised a good many people after A. P. F. Chapman's successful tour in Australia in

1928–9, when the M.C.C. team won the first four matches of the Rubber off the reel.

Whatever may befall the Australians in England, I am inclined to think that a side representing England in Australia is likely to be more formidable than an eleven chosen for one match only from our scattered Counties at home.

Frequently men chosen for a Test match at home have never before played together. Picture the feelings of a wicket-keeper "taking" a spin bowler whom he has never seen in action before. Nor will an opening pair of batsmen, with no previous experience of each other's running and calling, have that reliance and confidence in each other which is half their battle.

The individuals of a team can be regarded as threads which need a hand to fashion them into a composite fabric. That hand is the captain's. Personally, I have nothing but sympathy for the man whose duty it becomes, at a few days' notice, to improvise a design which will set off each separate strand to the best advantage and yet secure the maximum strength to the material as a whole.

In this, I know, many good judges are all against me. Their theory is that, of all sides, the one playing at home should be the easiest to captain. This may have been true twenty or thirty years ago. Then the play of each individual was apt to be better known than today, and each individual was a cog in the machine. If the cogs worked, the machine worked. If they did not, there was little remedy.

With the advent of spin bowling, and by spin bowling I mean leg break and googly bowling, a new set of values came into being.[1] And this applies with equal strength to the pronounced swervers, who for the most part were then only just coming into their own.

The ablest, the quickest, and the most enterprising cricket brain with which it has been my fortune to come into contact is that of my old captain, Mr. P. G. H. Fender.[2] For years Mr. Fender was called upon to take wickets without bowlers. His manner of making bricks without straw was a liberal education. He could at any time produce

[1] Leg-break and 'swerve' bowling both made their appearance around the turn of the century.

[2] Jardine took over from Percy Fender as captain of Surrey in 1932.

three entirely different plans of campaign. Though we occasionally differed – generally, I think, because I was too conservative – we always agreed that in nearly every game there comes a crisis when gambling is necessary. True, we used to differ over the precise moment of crisis.

I take this opportunity of saying that he was nearly always right. I am sure, however, that he would be the first to agree with me that if a gamble becomes necessary, it can be taken at far more favourable odds, with a lighter heart and a far greater chance of success, if a captain knows each member of the team and his play intimately, and the team know each other and trust their captain.

As a race, we run ourselves down and write ourselves off at any mention of efficiency and rationalization. "We muddle through" has become almost a boast, but anything less like muddling than the manner in which the Marylebone Cricket Club set about recovering the Ashes would be hard to imagine.

In 1931, as I have already said, the M.C.C. appointed a Selection Committee. The counties backed up the M.C.C. loyally, and guaranteed to release their players for trial matches as well as the Test matches against the New Zealanders and Indians. Both these teams, new as they were to International cricket, won their spurs worthily, and gave the Selectors an invaluable substitute for Ruff's Guide to Form. The Selectors took infinite pains, and for once in a while encountered comparatively little criticism.

Before the side for Australia was selected, Lord Hawke was added to the Committee of Selection as chairman. Proceedings at a Selection Committee are an inviolable secret, but I do not think I am opening any Bluebeard's cupboard if I illustrate the thought and care bestowed upon the selection of the side for Australia by one small instance.

The majority of the Committee had travelled many miles to attend a meeting. We met at 10.30 a.m., with only three places to fill. At 1.30 p.m. we adjourned for an hour for lunch, and at five o'clock we had filled only two places. The cynic may say that this displays divergence of opinion. Not so. We wanted only to *mak siccar,* as they say in Scotland, and to be as sure as possible that we did nothing in a hurry and forged no link which would not strengthen the chain. I do not think that this Selection Committee has ever had the credit which was its most just due.

Averages are no infallible guide to good selection. The place in the batting order occupied by a majority of a bowler's victims will frequently give a clearer index to his capabilities than the number and cost of his wickets. Nor must the locality in which any bowler plays be forgotten, nor yet the strength of his team.

Speaking only for myself, I like to look up a cricketer's record of performances in the north. A batsman's record against Yorkshire, if good, is no mean passport.[3] In the late tour we had more than one outstanding example of the reliability of this test. I pass it on for what it may be worth.

If it were possible to imagine two cricketers whose claims for inclusion, while being mutually exclusive, are so even that a spin of the coin might settle their fate, I would unhesitatingly choose the Northerner in preference to the Southerner for the exacting business of an Australian Tour.[4] The Bank Holiday Battle of the Roses is the nearest approach England can provide, for tenseness in cricket, to the atmosphere of Sydney or Melbourne when the crowds are orderly.

Trial matches are usually regarded as useless indexes to form. They are neither popular with the players nor with the counties deprived of their players' services. Such trials, however, are invaluable in two ways. They provide an opportunity for an individual star to expand in magnitude with added lustre, and for members of the sides to grow accustomed to each other's play and fit into their places on the field.

Opinions will always differ as to the ideal number which constitutes a touring side. It is a question about which it would be

---

[3] Between 1920 and 1940 Yorkshire won the county championship eleven times. Yorkshire was the first county to inaugurate a system of League cricket, the fixtures of which were considered more competitive than those between the counties. Many of the stars of the County team were 'blooded' in the League.

[4] Eight of the sixteen members of Jardine's squad were from one of the three 'Northern' counties (Yorks., Lancs., and Notts.). Gubby Allen (Middx.), was the only 'Southerner' among the bowlers.

foolish to be dogmatic. So much depends on the personnel of any particular side.

Australia is, par excellence, a country for the versatile cricketer; and assuming that one was in the fortunate position of being able to place one's hands upon five really good all-rounders, it would be both possible and desirable to tour with a far smaller number than could be contemplated with only two all-rounders available. Through sheer contrariness it usually happens that if the side takes a full complement of spare parts, no one breaks down. While Australia is the Mecca for this invaluable type of player, it is the worst place I know of for one who is only a batsman, and who is not playing matches constantly. With all their virtues, Australian grounds, with the exception of Sydney, are sadly and singularly deficient in arrangements for net practice.

Right up to the last moment we had hoped that that great cricketer and charming fellow Kumar Shri Duleepsinhji[5] would be able to join us in Australia, and I am sure that our disappointment and our sympathy for him were shared by a large number of Australians.

I give the names of the side we took, with their recent records in first-class matches:

[5] Prince Duleepsinhji (1900–59), the Sussex and England batsman, was prevented by ill health from taking his place in the team. The loss was significant: Duleepsinhji's Test average was 58.52, and included an innings of 173 against Australia at the Lord's Test in 1930. In 1950 he was appointed Indian High Commissioner to Australia.

Batting

* Signifies not out. In England the averages given are those of ten runs or more.

Name	Season		Innings	Total Runs	Highest Score	Average
G. O. Allen	England	1931	14	401	122	30.84
	"	1932	11	113	57	11.30
L. E. G. Ames	England	1931	50	1711	172	39.79
	"	1932	50	2482	180	57.72
	Australia	1928–9	8	295	100*	59.00
W. Bowes	England	1931	–	–	–	–
	"	1932	–	–	–	–
F. R. Brown	England	1931	34	416	100*	12.60
	"	1932	39	1135	212	32.42
G. Duckworth	England	1931	34	254	22	12.09
	"	1932	38	221	21*	10.04
	Australia	1928–9	13	84	39*	12.00
W. R. Hammond	England	1931	49	1781	168*	42.40
	"	1932	49	2528	264	56.17
	Australia	1928–9	18	1553	251	91.35
D. R. Jardine	England	1931	30	1104	106*	64.94
	"	1932	39	1464	164	52.28
	Australia	1928–9	19	1168	214	64.88
H. Larwood	England	1931	36	825	102*	25.00
	"	1932	38	643	67	18.91
	Australia	1928–9	14	367	79	26.21
M. Leyland	England	1931	41	1228	124	38.37
	"	1932	40	1980	189	52.10
	Australia	1928–9	17	614	137	43.85
T. Mitchell	England	1931	–	–	–	–
	"	1932	–	–	–	–
Nawab of Pataudi	England	1931	25	1454	238*	69.23
	"	1932	18	746	165	46.42
E. Paynter	England	1931	49	1235	102	28.72
	"	1932	55	2035	159	37.68
H. Sutcliffe	England	1931	42	3006	230	96.96
	"	1932	52	3336	313	74.13
	Australia	1928–9	16	852	135	53.25
M. W. Tate	England	1931	40	777	142	26.79
	"	1932	37	458	50	14.77
	Australia	1928–9	17	322	59	20.12
H. Verity	England	1931	25	234	28	12.31
	"	1932	33	494	46	19.00
W. Voce	England	1931	45	618	129	16.70
	"	1932	37	445	48	18.54
R. E. S. Wyatt	England	1931	49	1764	161*	42.00
	"	1932	49	1808	171*	43.04

Bowling

Name	Season		Overs	Runs	Wkts.	Average
G. O. Allen	England	1931	341.3	751	40	18.77
	"	1932	245.2	634	25	25.36
W. Bowes	England	1931	949.5	2131	136	15.66
	"	1932	1194.2	2877	190	15.14
F. R. Brown	England	1931	864.3	2424	107	22.65
	"	1932	989	2456	120	20.46
W. R. Hammond	England	1931	591.3	1457	47	31.00
	"	1932	627.5	1483	53	27.98
	Australia	1928–9	229.6	661	11	60.09
H. Larwood	England	1931	651.3	1553	129	12.03
	"	1932	866.4	2084	162	12.86
	Australia	1928–9	411.2	1258	40	31.45
T. B. Mitchell	England	1931	1043	2470	120	20.58
	"	1932	1193.5	2879	132	21.81
M. W. Tate	England	1931	1253	2179	141	15.45
	"	1932	1380.1	2494	160	15.58
	Australia	1928–9	892.2	1325	44	29.88
H. Verity	England	1931	1137.3	2542	188	13.52
	"	1932	1117.5	2250	162	13.88
W. Voce	England	1931	1006.5	2373	123	19.29
	"	1932	973.4	2295	136	16.87
R. E. S. Wyatt	England	1931	597	1734	59	29.38
	"	1932	832.3	1907	68	28.04

3

A Study in Australian Conditions

Many difficult decisions await a touring side in Australia, both as a team and as individuals. Individually, those of the team who are batsmen must realize the difference between the conditions obtaining in England and Australia.

In the latter country it has always seemed to me that an English batsman has a perfectly clear choice before him. Either he must attempt to counteract the changed conditions by being sounder, and, if necessary, even more orthodox than he is at home – or, alternatively, he may model himself on one or more good Australian batsmen, and depart from the strict English orthodoxy. By this I do not mean that there are not many orthodox batsmen in Australia, but only imply that what is orthodox in Australia is not necessarily orthodox in England.

One outstanding example is to be seen in the different way in which Australian batsmen appear to lift their bats as compared with the majority of English players. While the latter are in many cases far from straight, they seldom appear to lift their bats in a direction wider than an imaginary line drawn between themselves and second slip. The best Australian batsmen frequently lift their bats up towards the gully or fifth slip. There is no denying that this is frequently of assistance in hooking or forcing the ball on the leg stump.[1]

[1] In the *Cricketer* of 20th May 1933, Pelham Warner criticized DRJ himself for bringing 'his bat up in the direction of the slips instead of over the stumps'. Perhaps this was one reason for his renowned skill on the on side.

For cricketers who have been brought up only on the perfect wickets of Australia, there is no doubt that this method has been singularly effective in the past, but it takes some time to master the new technique. In the meanwhile the pace and difference of the wickets may well prevent an Englishman touring in Australia from getting the big scores which are of so much assistance to the process known as getting into form, and which are so valuable an aid to confidence.

It should not take a bowler new to Australia long to find out that he must abandon his hopes of swerving a ball to anything like the same degree as he can in England. In addition to this, he will have to accustom himself to a different idea of what constitutes a good length ball. In spite of the lack of opportunity to swerve, Australian wickets have often suited fast bowlers, owing possibly to the additional pace of the wickets.

But probably even more curious than the question of swerve is the extra margin of error which a slow bowler finds he has got in Australia. Both J. C. White and Verity were quick to discover and exploit this for all it was worth. Instead of a patch of approximately five feet in length, they are afforded nearly double that distance as a target for their good-length balls.

But while I do not imagine that fast or slow bowlers are in serious danger of becoming enamoured of Australian wickets, the way of the medium-pace bowler is hardest of all, for he falls between two stools. The extra pace merely seems to make his bowling come on to the bat more easily, and the extra margin of error does not appear to apply to his good-length ball: in his case it seems a smaller, instead of a larger, margin of error.

Indeed, unless Australian wickets change again, the prospect for medium-pace bowlers must remain a disheartening one.

But the mere recognition that these problems exist and demand some attempt at definite solution helps to dispel some of their difficulties.

The Australian cricketing authorities give nothing away. While, therefore, they are ready and willing for any of the "probables" among their batsmen to play frequently against the visiting team, they are exceedingly reluctant to show their hand by playing their own potential Test Match bowlers. Familiarity with a bowler's methods tends, in their view, to breed contempt in the batsmen.

To my mind this is perfectly sound. Though one should never formulate the general rule from a particular instance, the truth of this was brought home to us with singular force during the 1928–9 Tour.

Larwood and Tate, who began that Tour so destructively, gradually lost their sting. This was not primarily, I feel convinced, because there was any marked falling off in form, but because their methods had become familiar. Their figures in the Fifth Test Match in 1929 may be quoted as an extreme instance of this. In that game, between them they captured one wicket for no fewer than 348 runs!

A visiting captain, then, must try to keep some bowling in reserve; a strange bowler or two to "slip" at each batsman when the time comes. This sometimes does not appear as easy as one might be tempted to imagine. For example, before the First Test Match Bradman had played six innings against us.

The direct object can be attained in the field of play, at any rate to some extent, by making such dispositions as will avoid rencontres between particular bowlers and batsmen. A captain must be prepared to face criticism for not using his bowling to the best advantage; yet let him not be sensitive on that account, for the critics are not always in a position to know what is passing through a captain's mind, though that will not prevent them from criticizing.

In a Test Match series which I remember as a child, C. B. Fry was freely criticized for not bowling Woolley sufficiently against the Australians in a particular match.[2] He kept Woolley up his sleeve. I do not remember anyone giving him credit when, in the last Test Match of that series, Woolley helped England to an easy victory by taking 10 wickets for 49 runs.

However, there can easily be over-refinement in these schemes. If faced with the choice of disclosing one's hand or robbing a member

---

[2] This was during the 'Triangular Tournament' in 1912, when South Africa and Australia both visited England.

of the team of valuable match practice, I am inclined to think that it is best to play the bowler. He may have an early success against the batsman, the moral value of which may more than offset the familiarity gained by the batsman.

Before we sailed, M.C.C. had appointed a Selection Committee for the Test matches consisting of Messrs. Sutcliffe, Warner and myself. At my suggestion we added Wyatt and Hammond to our strength, with excellent results.

I am not disclosing any secret not known to all the side, when I say that only twice did I find myself in frank disagreement with the rest of the committee. For both the third and fourth Tests I advocated the exclusion of myself from the team on the grounds that (a) I was out of form with the bat, and (b) I fancied that the team would get a better deal from the crowd if I was not in the field.

The committee would not hear of the suggestion. I insisted that they should discuss it, and left the room, only to learn on my return that they had confined their attentions to discussing the price of beer or its equivalent.

Any captain who can handle his team throughout a single Test match without consulting anyone is indeed fortunate. There is much to be said for singleness and unity of control and responsibility, but I doubt if many such captains exist. Even if they do, it might well be advisable for them to consult a colleague from time to time, if only for form's sake. People like being consulted. Personally, I found it quite impossible to concentrate on my own fielding and yet pretend to see all the game. I therefore consulted freely and frequently. Nor could any captain have received sounder advice than that which was offered by Sutcliffe and Hammond. Necessarily, Wyatt had to field in the deep, and, since a captain must be near the scene of action, I really had little opportunity of consulting him.

Again, things frequently look quite different from the ringside.

There is no keener cricketer or sounder judge than Duckworth.[3] He has in a unique degree the capacity to say exactly what he means

---

[3] Duckworth was a member of the squad, but despite his tactical acumen took no part in the Test Matches. Though a superb wicket-keeper, he was mediocre with the bat and was superseded behind the stumps by the more versatile Ames.

with forceful brevity. He misses nothing, and was an invaluable counsellor from off the field. Allen, too, is no mean judge, and I am indebted to him for some exceptionally good suggestions.

The supreme test of the desirability of advice depends upon those who give it. Only one consideration might induce me to refrain from seeking advice – the fear that the adviser might feel hurt if I did not accept it. In the late tour I had no such grounds for anxiety. But unless that cordial feeling exists, I would suggest that a captain would be well advised to confine himself to his own errors of judgment: they will in all probability be sufficiently numerous.

Ordinarily speaking, there is no Absolute in the matter of right or wrong policy. What may be intrinsically wrong is hailed as right or even brilliant if it comes off.

Most people know the story of the captain in the Eton and Harrow match who received a message bidding him put X on to bowl (in those days the school sides were, in effect, captained by means of messages from the pavilion, sent by an old Etonian and Harrovian respectively).

Now X had never been known to bowl, but the obedient schoolboy captain put him on, and, to the surprise of everyone, including X, he got an immediate wicket! A brilliant stroke of genius! The captain's satisfaction was, however, short-lived, for at the fall of the wicket he received the following frenzied and sarcastic note from the pavilion: "Are you captaining the side or am I?"

Messages by word of mouth are liable to become garbled in transmission. Indeed, rumour has it that the only message which was ever successfully passed down the length of a whole battalion and reached its destination word-perfect was to the effect that "at the next halt each man shall have a glass of beer".

4
Organization of Australian Cricket

It would take a brave man to suggest that the organization of Australian cricket was anything but effective. There is no getting away from results, which speak for themselves. Australia regularly produces International cricketers of the highest class, with a genius or two at frequent intervals.

The policy of catching them young, giving them their chance and trusting them, has paid handsomely. Victor Trumper, Clem Hill, Archie Jackson[1], and Bradman were all playing International cricket at an age when they would have been regarded as mere schoolboys in England. That the climate and environment play an important part can scarcely be doubted, even if one does not subscribe whole-heartedly to the doctrine of that Australian character who in the early days poured scorn on any of his compatriots who had not shot their man and begot their man before attaining the ripe age of sixteen summers.

Whatever the explanation of this early maturity may be, the system which brings talent, however promising, to so high a pitch at such an early age, must be entitled to a very large share of the credit.

Success is vital to this scheme in order that cricket may be a financial success in the Dominion. The upkeep of the major cricket

---

[1] Trumper played in his first Test Match in 1899, aged 22; Hill in 1896, aged 19; and Jackson in 1929, also at the age of 19 (see footnote p. 49).

grounds involves very large annual expenditure. The first thing to realize is that mere numbers count for very little. As outstanding instances of this fact we need go no further afield than the ability of Scotland and Wales to hold their own with England at football, and Australia's own success against the world at lawn tennis.[2]

The centres of population, Melbourne, Sydney, and Adelaide, form the nucleus of the system, with cells in the shape of various "Grade" teams making up that nucleus. Grade matches consist of two half-day cricket matches played on successive Saturdays. The pitches, judged by English standards, are extremely good, and the time factor is very essential to the game.

In addition to these Grade matches, a country week is always arranged in each State. Teams come from near and far to compete with each other in the State capital. In this way little talent is allowed to escape the notice of someone sufficiently interested or influential to see that merit should have its chance. If the chance given is duly seized, promotion to State, and ultimately to Test cricket is the prize dangled before the eyes of the aspiring Grade cricketer. Frequently a promising colt from "way back" is found a job in town which will enable him to assist one of the Grade teams of that locality.

The only possible objection to the system is its over-centralization, and the difficulty caused thereby in raising the standard outside the immediate neighbourhood of the capitals.

Just as the counties at home and the Dominions occasionally lose good talent to the cricket Leagues[3], so do States, such as Western Australia and Tasmania, lose the cream of their cricketers to Melbourne and Adelaide. Club cricket, as we know it in England, is non-existent, for over the entire system the State cricket associations stretch out their hands; hands encased in iron gloves. To them, all clubs must render obedience and tribute, sometimes to the extent of having their own fixture list approved, and the State associations are not given to approving casual fixtures with teams owing them no

---

[2] An Australian, J.H. Crawford, won Wimbledon in 1933. No British player had won the Gentlemen's Singles since 1909, although the age of Fred Perry was about to dawn.

[3] The League games of the Midlands and the north were, compared with the 'gentlemanly' encounters of county cricket, fiercely competitive.

allegiance. One result is the almost complete absence of Public School and University cricketers from the State teams, though I am assured that there is plenty of suitable talent available. The authorities, it seems, have rather a "skite" against clubs formed from such sources, as being likely to be more independent in their outlook and finances than the average Grade team. School and University players for the most part give up serious cricket on leaving and take up golf and lawn tennis.

Various Grade teams elect representatives to the councils of the State cricket authorities. One result of this concentration of cricket in Australia is the comparative ease with which it is possible to choose an Australian Test Match team. In an ordinary domestic season no player gets more than six first-class matches – three at home and three away – among the four Sheffield Shield States, Victoria, New South Wales, South Australia, and Queensland. Nor do most players perform in all these. The journey to Brisbane is no mean undertaking at any time, and the weather after November holds out little inducement to cricketers.

Nearly every inter-State player by the time he has played a couple of seasons knows the form of his team-mates and opponents far more intimately than county players at home know their opposite numbers. Many counties do not play each other, and the weather spoils so many of our games. Two or three players from South Australia and Queensland may "pick themselves" for the Australian XI, but the remaining eight or nine must come from the two premier cricketing States. In consequence, the veriest ignoramus can nearly always be relied upon to pick eight or nine certainties for the International team.

This takes us out of the limits controlled by the Grade and State cricket authorities into the realms wherein the Board of Control holds sway.

Though composed in most instances of many of the same members, the Board and the State authorities have little in common. Both need money, and there is occasional clashing in this respect, but both rule their particular roost and their players with the same autocratic hand. At home, cricketers who compose our various teams are important factors; in Australia, quite clearly, it is otherwise. The controllers of cricket come first every time, and the arrangements made for them on the ground, by comparison with those made for the players, reveal and emphasize this rather startling difference.

The history of the Board of Control has been a stormy one. At one time or another the Board has succeeded in alienating the sympathies of players, public, and Press, and sometimes all three at one and the same time.

The birth of the Board was not auspicious. Brought into being shortly before the triangular tournament in 1912 (when both Australia and South Africa had representative sides touring England at the same time), the Board took over from the justly famous Melbourne Cricket Club. The Melbourne Cricket Club had been the pioneer of the early International encounters with England[4], and it acted as host to all our early touring teams. A sadly undignified squabble between the newly-created Board and several of the players who should have made the trip to England immediately ensued.

The late Mr. S. H. Pardon, writing in the 1913 "Wisden", thus described the result:

"The Australians, who had been allowed to have everything their own way in choosing a time for the first trial of Sir Abe Bailey's ambitious scheme (the triangular tournament) quarrelled so bitterly among themselves that half their best players were left at home. . . .

"It is no business of mine to go into the details of the squabbles and quarrels in Australia. Under the special circumstances I think all personal considerations should have been put aside and made subordinate to the prime need of sending over Australia's best men for the tournament. The personal differences were too deep to admit of adjustment. The Board of Control carried its point, but as regards the prestige of Australian cricket, the victory was dearly won."

Belief has it that the question of the appointment of a manager for

---

[4] The first England Tour of Australia was in 1861–2, but the matches were played 'against odds' (using a system of handicaps), and so did not qualify as first-class. The first bona fide Test Match between the two countries was in 1877.

the team was the bone of contention. In the past it had been an invariable rule that the players selected should in their turn choose a manager. The Board's juggernaut rode roughshod over this custom and achieved its first iron victory, but at a price. Half a dozen of the best-known and best-liked Australian cricketers refused to be trampled upon, and, rather than submit, such great players as M. A. Noble, V. Trumper and W. W. Armstrong declined to make the trip to England.[5]

Certainly in Australia the strength of local feeling and local pride is a fearsome and wonderful thing for a country so sparsely populated. South of Suez one never meets an Australian, only New South Welshmen or Victorians, etc., and even in faraway Tasmania intense feeling exists between the northern and the southern half of the island. There is, I fear, no disguising the fact that feelings of mistrust between players and the Board, and even between members of the Board themselves, are distressingly common. Many people have expressed surprise that out of the whole Board only two of its members can claim to have played first-class cricket at all regularly, and that only one has ever played against England in a Test match.

If the members of the Board were prominently distinguished for activities outside cricket, a mistrust for too many cricketers with no outside qualification as suitable guides for its destinies might be understandable. The Board, however, would not venture to make any such claim. The omission, therefore, from its numbers of such names as Noble, Hill, Macartney, Bardsley, Gregory, and many others is an enigma which seems to require some explanation. Whatever the explanation may be, it is at least curious that an Australian captain either should not be invited to be a member of the Selection Committee which picks the team he is to captain, or, having been invited to serve as a Selector, should prefer to dissociate himself from this sub-committee of the Board of Control.

---

[5] M. A. Noble (1873–1940): all-rounder who played 42 Tests for Australia in the first two decades of the 20th century; V. Trumper (1877–1915): batsman of genius, especially on difficult wickets, rated by some as highly as Bradman; W. W. Armstrong (1879–1947): all-rounder renowned for his immense physical stature and fine captaincy as well as his prowess with bat and ball. Australia was undefeated under his leadership.

By comparison with the contract which English players sign before making the Australian tour, the contract extracted from Australian players is diffuse and onerous to a degree.

In practice I do not believe that the English contract has been broken in any single instance, but if such were to occur, I doubt if it would be given publicity. When, however, the Board found it necessary to reduce by £50 the payment which it was making to Bradman after his triumphal English tour in 1930, many of the newspapers had headlines on the subject, and men in the street took sides over the question, as one would expect people to do over a *cause célèbre* or an election.

However, it is easy to be hypercritical, and, as I have already said, the quality of Australian cricket is no mean advertisement for its organizers. Moreover, the members of the Board, drawn, as they are, from places so far distant as Perth and Brisbane (which are nearly 3,000 miles apart), must necessarily have limited chances of getting acquainted and discussing their several points of view. Though founded on a democratic basis, the Board finds it easier and more expeditious to act autocratically. A single meet of the Board of Control, it may be added, is estimated to cost between £300 and £400, and necessitates a week's absence from home on the part of those members who have farthest to travel.[6]

---

[6] This is equivalent to between about £10,000 and £15,000 today.

5

Captaincy and Problems

If a captain expects his men to do their best for him, it goes without saying that they will only do so if they are convinced that he is doing his best for them. As the Lonsdale Library volume on cricket has it: "A captain must have confidence in every man of his side, and every man on his side must have confidence in him."

There is an old, but scarcely modest, adage to the effect that if you want a thing done well you must do it yourself. A captain therefore should not delegate his duties to anyone else. He may take someone out with him, for consultation, to inspect the wicket, but there is no substitute for seeing the wicket himself. He should himself see the balls to be used in a Test Match put through a gauge by the umpires.

In the excitement of the big day it is not always easy to remember such little things. Woodfull and I even forgot upon one occasion to exchange the names of the sides finally selected before tossing, as the rule lays down. I hope that some will profit from my mistakes. One thing is certain in this world: one learns more from one's own mistakes than from those of others!

By the time a man is good enough to play for England or Australia, many people are tempted to think that he must have progressed so far that there is very little left for him to learn about cricket, though he will naturally have to learn how to face and cope with new problems when playing abroad under different conditions to those to which he is normally accustomed. I can assure readers that this applies with greater force to the captain than to any other member of the side. There is far more attention paid to cricket education and tactics in the north than in the south of England. Up north they are not content with bowling you out: they think you out as well – one reason, perhaps, why the county championship has gone north so regularly of recent years.

There are, however, a good many rules, almost first principles, which we have all learned at one time. Some of these are so elementary that they are forgotten, or relegated to the limbo as of such little importance as to be hardly worth observing. True, the usefulness of these rules is not always apparent, but their neglect is apt to be attended by devastating consequences.

In my limited experience I have seen Test matches won and lost by their observance or the reverse. The time to test and analyse the true worth of such details is after the game has been won or lost by a trifling margin of, say, from one to twenty runs. Let me give some actual examples.

The calling of runs by batsmen at the wicket should be simplicity itself. When we were young we were all told that there were only three calls: "Yes", "No", "Wait". How often is this strictly observed in first-class cricket today?

In a recent Test Match the striker called "yes". The non-striker, instead of responding to his call in silence, signified his agreement in American slang: "Okay", said he, pronouncing it "Oke". The striker thought he said "No", and turned back while the Yankeephile continued merrily on his course. Eventually he realized that something was wrong. Fortunately there had originally been a run and three-quarters "in the strike", and by dint of throwing himself to the full stretch of his by no means negligible length, he just managed to regain his crease with nothing worse to show for it than a skinned elbow, one run lost to his side, and a total loss of confidence between himself and his batting partner.

On another occasion, when a new ball had been requisitioned at 200, and promptly despatched to the boundary, the fieldsman returned it to the wicket-keeper along the ground. There is no quicker and surer method of removing the shine from a ball than this. The shine lasts all too short a time in Australia in any case. On this occasion I was saved all embarrassment, for just as I was thinking out some mild suggestion to the effect that for the future it was most desirable that a new ball should be returned at full pitch to the wicket-keeper, a voice, the dialect of which I shall not attempt to reproduce, informed the delinquent that his error would have earned him the sack from a county side which I do not propose to identify. He never offended again!

In contrast to these mistakes let me recall what is one of the most vivid, if not actually *the* most vivid mental picture which the last tour left with me – an example which illustrates, from one side's point of view at least, the importance of observing first principles, the execution of which could not have been bettered by the King's Company of the Grenadier Guards on ceremonial parade.

Love and Darling, a curious combination of names, were batting in the second innings of the Fourth Test match at Brisbane. Larwood was bowling to Love. I had just dropped back some 15 yards to very deep mid-on, largely with the idea of offering Love an easy single, and thereby bringing Darling to face Larwood's bowling.

Darling, I should add, was the last reputed batsman on the Australian side whom we had still to get out.

The only other fieldsman necessary to mention was Mitchell, joint hero with Larwood of this particular episode.

Mitchell was fielding midway between where cover and mid-off would ordinarily field, and close enough to foil any attempt at stealing short runs on the off side.

Love pushed the ball very gently in front of square leg in the direction of deep mid-on and called his partner for the run. Larwood was after the ball like a flash, and, appearing to cover an incredible amount of ground, just reached it at full stretch.

As Larwood started his dash, I saw Mitchell coming up to the bowler's vacated wicket like a racehorse. These things take some time in the telling; on the field they happen in the twinkling of an eye.

Darling had backed up well, and was nearly halfway down the wicket, when Love, seeing that Larwood had fielded the ball, and realizing that the wicket-keeper's end was by far the easier end for Larwood to throw, sent Darling back, at the same time returning to his own crease.

Darling either did not hear this second call, or could not check his headlong progress in time, but above this call and counter-call, with two batsmen nearly in the same crease, Larwood heard the shout, "This end, Lol". He turned in an instant, and instead of hurling the ball as hard as he could or indulging in a wild shot at the wickets (which is all too common an error at such moments) deliberately tossed the ball underhand at full pitch to the waiting Mitchell, who whipped the bails off.

Love was blamed for not sacrificing his wicket for Darling's — unfairly, I maintain, since, admitting the original error of his call, it seemed to me that he took the only possible chance of saving both wickets.

We are not concerned with that, however; we are only concerned with the principle that the nearest fieldsman to a vacated wicket should take charge of that wicket as promptly as he can, and that, where possible, the fieldsman with the ball should receive instructions directing the end to which he should make his return throw.

I always felt that this was in reality the last crisis of the Rubber Test match, and that by their promptness and ability to keep their heads and remember first principles, Larwood and Mitchell robbed Australia of her last chance of retaining the Ashes.

Lose a match by one run, and how many batsmen on the losing side who have made a few runs can honestly say to themselves, "I missed no runs by not running the first run as quickly as possible, just in case the fieldsman fumbled!" How many times have catches been missed by fieldsmen straying from their appointed places even by a yard or two!

A captain, who has always to be on the outlook for wandering sheep, is very apt to be caught napping himself, and another missed catch is the result. But enough of this. I hope I have made it clear that Test cricketers of all countries have still much to learn, and many things to remember. Were it otherwise, cricket would lose a very vital part of its charm and uncertainty.

Cricketers are often temperamental to a degree, and here again one could hardly wish to eradicate temperament, even if at times it is a sore trial to the individual who suffers from nerves, or to the captain who sees one of his team lose his head. I doubt if there has ever been a great cricketer who had "no nerves". Nerves are, after all, only a form of over-anxiety to do well for a side, and to justify the faith reposed in the individual. Even cricketers who only play from the pavilion have been known to suffer from acute attacks of nerves – though, of course, we know that they never make the futile and asinine mistakes that the players on the field are so prone to commit in the excitement of the moment.

Under Australian conditions for Test Matches, time is theoretically of no consequence, since matches are played to a finish. There are not, however, so many differences between limited and unlimited cricket as might be supposed. In the first place, the hours of play in Australia are considerably shorter than at home: 12 to 1.30, 2.15 to 4, 4.15 to 6. Under these conditions there is rarely the same temptation to go for the bowling and knock it off, as is the case at home.

The crisis of many a day's cricket in Australia. comes in the last hour's play. The captain can do much to ease this all-important hour for his side when in the field. With the short hours of play, it is very rarely possible for the batsman to get right on top of the bowling, for the simple reason that in order to do so he must make such short work of the change bowlers that the original bowlers have to be put on again before they have had a sufficient spell of rest.

After the last interval of the day the batsmen, obviously, have had a better chance than at any other time. Throughout the tour we adopted the principle of nursing one good bowler to bear the burden of the last hour's work. It usually fell to Verity and Hammond to keep one end going for this last trying hour. Again and again they did it at trifling cost, thus enabling us to retain the initiative at one end at least.

And those who have not encountered the heat of an Australian summer can rest assured that there is a world of difference between working a pair of fast bowlers for spells of three, instead of five, attacking overs at the close of an exhausting day.

We made arrangements in advance for our drinks to be sent out on the tick. This again means much to the bowlers. As a general rule we tried to keep a little something in the way of initiative up our sleeves: (1) to launch at each new batsman as he came in, (2) with each new ball, and (3) after each interval. We proved by experience that on hot days it is better for a fast bowler to bowl one over before the drinks arrived, instead of waiting to bowl until after he had had the drink.

But, as I have said, this implies clockwork punctuality in bringing out the drinks.

6

Review Previous to First Test

As soon as we landed in Australia, and during our visit to the various States, two things were made extremely clear to us. The first was that our chances of winning the Rubber were hardly worth considering. Now the Australian temperament, whether from sunshine or other causes, is nothing if not sanguine. In some respects, at least, it is fortunate for Australia that this is so.

As an Australian wrote to me: "If it were not for our optimism and talk of vast unexplored resources, we should never have gone as far as we have in developing the country – a country the centre of which was accurately described by two of our intrepid airmen as being the best place in the world for parking old razor-blades." Anyone who has fielded out for a day in Melbourne, with "a northerly" blowing, will readily subscribe to the belief that this most unpleasant wind does in fact hail from thousands of square miles of desert, whether carpeted with sand or razor-blades, or both. It is like the blast from a furnace door which is opened in one's face.

But if our chances of winning the Rubber were not worthy of consideration, we had, it appeared, one important function to perform – we were to supply opportunities for the cream of Australian cricketers to make and break records. Everywhere the man in the street tends to bow down and pay lip service to the spectacular. This is perhaps surprising in cricket, a game which from its very nature requires the subordination of individual interests to those of the team as a whole.

Few will be found to admit that the hero-worship, almost amounting to idolatry, to which, for example, Bradman was subject, is desirable for the game's good, or fair to the individual. It encouraged the feeling that Bradman was a run-making machine of almost superhuman powers – in short, that he was a team in himself; and this habit of extolling one man must naturally lead to the lack of appreciation of others. For example, Woodfull is equally invaluable to his side, but being less spectacular has never received anything like the appreciation to which he is entitled.[1]

The second fact which we were to learn was that the Australian cricket authorities were extremely upset by the M.C.C.'s decision that its side should return home by way of New Zealand, playing cricket on the way in that Dominion. As the date of our departure from Australia (March 16, 1933) had in no way been affected by the decision to return through New Zealand, I could not see any possible grounds for objection which the Australian authorities could have on this score. The English cricketing authorities would not complain or cavil were an Australian team touring in England to return to Australia by any route they might select, playing cricket on the way, whether in South Africa or elsewhere. Nor, I feel sure, would offence be taken, since this would be a matter of purely domestic arrangement between South Africa and Australia, and nobody else's concern at all.

It seems inconceivable that our return through New Zealand could be held to imply any criticism, however indirect, of Australian dealings with the neighbouring Dominion.[2] On more than one occasion I was left with the unpleasant impression that by visiting New Zealand we were in some way flouting or slighting Australia. I only trust that a very small number of Australians are still labouring under this delusion. It must surely be common knowledge that a

---

[1] A short account of W.M. Woodfull's career appeared in 2000 in the 'Famous Cricketers' series, published by West Bridgford: Association of Cricket Statisticians.

[2] Even before the team left England, there had been a terse exchange between the Board of Control and the M.C.C. on the subject of the New Zealand visit. The Board were concerned that it would detract from the importance of the Ashes fixtures.

team is responsible neither for its programme nor its itinerary. Nor should the Australian authorities be anything but sympathetic to New Zealand's desire to see a fully representative English team.

No such team had visited New Zealand for forty-six years, and the desire to see in action cricketers of the old country, who hitherto were only names, was surely as natural as it was worthy of encouragement.

Moreover, cricketers who go to New Zealand receive so much kindness and such a warm welcome that anything they can do in return seems quite inadequate. I hope that any future M.C.C. Australian team will have the good fortune to return, as we did, via New Zealand.

By the time the team has played the Sheffield Shield States for the first time, it should not be difficult to form within limits some reasonably accurate forecast of its chances. Barring flukes and rain, if the touring team is beaten by any of the States when playing anything like its full strength, it is safe to assume that its prospects of being successful in the Test matches are the reverse of encouraging. I say this not only for the obvious reason that an Australian eleven is a much stiffer proposition to tackle than any State team, but also because, on the first tour through the States, the Australian players are far from being in full practice.

J. W. H. T. Douglas's team in 1920–21 was defeated by New South Wales, which State's team at that time contained three-quarters of the Australian eleven. The writing on the wall was clear, and this team failed to win a Test match.

Again, in 1924, Gilligan's team lost to Victoria. On this occasion it is true that the game was lost only after the English captain had seen fit to permit play to continue after the time agreed upon for the drawing of stumps. But again this early reverse proved a reliable augury for an ultimate Australian triumph of four matches to one.

There can be no doubt that outright wins hearten a side, and do it much good, but it is a moot point whether it does not pay better to indulge in batting practice even at the expense of sacrificing an occasional win. The opportunities of getting all the batsmen on a touring side into form in Australia are all too few. A. P. F. Chapman pursued this policy of affording his team all the batting practice possible in 1928, with the happiest results.[3]

However, in our case we had every reason to be satisfied with the results obtained. Before playing the first Test match we had already defeated each of the three leading States in a single innings: a sufficiently cheering indication. It must be admitted we did not put up a very convincing performance against an Australian eleven at Melbourne, but the side was not then at full strength. It is, moreover, my experience that every side, be it school, club, university, county or international, does, in the course of a season, play well below its true form at least once or twice. We were, if anything, relieved to have that particular performance behind us. It was our batting which had broken down. At that time, though exercised about our bowling, we were fairly confident of our batting strength. The favourable impression created by our bowling, however, encouraged us not a little, and must have had anything but a similar effect upon our opponents.

We had, moreover, made a discovery. To our surprise, we found an almost totally unsuspected weakness on the leg stump in the play of several of those leading players who were bound to be opposed to us in the representative matches.

This had been particularly apparent in the case of Bradman as early as the second match of the tour, when he came to Perth to play against us and encountered Allen bowling really well, even at this early stage in our tour. No such weakness was apparent in McCabe or Richardson; and Fingleton, though rather foot-tied and slow, seemed more likely to make runs off leg-theory than any other sort of bowling.

Fortunately for us, these last three batsmen occasionally gave the bowlers grounds for hope when attacking the off stump, and though they made a lot of runs – and made them well – I think that secretly they were inclined to welcome leg-theory. Our ultimate policy,

---

[3] England won the Rubber 4–1, despite two 50s and two 100s in four matches by a young, if not callow Don Bradman in his first Test series. The English team's mean first innings total was 483.25, with Jardine himself averaging 42.62.

therefore, when bowling to them, involved very little leg-theory, and then only for variation's sake.

In contrast, Ponsford and Kippax, whom we considered certainties for most of the Test matches, revealed a marked weakness on the leg stump; in very different ways, however, for whereas Kippax, with his correct and beautiful style, was inclined to edge away and spar, Ponsford was inclined to move too far over on to the off-side, leaving his wicket uncovered. Indeed, we got Ponsford out round his legs three or four times during the course of the tour.

It seemed to me that Woodfull had lost something of his amazing ability to play the ball in the exact centre of his bat at the very last fraction of a second, even when it appeared to have half-beaten him. Throughout the series I did not think that either Woodfull or Bradman was physically fit, but there is no doubt that, as time went on, they improved with practice, and familiarity with our bowling restored both to something very like their old form. I doubt, however, if Australian wickets, which have changed so noticeably in the short period of four years, are likely in the future to encourage scoring on the scale to which onlookers were once accustomed.[4]

Even before we left England, I thought we had more than a good chance of winning, and I arrived at this conclusion by comparing the strength of the two teams from numbers 6 to 11.[5] I thought there was very little to choose between the two probable teams so far as numbers 1 to 5 in the batting order were concerned, though I was prepared to concede to Australia any slight advantage that there might be here. From numbers 6 to 11 the dice were very heavily loaded in our favour. I doubt if Australia has ever had such a tail as fell to her lot to carry in this last series, while England can rarely have had a better, and certainly never a more courageous, lower half to her batting order.

[4] Many observers commented that the wickets were less fast and less consistent than during the 1928–9 Ashes tour.

[5] Jardine's forecast was borne out by the results: during the series the English Nos. 6 to 11 batsmen averaged 26.31, compared to 14.67 among their Australian counterparts. There was far less to choose between the two teams' first five batsmen: the Australian Nos. 1 to 5 averaged 33.77, and the English 39.40.

7
Leg-theory

Australia's writers showed their claws,
Her backers raged, her batsmen shook,
Statesmen consulted – and the cause?
Our bowling was too good to hook.[1]

This book would scarcely be complete without a chapter on this most highly skilled form of bowling.

There appears to have been so much misconception as to what is meant by leg-theory that it may not be out of place to offer some explanation of its nature and objects.

Those who know, or have always known, all that there is to be learned about leg-theory are advised to skip this chapter.

The great heart, however, who continues to read in patience should at once clear his mind of preconceived ideas, from whatever source they may have been derived, and he must not be disappointed if he finds the theory and practice of leg-theory both simple and elementary, whatever the degree of skill which its application and execution demand.

To begin with, there is nothing new about leg-theory. Whether the credit for its introduction into cricket is due to George Hirst, for many years Yorkshire's and England's fast left-handed bowler, or to W. W. Armstrong, the slow Victorian and Australian bowler, need

[1] Jardine himself appears to have been the author of this acerbic quatrain. The Australian satirical weekly *Bulletin* lampooned overblown English claims to good sportsmanship thus: "At 'Ome, of course, we Play the Game,/ The crowd behave decorously;/ They never criticize or blame,/ But say Bravo sonorously;/ 'Played, sir!' they chirp, or cry 'Well run!',/ But barrack, haw! – it isn't done!"

not concern us, unless it is to establish the fact that leg-theory is considerably more than a quarter of a century old.[2]

All bowling, irrespective of pace and type, may for all practical purposes be divided into two, and only two, types.

The first aims at getting wickets, with the restriction of run-getting as a matter of very secondary importance. The second aims at restricting the scoring of runs, with the taking of wickets as a minor consideration.

Obviously the ideal is to be found in the bowler who can take wickets and restrict the rate of scoring at the same time. As a matter of practice, however, the bowler must have either the one or the other of these two objects clearly in mind – in other words, the one plan of attack must be definitely subordinated to the other.

At one time, judging from certain newspaper reports, one might have been tempted to imagine that the bowler had a totally different object in view – that of causing physical harm to the batsman! That such a misconception was almost entirely due to the coining of the phrase "bodyline bowling" can scarcely be open to doubt. Apart from commenting on the stupidity of bringing any such charge against England's bowlers, we need not concern ourselves further with its patent untruthfulness.

Like all other bowlers, our bowlers bowled to take wickets, and occasionally to keep down runs, but the latter was a duty which no sane captain would depute to a fast bowler in Australia.

Most people are familiar with off-theory. In off-theory it is the off stump which is attacked, when the bowler's margin of error will be limited to the off-side for the sufficiently obvious reason that nearly all his fieldsmen are stationed on that side of the wicket. Off-theory bowling can be exceedingly dull for players and spectators alike. The bowler has only to err, say, nine inches within his margin of error (that is, to bowl nine inches outside the off stump), and the batsman, under ordinary circumstances, will be under no compulsion to make any shot whatsoever.

[2] G. H. Hirst is credited with being the first to master 'swerve' bowling. See p. 27 for note on W. W. Armstrong.

It can easily be understood how disheartening this is to any bowler, and particularly to a fast bowler, to whom, especially, stamina is always a matter of prime importance.

Now, in leg-theory it is the leg stump which is the object of the bowler's attack, and since the majority of his fieldsmen are employed in various positions on the leg side, the margin of error in this case must be limited to a few inches outside the leg stump.

I may be wrong, but I have a strong suspicion that it is easier for the batsman to decide what ball is just outside the off stump, and consequently need not be played, than for him to make up his mind about the course of the ball which pitches the same distance outside the leg stump.

Apart from technical considerations which I need not enter into, there is the obvious danger of the batsman being bowled off his pads – an additional reason why the leg ball demands active treatment.

Bradman has paid tribute to the amazing accuracy of Larwood and Voce when bowling off- or leg-theory. No doubt he realized the immense saving in stamina which accrued to two such bowlers, who could, when bowling leg-theory, force the batsman to play nearly every ball they bowled, instead of allowing him to watch three balls in an over pass by outside the off stump, and remain passive.

A few notes on the history of leg-theory may not be out of place. The first is taken from an article entitled "Warning to Legislators of the Game of Cricket". I will respect the anonymity of the author of this excellent article which appeared in the *Christchurch Star,* though his identity is an open secret to the cricket world.

ORIGIN AND DEVELOPMENT OF LEG-THEORY

To acquire a fair and unbiased view of leg-theory bowling as now practised it is necessary to review the origin of this method of attack and the various stages of its development. From the very beginning of leg break bowling it has always been the practice, if the batsman was inclined to be weak on the leg side, to put additional men over and bowl more on the legs. But it was not until Armstrong came along with his leg breaks that a definite leg-theory policy by a leg break bowler was evolved.

For years Armstrong bowled with all his men on the leg side except two. These tactics were certainly irritating, but no one suggested they were unfair.

One of the brightest memories of Armstrong's leg-theory bowling comes from the way Johnnie Tyldesley dealt with it.[3] He used to jump back and square cut and drive through the covers, and the vigorous manner in which he did this was a delight to the public and disconcerting to the great Armstrong.

Noble recently stated in Australia that it was he who induced Armstrong to give up the leg-theory bowling, but it must be remembered that the change was not made on account of its being considered unfair, but because it was found that Armstrong was a better bowler when concentrating on the middle and leg stumps.[4]

TRUMBLE SOWS THE SEED

Turning to the faster bowlers who adopted leg-theory tactics, it is probable that Hugh Trumble – pure medium pace – was the first to attempt this as a varied method of attack.[5]

In the Second Test match at Melbourne in 1901, when bowling to MacLaren, who was a magnificent player on the off side, Trumble packed a leg field and bowled on the leg stumps and the pads. But MacLaren was too clever, and the frequency of the ones and twos he scored on the on side prevented Trumble from persisting.[6] But he was

---

[3] Johnnie Tyldesley (1873–1930) was a Lancashire and England batsman noted in his obituary in Wisden as having been 'exceptionally quick on his feet'. In the Oval Test Match in 1905, he scored 112 against an Australian attack dominated by Armstrong, who bowled 30 overs of off-breaks down the leg side.

[4] See note on p. 27.

[5] Hugh Trumble (1867–1938) played 31 Tests against England, taking 141 wickets at an average of 20.88. In the first innings of the 3rd Test in 1902, he bowled 18 overs for only 21 runs, largely against the 20-year-old Fry, whom he dismissed lbw for 4 in the second innings.

[6] The Christchurch Star's account is a little awry. The Test, which Australia won by 229 runs, was played in the first four days of 1902. In the first innings England were bowled out for 61, of which MacLaren made 13 before being dismissed by Trumble. He made 1 in the second innings, and was then caught off Noble's bowling – by Trumble.

more successful the following year in England, when he bowled a definite leg-theory to C. B. Fry, then the best "on" player in England.

Trumble has always been considered one of the shrewdest players the game has ever produced, and it was thought extremely clever to attack a man on his strongest point, but no one ever suggested such tactics were unfair. As a matter of fact, the Englishman at the time joined in appreciating this form of strategy.

It is true that Fry was terribly upset to find his best shots on the on side bringing him no runs, but his discomfiture was only a personal one, and no protest came from any quarter against Trumble's methods.

FASTER BOWLERS AIM AT THE PADS

Then we come to bowlers of more pace using the leg-theory. Hirst, until the beginning of this century, was just an energetic fast left-hand bowler, but when he developed the great swerve, for which he afterwards became famous, the natural sequence to it was an on-field, for his left-hand swerve was always making into the batsman, and a straight-pitched ball would often go outside his legs.

The result was that for years Hirst only had mid-off and point on the off side. He had two or three short-legs, a short fine-leg, a deep fine-leg and a deep square-leg: in fact, a field very similar to Larwood's. There is no doubt this form of bowling at that pace was something new to England, and carried with it great misgivings among the batsmen at that time.

The Australians in 1902 found it very troublesome, and a good story is told of their match at Leeds against Yorkshire. Hirst quickly bowled Duff, and Clem Hill, taking his place, found it difficult to negotiate Hirst's last leg-theory.[7]

At the end of the over Victor Trumper walked down to the wicket and said:

"He's worrying you, Kruger," as they nicknamed Clem, and Victor said: "Leave him to me for a while," and so, making sure of getting singles at the end of the other bowler's over, Trumper stayed at Hirst's end.

[7] Clem Hill (1877–1945) was an aggressive left-handed batsman, who played 49 Tests. Better on Australian than English wickets, he made successive scores of 99, 98 and 97 against England in the 1901–2 Ashes.

HIRST EXPRESSES HIMSELF

In the first over he hit him through the leg field to the fence: two balls later he stood back and chopped him past third man for four, and then hit him outside mid-on for another four; and as Hirst walked back past the umpire he quietly exclaimed, "Well, I'm d – d," pronounced in his broad Yorkshire dialect.

And so they were able to get humour out of the leg-theory nearly thirty years ago. No one, either Englishman or Australian, ever accused Hirst of bowling unfairly, and he was certainly a pretty fast bowler, although not as fast as some of the really fast bowlers who have made their reputations in the history of cricket.

THE WHIRLWIND KNOX

Many of the fast bowlers of the past intimidated the batsmen just as Larwood has been doing lately. Knox, the Surrey express bowler, in his one brilliant season of 1906, played havoc during the dry season in England.[8]

In the Gentlemen-Players match at Lord's[9] he had most of the professionals absolutely scared, and those who saw it will remember how John Gunn[10], the Notts. player, kept jumping out of the way, reminding one of the remark made recently in Australia that this present-day fast bowling is comparable with the old-fashioned "coconut-shy".

Knox's bowling figures in this match were five for 73 and seven for 110; but in another Gentlemen-Players match, three weeks later,

[8] Neville Knox's 1906 county season was brilliant indeed: he took 144 wickets at an average of 19.63 runs apiece. It is a measure of DRJ's high standards that he chooses not to apply the epithet to Knox's performance the previous year, when he took 121 wickets, and averaged less than 22. Perennial shin complaints brought his career to a premature end.

[9] This fixture was inaugurated in 1806. The distinction was between amateurs and professionals, with the Gentlemen generally being from the south and the Players from the north. The Players almost always won, mainly due to a widespread preference for batting over bowling among the Gentlemen of the time. The importance of the match declined with the growth of county and Test cricket.

[10] During his 29-year association with Nottinghamshire C.C., John Gunn scored 24,601 runs, took 1243 wickets, and held 233 catches. In 1903 he scored 294 runs against Leicestershire in under four and a half hours.

when the professionals had recovered their equilibrium, his figures were one for 83 and one for 110!

Knox, like Cotter[11], the Australian fast bowler, was never quite accurate in his direction, and it is safe to say that both these bowlers banged down at least two balls an over which went straight at the batsman.

Larwood, on the other hand, is more like Richardson.[12] He is an accurate fast bowler, and, what is more, he has a body action which makes the ball go into the batsman just as Richardson used to do. Some thought this an off-break, but a fast bowler, to get all the pace he can, must keep his fingers behind the ball at the moment of delivery; and only a few of the right-hand bowlers have made the ball swing inwards.

This characteristic of Larwood's bowling makes it necessary under any circumstances to have additional men on the leg side. It must be disconcerting to batsmen, especially those who pull away, to find that as they draw away the ball still comes on towards them.

INCREASES BATSMEN'S DIFFICULTIES

The chief trouble for the Australians today is that Larwood is a really first-class fast bowler, and that he has developed leg-theory better than anyone else in the past, except, perhaps, George Hirst; but his advantage over Hirst is that he is considerably faster, and this has added to the batsmen's difficulties.

The Australian batsmen appear to be making the most of their own troubles: it is impossible to be moving away from a ball and to play it properly.

Pictures which have been shown in Christchurch on the screen show that Bradman on two occasions was at least two feet away from the leg stump when he was bowled. This was in his earlier innings when he failed, but people who witnessed his fine innings in the second Test match at Melbourne say that he had recovered his

[11] Albert Cotter was killed in 1917 at Beersheba. His obituary in Wisden describes his bowling in the early part of the 1905 Ashes Tour as 'a quaint mixture of long hops and full pitches', but concludes that 'on his day he was deadly.'

[12] Arthur J. Richardson, the Australian medium-paced bowler of the 20s. According to his Wisden obituary, Hobbs feigned discomfort while Richardson was bowling during the Oval Test of 1926, in order to prevent a change of bowling.

confidence, and he was never once hit by the leg-theory in that great fighting innings.

We in this country know how Ponsford shapes at fast bowling: he palpably flinched away from our own Dickinson, who bowled him neck and crop in Dunedin, and altogether his displays here showed us that he did not like fast bowling. How much more difficult must he find it negotiating Larwood. In three out of his four innings in the present Test series he has walked across to the off and been bowled behind his legs.

In spite of all this, I would not suggest that leg-theory, if bowled by a hefty lad of eighteen to a fourteen-year-old on a bumpy park pitch, might not be legitimately described as "rather strong meat", but, in these circumstances, any fast bowling might be so described, and the same term might also be applied to shots such as the leg glance or the late cut.

No one, however, would seriously suggest that because these two shots, when played under circumstances which are far from ideal, are "strong meat" for a fourteen-year-old, legislation should be brought in to bar or curtail their use.

Any batsman who is fortunate enough to get a few runs on a sticky Australian wicket against medium-pace or fast bowling faces the absolute certainty of being hit.

Those of us who in 1929 were privileged to see Hobbs and Sutcliffe make a hundred on a Melbourne glue-pot in the Third Test match saw those two batsmen hit all over the body, and it would be futile to suggest that this, if they were to make runs at all, was anything but inevitable.

It has yet to be suggested that, since it is quite inevitable that a batsman making runs on a sticky wicket in Australia will be hit with the ball, cricket should not be played upon a sticky wicket. Had we had the fortune to bowl against Australia on a sticky wicket, we should not, I imagine, have bowled leg-theory, for obvious reasons.

In the first place, our slow left-hander, Verity, would in all probability have bowled unchanged at one end; secondly, we should not have willingly incurred the risk of a courageous hitter making a dozen runs in a single over or knocking one of our bowlers off, as he might most easily have done (and with less risk of getting out), so long as leg-theory was being exploited upon such a wicket.

I venture the opinion that upon good wickets if a good batsman is hit when playing leg-theory he has no one to blame but himself.

Let me instance Bradman in support of this; for Bradman, against whom leg-theory was popularly supposed to have been largely aimed, was hit exactly once in the course of the numerous innings he played against us during the tour. This was in the last innings in the last Test Match, when Larwood hit him on the arm with a ball some six or nine inches outside the leg stump which Bradman was attempting to cut square past cover-point.

Bradman had already succeeded in making this shot several times; but Bradman himself, I feel sure, would be unwilling to assign any blame to anyone but the batsman attempting a shot so unorthodox.

That brilliant Australian batsman, the late Archie Jackson[13], writing not long before his lamented death, said that if Ponsford and Fingleton had been battered about the body "that is mostly their own fault". He added:

"For the sake of Australia's sporting traditions, may it be left to the cricketers themselves to furnish the only answer to the legitimate tactics employed by the Englishmen."

If Hirst and Armstrong share the credit of introducing leg-theory, it must not be imagined that they had not many imitators. W. B. Burns, the Worcester fast bowler, under the captaincy of H. K. Foster, bowled at Lord's more than twenty years ago with seven men on the leg side, without earning the epithet "unsportsmanlike" for himself, his captain, or his side. Before the war, A. Jaques, of Hampshire, and B. J. von Mele, the South African and Oxonian, both favoured this form of attack. In recent years MacDonald the

---

[13] Archie Jackson is to cricket what Keats is to poetry. He was just 23 when he died of tuberculosis on the final day of the Brisbane Test – the day his country lost the Ashes – and was much mourned by players and spectators alike. By contemporary accounts a dazzlingly stylish batsman, he scored 164 in his first Test Match in 1929, and was a member of the side which toured England the following year, sharing what was then a record 4th-wicket stand of 243 with Bradman at the Oval.

Australian Lancastrian, Root of Worcestershire, and Bowes of Yorkshire, have followed the same tradition, and, with one exception, without protest.

To me it seems that the chief reason for the development of leg-theory bowling is supplied by the modern batsman: I refer to the methods and style of batsmanship universally employed today, coupled with the easiness of the wickets provided.

With the increase of swerve bowling – and I am credibly informed that in the nineties there were not three bowlers who could swing the ball away from the batsman – a decline in off-side play was almost inevitable.

Batsmen, for their own as well as for their side's good, have tended – and in my submission rightly so – to eliminate dangerous shots from their repertoire.

One open and visible sign of this tendency has been the frequency with which the batsman plays in front of and even right across his wickets, placing most of his body in the path of the oncoming ball.

Incidentally, this habit on the part of the batsman frequently robs the bowler of so much as a sight of the "promised land", by which I mean the wickets. The two-eyed stance is commonly blamed for this practice – unfairly, I think. Many who do not adopt the two-eyed stance bat in the manner I have indicated. The cardinal point which emerges, however, is not the iniquity or the reverse of the two-eyed stance, but the certainty that the batsman will be hit with the ball should he miss it with the bat, whether the ball pitches six inches outside the off stump or on the wicket.

It was a ball outside the off stump which hit Woodfull in the third Test match while he was in the act of playing just the type of shot which I have endeavoured to describe.

A well-known Australian writer, in speaking of leg-theory, makes an unintentional admission when mentioning Woodfull and Ponsford:

Woodfull, never quick on his feet, faced it, but ducked his head and often his body. Twice he was hit over the heart, but in each case it was by a ball well pitched up which "fizzed" and kicked, and he could not avoid it. Hour after hour he faced an attack which was directed against him. . . . Ponsford, too, ducked, but also moved across in front of his wicket, only to find that the ball, coming in behind him, took his leg stump.

It is hard to know what the writer means by "directed against him". In point of fact, the attack was never directed against Woodfull or Ponsford, but against their wickets. Woodfull remained in front of his, and, if he was occasionally hit, I hope that the critics of leg-theory were not suffering from myopia when Ponsford did not leave sufficient of his bat or pads in the way to prevent the ball from breaking the wicket.

I can, however, satisfy this gentleman on one matter, since he refers to me personally. In reference to the Surrey and Yorkshire match in 1932, he writes: "I wonder what Jardine would have said if one of those two fast full pitchers from Macaulay had struck him on the head."

Owing to the publicity given to this match in certain quarters, I would remind those who made so much of it that if there had been any ground for complaint, the obvious and, to my mind, the only person to make those complaints was the Surrey captain (myself). Had either of the two full-pitchers mentioned (aimed not at my head, as is suggested, but at the top of the wicket), hit me or the wicket, I should have said that it was a case of poor batsmanship on my part and that the time had come when I should very seriously consider the desirability of ceasing to play first-class cricket owing to my obvious lack of skill.[14]

To digress for a moment, I notice that this same critic has seen fit to accuse a member of the English team (Voce) of "catapulting". Beyond suggesting that the bowler should be no-balled under Law 48, he is discreet enough not to define further what "catapulting" may be.

I am as much in the dark as anyone else. It will, however, come as a shock to everyone in England to learn that Voce's bowling action

[14] In the 2nd Test at Old Trafford against the West Indies in 1933, Jardine backed up his assertion that a skilled batsman could cope with 'body-line' tactics. Faced with a barrage of short, fast deliveries from Constantine and Martindale, he scored 128 runs – his first and only Test century.

has ever been the subject of comment or criticism of any kind. As far as Voce is concerned, we may safely leave it at that, but, if there is to be any discussion on fair and unfair bowling actions, it is surprising to find that this critic makes no mention of Ironmonger's.[15]

Everyone knows the value of a slow left-handed bowler to any side touring in England. For years, Ironmonger has been the outstanding left-handed bowler in Australia. In the circumstances, it is a little peculiar that Ironmonger has never been selected to fill one of the fifteen or sixteen places on the touring side, in spite of the fact that he has been good enough to gain a place time and again amongst the eleven chosen in Australia.

Players and members of the various controlling bodies alike make no secret of the reason for this curious omission. All were convinced that Ironmonger's action would not be allowed to pass unchallenged for one single over in England.

One point in the leg-theory controversy has never, as far as I know, been adequately realized. I refer to Larwood's extraordinary record of victims clean bowled or its equivalent, l.b.w.

He obtained 18 wickets out of his 33 wickets taken in Test matches – that is, over 50 per cent – in this manner, a record which for fairness as well as effectiveness will bear comparison with any bowler of the past, and, in all probability, any fast bowler of the future.

Critics are apt to forget that the elimination of certain strokes by certain batsmen are just as much a part of batting skill and duty to the side as the production of other shots. I am not suggesting that there is not a time and place to exploit every form of technique, but for ordinary purposes and in ordinary circumstances certain shots prove to be an all too expensive luxury in individual cases.

A little clear thinking and honest analysis will soon prove to any player which of his shots over a season are a gamble which is or is not worth taking.

If the standard of batsmanship of the players who fill the first four

---

[15] Ironmonger's unorthodox left-arm action may have had something to do with the fact that he had lost the forefinger of his left hand.

or five places in an England or county eleven may not be so high as it used to be twenty or more years ago, after No. 6 in the batting order in first-class cricket there has been a very marked improvement. In most cases even Nos. 10 and 11 can keep up an end in emergencies, though they frequently do not trouble to do so, unless there is a good batsman set at the other end.

In these days there would be many a welcome wait for the horses, who, if we may believe the old story, would of themselves start their weary journey between the roller-shafts as the tail-enders went in to bat.

I imagine that one of the best examples of a player adapting his methods to modern conditions is Hobbs. Though I cannot speak from personal knowledge, there can be little doubt that, by the reduction of much of his pre-war brilliance on the off side, Hobbs added much to the soundness of his play and the total number of his runs.

As long as the bowler can make the ball move away from the bat, whether from atmospheric conditions or the newness of the ball, there will always be a tendency for the batsmen to walk across, covering their wickets with their legs and leaving the ball severely alone.

Chiefly, I imagine, on account of this tendency, Larwood during the 1928–29 tour in Australia from time to time attempted a form of leg-theory, though without packing the on side. The results, judged either as a means of taking wickets or retarding the rate of scoring, were the reverse of satisfactory. In the words of a member of the Australian Board of Control, "Whenever he [Larwood] started bowling leg-theory four years ago we reckoned he had shot his bolt."

Now, leg-theory is more effective in Australia than in England for two reasons. Owing to the atmospheric conditions, it is not possible to make even a new ball swerve to anything like the degree that is possible in England; and the new ball itself loses all its shine after three or four overs on an Australian ground. There is, therefore, more call and scope for any substitute for off-theory.

As a striking instance of this fact it may be interesting to recall that in 1928–29 it was not until the fourth Test match of that series that we got a catch in the slips – this with Larwood, Tate, and Geary, all of whom can make the ball swerve away from the batsman in England, even after 50 or 100 runs have been scored with it.

Though I did not take part in the last Test match against Australia at the Oval in 1930, I have been told on all sides that Bradman's innings, impressive though it was in the number of runs scored, was far from convincing on the leg stump whilst there was any life in the wicket – this in very marked contrast to Jackson, who was batting at the other end.

I am sorry to disappoint anyone who has imagined that the leg-theory was evolved with the help of midnight oil and iced towels, simply and solely for the purpose of combating Bradman's effective-ness as a scoring machine. However highly Bradman may have been rated, this view is exaggerated.

It did, however, seem a reasonable assumption that a weakness in one of Australia's premier batsmen might find more than a replica in the play of a good many of his contemporaries, some of whom had doubtless modelled their play on his.

In view of our experiences in 1928–29, I myself was not inclined to rate the possibilities of leg-theory very highly. Although, as I have

THE FIELD FOR LEG-THEORY

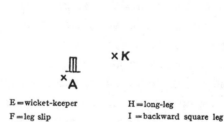

A = bowler	E = wicket-keeper	H = long-leg
B = cover mid-off	F = leg slip	I = backward square leg
C = third man	G = 2nd leg slip or deep square leg	J = forward square leg
D = gully		K = mid-on

already said, I was not present at the last Test match at the Oval in 1930, my past experiences of the Australians had given me a very healthy respect for their play off the leg stump. I had never imagined that leg theory would stand such a test as would prove its effectiveness throughout the whole tour, but I did hope that it might occasionally prove a profitable variation when two batsmen were well set.

Accordingly, I impressed two important facts upon our bowlers. The first, sufficiently obvious, was that in the event of their giving leg-theory a try, it was folly to have anything but a skeleton field on the off side.

No bowler yet has been able to set his field for both off and leg-theory, without losing half the efficiency of both systems. If there is any attempt at compromise, gaps in the field must be the inevitable result.

The second, and only other principle I ventured to suggest was that it was all-important that they should not jeopardize the safety of the death-or-glory fieldsmen – the so-called "suicide-squad" – for the only danger which I saw in leg-theory was the perilous position in which the nearest fieldsmen, stationed respectively in front of and behind square leg, were necessarily placed.

I impressed upon our bowlers that an in-fieldsman had only to be cut over once, to rob him of the confidence which enabled him not only to stand close to the bat, but to do so on the tips of his toes. Once let him lose this confidence, and he would always be tending to edge away with his weight on his heels.

Larwood's accuracy was almost miraculous, and never once was a fieldsman cut over through any fault of the bowler.

While Australian wickets have changed considerably, even in the four years of my experience, they are still better than the best English wickets.

Partly, it may be supposed, with the idea of rendering them more receptive to spin, or, perhaps, with the idea of toning them down, a top dressing of Glen Roy soil has, in many cases, been added.

Where four years ago the ball seemed to slide or skid off the wicket, now there is more tendency for it to bite and pursue a parabolic course. That this assists the very best type of fast bowler seems probable, just as it tends to assist the slow spin-bowler.

What, then, were the main objections to leg-theory? Generally speaking, I think they amounted to three – (1) that the batsman objected to the short ball which gets up, (2) to the length ball which lifts, and (3) that leg-theory slowed down the game by depriving the batsman of opportunities to practise his repertoire of attractive strokes.

Let me take these objections *seriatim*.

First, then, if a batsman of International class seriously objects to a short ball bumping, one can only suggest, with great deference but in all sincerity, that if he cannot cope with this ball with the bat, or leave it alone, he would be well advised to consider the desirability of making way for rising talent which not only can, but will, deal effectively with this type of ball.

Secondly, if his objection is to the good-length ball which lifts, one is, I think, entitled to ask what, if anything, he would allow a fast bowler to do, or try to do? The ability to make a good-length ball lift on modern wickets, apart from its rarity, is one of the strongest suits in any fast bowler's hand. If he is to be deprived of this, cricket really should not be played with a hard ball. Nor does it seem to matter if leg- or off-theory is being bowled, since the modern batsman's tendency to cover up his wicket will bring him into the danger zone in either case.

Some people suggest that the batsman has no right to do this.[16] With these critics I am, I am afraid, at utter variance, but I will go far down the road with them when they say that if the batsman covers up, and does not use his bat for the purpose for which it is presumably intended, and in the process is hit with the ball, he should be the last person in the world to complain.

Finally, on æsthetic grounds, let me say once and for all that leg-theory, properly played, entails no subtraction from the batsman's repertoire of strokes.

---

[16] In 1933, batsmen could not be out lbw to a ball not pitching directly between the two sets of stumps; two years later, after half a century of debate, the law was altered to its present form.

The rate of scoring off leg-theory bowling is appreciably greater than the rate possible with the same degree of safety when the bowler is exploiting off-theory, but, if this assurance is not enough, it may comfort the critics to know that very few bowlers can hope to bowl the leg-theory which we are discussing with success, on account of the great pace, and the tremendous accuracy of direction and length which this theory demands. Even then the Tyldesleys, McCabes and Bradmans can overcome all this, and from the alarming rate of scoring and the variety of shots possible against leg-theory force the fielding side to abandon it and return to off-theory in less than two overs.

Badly bowled leg-theory, consisting of occasional long-hops, full pitches, and half-volleys, must surely be the batsman's dream come true.

With the realization of the batsman's dream the fieldsman's nightmare begins!

Few lovers of the game have more respect for Australian batsmanship than myself. Few have better cause or surer grounds for this respect; but, while holding these views, I hope I am not being ungenerous or over-critical if I say that the Australian batsman of today is scarcely equal to the representatives of past generations in his ability to play fast bowling.

Macartney, Ryder and Bardsley[17], to take at random only three names from recent cricket history, would, in my opinion, have made very short work of leg-theory.

I doubt whether the present giants would claim to be great players of fast bowling in a year in which Wall, the Australian fast bowler, could bowl out the whole of the strongest batting State in Australia (New South Wales, winners of the Sheffield Shield), taking all ten wickets for a paltry 36 runs.[18]

---

[17] C.G. Macartney (1886–1958) reached his peak as a batsman in the years following the First World War. His diminutive stature belied the power of his stroke-play: in 1921 he scored 345 in a single day against Notts.; J. Ryder (1889/90–1977), an attacking right-handed batsman, once caused a fielder who had tried to catch one of his on drives to faint with pain; W. Bardsley (1883–1954) was a left-handed batsmen who performed notably well during Australia's 1909 tour of England: in the 5th Test he scored a century in each innings.

[18] Wall was the best Australian bowler of the series, with 16 wickets at an average of 25.5; he dismissed DRJ twice.

In order that the reader may have an opportunity of judging whether or no these views are peculiar to myself, I am quoting some extracts, the first from an interview with the old Australian captain, Jack Ryder, who captained Australia on the occasion of the M.C.C. visit in 1928, and an interesting article by Arthur Mailey, in which leg-theory and off-theory are compared and contrasted.

The *Sporting Globe,* of Melbourne, contained the following:

Ryder does not see how leg-theory can be abolished. "Slow and medium-pace bowlers can exploit it, so why not fast bowlers?" he asked. Jack realizes that a fast-flying ball on the leg stump is nasty, but he does not think that protests and squeamishness will do any good.

"I have not changed my opinion that leg-theory for any type of bowler is quite legitimate," he said. "A captain can place the field where he desires.

"England taught us a tactical lesson with the success of the leg-theory for the fast bowler, and we have to learn it."

Ryder has the greatest respect for the men who control English cricket and their judgment, and he does not think that they would condone any type of play that is contrary to the best interests of the game.

"Cricket is a duel between bat and ball. In recent years the bat has been well on top. Now that the ball has come back, the change has unsettled many people. Leg-theory has been overcome at times by our batsmen during the Tests, proving that it can be dealt with."

Ryder believes it is essential that men occupying big positions in Australian cricket control should have had a close association with the actual game. Then there would be little likelihood of anything foolish being done on vital matters.

He deplores the possibilities of young cricketers of the future growing up afraid of fast bowling because of the fuss that has arisen around Larwood.

"Our young cricketers have to stand up and face fast bowling. It does not matter what theory is being bowled," he stated.

He also contended that greater concentration was required by young men coming on, and that they should study the finer points. In Test cricket Australians had thrown away too many wickets.

It was his candid opinion that until our cricketers overcome the fast bowling bogy, Australian cricket would be at a standstill.

Arthur Mailey, of the *Sydney Sun,* wrote as follows:

After watching two days of the Brisbane Test I am convinced that cricket has changed with the times, and that fast leg-theory bowling is the aftermath of peace. I mean that no longer will thousands of people sit and watch futile-looking off-side deliveries pass without some outward sign of indignation.

On Saturday we had good samples of the much-discussed body-line bowling, and the more sedate off-theory attack. I really should not call it "attack"; "compromise" would be a much better word.

On Friday the air was electrical; everybody was on the tiptoe of excitement, waiting for something dramatic to happen. They did not want sedate and apologetic glances between slip fieldsmen; they merely wanted action, something new, something that had a flavour of modernity about it. When Larwood took up the ball to bowl his first over, one felt it difficult to suppress a peculiar feeling that comes before every climax.

A moment before, in the Press box where I was sitting, journalists had their heads down, shooting thoughts to all parts of the world; typewriters and telegraph operators were tapping merrily. But when Larwood picked up the ball to bowl the noise suddenly stopped. Spectators, who a moment before were fiddling with cushions and discussing subjects far removed from cricket, sat upright and stared at the arena as though they expected the end of the world, or something.

I could go on in this strain indefinitely, and describe an atmosphere which can be felt nowhere excepting at a cricket match, but it would not help the story.

Larwood bowled, and each ball was received with enthusiasm, whether it had been clouted, played with an undesigning bat, or allowed to whistle past without notice. And this went on right throughout the Australian innings.

Friday's cricket was the most interesting day's cricket I have seen, not because many runs were made – in fact, it was a low-scoring day – but because a new interest had forced its way into cricket, and that interest was fast leg-theory bowling.

Let us forget, if we can, the drama of Friday's cricket, and think of lion-hearted Tim Wall opening the attack on Douglas Jardine and Herbert Sutcliffe on Saturday.

Saturday's cricket lacked that intensity that was so apparent on Friday. It drifted down into a negative affair that merely meandered on until darkness happily put an end to the proceedings. I have never appreciated a premature sunset so much before; the game literally died on the players' hands, and they carried the corpse into the dressing-room and left it there, to be forgotten for the time being.

The introduction of fast leg-theory has done all this. It has whetted our appetites for something sparkling, virile, and risky.

After watching the Brisbane test, I am inclined to think that a certain amount of money has been wasted on cables lately[19] – I am not referring to those used for newspapers, business deals, or for birthday messages!

Just for the moment I am trying to express the spectators' subconscious reaction to leg-theory rather than ridicule off-theory.

Off-theory has had its uses, just as crinolines had, some fifty years ago. Whether we go back to crinolines is a matter for the Board of Control.

---

[19] After the 3rd Test, the Board of Control sent a cable to the M.C.C., accusing the English players of bad sportsmanship. See Appendix (p. 173) for this and the ensuing 'Cable Rubber'.

8

The First Test Match

(At Sydney, December 2–7. England won by ten wickets)

There is no pretending that the First Test Match of an Australian Tour is not a nerve-wracking affair, perhaps even more for the old hands than for the new. The former have more of the anxiety without the compensating excitement and novelty, which helps to take the edge off some of the new hands' nerves.

An Australian, famous not only for his prowess, but also for his manly form, has given it as his considered opinion that with anything like a normal distribution of luck it should be possible, before a ball has been bowled, for a good judge to pick the winning side nearly every time.

I only once asked him to put his theory into practice. This was before the First Test Match at Brisbane in 1928. On that occasion he preferred to hedge. He contented himself with saying that with two such indifferent sides anything might happen. As England won that match by no less than 675 runs he could at least claim that he was about the only successful prophet.

The sides finally selected for the First Test Match were:

AUSTRALIA: H. M. Woodfull, W. H. Ponsford, V. Y. Richardson, A. F. Kippax, S. J. McCabe, J. H. Fingleton, W. A. Oldfield, C. V. Grimmett, T. W. Wall, W. J. O'Reilly, L. E. Nagel, S. Hird (12th).

ENGLAND: D. R. Jardine, R. E. S. Wyatt, H. Sutcliffe, W. R. Hammond, Nawab of Pataudi, M. Leyland, L. E. G. Ames, G. O. Allen, H. Larwood, W. Voce, H. Verity, E. Paynter (12th).

In the capacity of a Selector it is extraordinarily interesting to try to put oneself in the other fellow's shoes, and, having made up one's mind what he is aiming at, to set about countering his moves to the best of one's ability with the available material. I analysed the Australian side as follows:

5 batsmen, pure and simple: Woodfull, Ponsford, Richardson, Kippax and Fingleton.

4 bowlers: Grimmett, O'Reilly, Wall and Nagel. i all-rounder: McCabe, and the wicket-keeper, Oldfield.

Against this, England took into the field:

5 batsmen, pure and simple: Sutcliffe, Wyatt, Pataudi, Leyland and Jardine (though two of these, Wyatt and Leyland, have from time to time bowled with a certain amount of success).

I bowler, pure and simple: Voce, and

4 all-rounders: Hammond, Larwood, Allen, and Verity, with a batsman wicket-keeper in Ames.

For the purposes of comparison, let us assume that a char-a-banc containing the first five batsmen on either side fell over a cliff, and that the remaining dozen players played the match six-a-side. I do not think that there can be any two opinions as to which side would have won, and won easily.

All of the six remaining Englishmen, with one solitary exception, were not only capable of making runs against the best Australian bowling, but, in fact, did so, whereas on the Australian side McCabe, the solitary all-rounder, was the only one who could claim any success with the bat.

On record, and particularly as Australia was without Bradman, we were, I think, stronger from Nos. 1 – 5 than our opponents but, be that as it may, on form at least, our strength from Nos. 6 – 11 was preponderating and decisive.

For the first and, alas, not the last time in the series, I lost the toss. Winning the toss in Australia is generally estimated as being worth between 100 and 150 runs to a side, except at Melbourne on what used to be a Melbourne wicket.

One of the Australian batsmen, who had played against us for the Australian XI in Melbourne, had been at great pains to assure our fast bowlers that they would be unable to make the ball rise knee-high at Sydney.

Ironmonger of Victoria, who had been a strong candidate for the Australian side, was omitted at the last moment, largely, I imagine, owing to his record on the Sydney Ground, which is not very convincing. As it turned out, there is little doubt that the Australian Selectors would have been well advised to include him instead of Nagel. Personally, I confess I was relieved by his exclusion.

Ironmonger, with his peculiar action, can keep on operating at one end for the better part of a day, and although he is not a dangerous bowler on an ordinary wicket, his accuracy saves him from being properly collared and punished; and while he keeps one end going the attacking bowlers can exercise their imaginations at the other end.

Had it rained during the course of the match, as was prophesied, the Australian Selection Committee would no doubt have suffered much caustic comment on account of Ironmonger's omission.

After our batting failure at Melbourne, we determined to strengthen our batting by playing Ames in preference to Duckworth. Had Ames struck a bad patch with the gloves we should, no doubt, have had our share of criticism. With this exception, I do not think that our selections were open to question.

THE FIRST DAY

Two performances stood out in Australia's first innings – Larwood's bowling and McCabe's batting.

The first two overs did little to encourage us. Neither Larwood nor Voce seemed capable of getting any assistance or life out of the wicket; but in his second over, Larwood made a length ball fly, which Woodfull was lucky to miss when playing a sparring shot on the off side in the direction of three hungry slips and a gully.

Voce, too, seemed to get more life out of the wicket as he loosened up, and was eventually responsible for the dismissal of Woodfull, who was playing a shot similar to the one I have already mentioned – a shot quite unworthy of Woodfull at his best.

That was the extent of our success before lunch, though neither Fingleton nor Ponsford was ever comfortable.

After lunch, things began to happen, and from 63 runs for one wicket at the interval, the huge scoring board read 87 for 4.

In an inspired spell, Larwood had captured the wickets of Ponsford, Fingleton and Kippax for 7 runs, his full figures being 3 for 20.

Here was the first crisis: Larwood was finished for the time being, and everything depended upon maintaining the pressure. I said as much to Allen as I gave him the ball. Now Allen did so well subsequently that I know he will not mind my saying that on this occasion he bowled far below his true form, and what appeared to be a decisive early advantage gradually began to slip away.

McCabe and Richardson, with their backs to the wall, played magnificent cricket, and never looked seriously like getting out, though McCabe survived a very confident appeal for leg before wicket in Larwood's last over before tea. These two batsmen were destined to stay together until very nearly the close of play, but just before the end Richardson played an unworthy shot and presented Hammond with an easy chance off Voce at square leg.

Many people were inclined to criticize Richardson for playing a schoolboy shot from over-anxiety to get his 50. Certainly, the ball was not a very good one, but it is so easy to play cricket from the pavilion; and, personally, I think that it was just one of those unaccountable things which happen, and that Richardson was the unfortunate one to whom it happened.

Oldfield, who came in and presented a very straight bat with every intention of playing out time, was out to a good catch at the wicket off Larwood, who, throughout the day, had bowled with wonderful stamina and determination.

Grimmett, who followed, gave hopes of a catch to the slips which did not materialize, and, just before the close of play, a better fieldsman than myself might have caught McCabe at square leg from a hook off Larwood.

290 for 6 was the score at "stumps" – a vastly different affair from 87 for 4, and, adding on at least a hundred runs for the advantage of winning the toss, it was clear that Australia had pulled herself out of a nasty mess and once again proved her capacity to fight back.

After tea, the crowd was in high fettle. Rounds of applause greeted each fresh score by McCabe and Richardson, the applause being in marked contrast to the volume attending Larwood's first devastating spell of success, when we experienced the nearest approach to silence which I can remember in an Australian Test Match.

McCabe had a thunderous and well-merited reception on his return to the pavilion, undefeated at the close of the day's play.

To sum up, then, the match at the end of the first day was very much alive. Our bowling, with the exception of Larwood and Voce, had scarcely been up to the mark. Allen, Verity and Hammond had presented little difficulty, though Hammond had on several occasions beaten the batsmen, narrowly missing the wicket.

The English fielding throughout the day had been excellent. Indeed, the improvement in this department had been very marked since the first Victorian match.

It was, of course, early in the season for Australia, and the grounds had in some cases failed to make their usual recovery from the football season. This is upsetting to any side, but while admitting that our fielding at Melbourne was too bad to be true, it was obvious that we should have to take steps, and drastic steps if necessary, to ensure an improvement. Several doses of practice, and a specialization of certain individuals in certain places, which they kept throughout the Tour, produced startling and highly gratifying results.

THE SECOND DAY

The second day was a batsman's day throughout. Continuing with his score from 127 not out, McCabe took his courage in his hands and went for the runs, which came at an alarming rate.

Nothing succeeds like success, and McCabe was on the crest of a wave. Two or three times the ball just cleared a fieldsman standing in the deep, but not quite deep enough. I was to blame for this, as, thinking that we were more likely to get him out off a mishit than from a full-blooded blow, I had placed the fieldsman some twenty yards from the pickets; but not, I should add, out of the range of any orange peel for which the spectators had no further use.

Our first success was not long in coming, for with the addition of two runs to his score and nine runs to the overnight total, Grimmett fell to a good catch at the wicket by Ames off Voce.

The addition of one run, which hoisted the 300 onto the scoreboard, saw Nagel clean bowled by Larwood, and five runs later Voce clean bowled O'Reilly for 4.

For Grimmett, Nagel, and O'Reilly, the slips were so crammed that I do not know whether a stickler for accuracy would describe the place in which I was fielding as the gully, backward point, or fifth slip.

With nine wickets down for 305, we appeared to have taken a firm grip of the game again, but there followed a truly magnificent last-wicket stand. These are the occasions, these the performances, such as McCabe's and Wall's, which give to cricket so much of its fitful and amazing charm. These two batsmen gave the spectators a treat which can hardly ever have been equalled, and certainly never excelled, on the Sydney Ground. The last wicket added 55 priceless runs, and though McCabe was taking many chances, there seemed no particular reason why he should ever get out.

In vain we switched from off- to leg-theory, only to find that he hit harder than ever, and, though we did our best to keep him away from the bowling, and managed to have several good spells at Wall, the latter remained as steady as a rock.

Both batsmen ran between the wickets with real intelligence. It is no exaggeration to say that Wall's 4 runs were worth as much as many another's 50. Eventually, Hammond succeeded in dismissing him, Allen taking a really good catch.

During this hectic twenty-five minutes there was every excuse for the fielding side to become rattled. The fact that we did not was about our only satisfaction, except for the thrill which every cricketer must feel in acknowledging a really outstanding performance of skill and grit, even if it is at his own expense.

I hope I am not detracting in any way from this performance when I say that, throughout the innings, after Larwood's first great spell on the field, our bowlers had been exceedingly unfortunate. With ordinary luck to help them, we might well have had Australia out for nearer 200 than 250 runs.

England's first innings, in contrast to Australia's, contained comparatively few major thrills. Three batsmen were destined to pass the century mark, but the general course of play must have seemed serene and workmanlike rather than sparkling and full of incident.

From the start, Sutcliffe scored freely. If, throughout the Tour, Sutcliffe, did not enjoy the unfailing success which has hitherto been his in Test match cricket, it was not due to any falling off of form.

Throughout the Tour it was clear that he missed his old partner[1] at the other end, and the responsibility of being the senior instead of the junior partner must often have weighed on his mind.

Sutcliffe was criticized for going slow during much of the second half of his innings. He was playing under instructions, and, though I am anticipating, I take this opportunity of saying that the responsibility for those instructions were mine, and mine alone, and right nobly did Sutcliffe carry them out to the letter. That this policy of caution proved right in the end is neither here nor there, and Sutcliffe can look back with a smile on being one of a select few to have been criticized for making only 194 runs.

That such criticism should rankle with Sutcliffe and many other Yorkshiremen seems only natural to me, in view of its source. Critics who have the courtesy of the dressing-room extended to them (and this means far more in Australia than in England) have no one to

[1] Sir John Berry (Jack) Hobbs (1882–1963), who had retired from Test cricket after the 1930 Ashes, at the age of 47. Altogether, he and Sutcliffe made 26 opening stands of 100 or more, including 15 in Test Matches.

blame but themselves if their words *gang agley*[2]; for, with access to the dressing-room, ignorance of the tactics to be employed cannot be pleaded.

The responsibility for those tactics can only be the captain's.

The first wicket produced 112 runs – a grand start, for which half the credit must be given to Wyatt, who played his usual steady game in his most assured manner.

Both O'Reilly and Grimmett bowled extremely steadily and had him in difficulties from time to time, but he rarely failed to meet the ball with the centre of a very straight bat. Eventually, he appeared to miss sight of one of Grimmett's flighty deliveries, and, giving the impression of tangling his bat with one of his pads, played outside the ball and was out leg before wicket.

Until Hammond broke the record Test Match score in New Zealand[3], he must have considered Sydney his happy hunting-ground. It was here, four years ago, in the Second Test Match of that series that he made his first double century against Australia.

I am not a believer in the popular superstition that cricketers are lucky on certain grounds – "Horses for courses," as they say in Australia – but, assuredly, Hammond's past deeds on this historic ground will stand him in good stead when he bats there again.

For a time he was unusually restrained. Just before Wyatt got out, Sutcliffe had played a ball from O'Reilly on to his legs, from where it had dribbled on to the wicket without disturbing a bail.

Perhaps Hammond felt that we should not further tempt Providence, but one over from Grimmett in which he punctured the covers three times, twice on the full drive and once with that amazing shot off his back foot – a combination of drive, cut, and slash – put him on good terms with himself, and from that moment until the new ball quietened him down at 200, he gave the Australian fieldsmen little peace, and the bowlers less encouragement.

One hundred and fifty runs had come in under 140 minutes.

[2] 'go awry' (Scots)
[3] Hammond made 336 in the Third Test at Auckland (31st March–3rd April 1933), breaking Bradman's record of 334, set at Headingley in 1930.

ILLUSTRATION

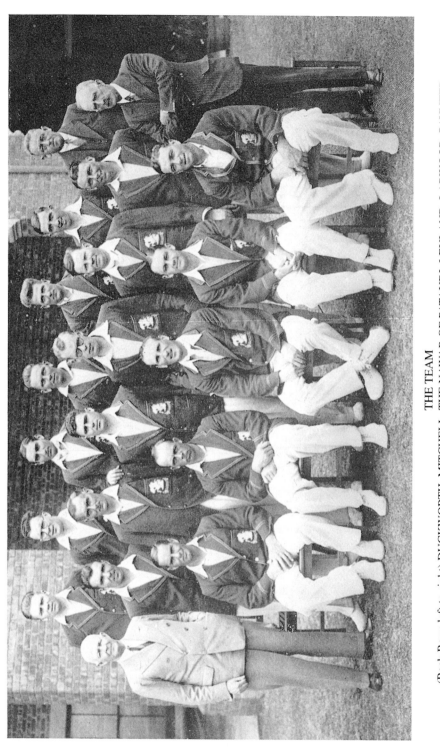

THE TEAM

(Back Row: left to right) DUCKWORTH, MITCHELL, THE NAWAB OF PATAUDI, LEYLAND, LARWOOD, PAYNTER, W. FERGUSON (Scorer)

(Centre Row: left to right) P. F. WARNER, AMES, VERITY, VOCE, BOWES, F. R. BROWN, TATE, R. PALAIRET.

(Sitting: left to right) SUTCLIFFE, R. E. S. WYATT, D. R. JARDINE, G. O. ALLEN, and HAMMOND

LARWOOD BOWLING – A FINE "ACTION" STUDY

WOODFULL, AUSTRALIA'S CAPTAIN, CAUGHT BY DUCKWORTH OFF LARWOOD FOR A "DUCK" IN THE MATCH BETWEEN THE MCC AND AN AUSTRALIAN XI AT MELBOURNE, NOVEMBER 22. THE WICKETKEEPER IS THROWING THE BALL UP IN DELIGHT

MR D. R. JARDINE

FIRST TEST MATCH – VOCE, IN THE SLIPS, JUMPS AT A BALL FROM THE BAT OF MCCABE, WHO MADE 187 NOT OUT

FIRST TEST MATCH – MCCABE ON THE WAY TO HIS CENTURY

[Central Press
Photo]

SYDNEY'S VAST CRICKET GROUND. AN AERIAL PICTURE DURING THE FIRST TEST MATCH. THE BIG SCORE BOARD IS IN THE BACKGROUND ON THE HILL, THE BARRACKERS' STRONGHOLD

FIRST TEST MATCH: CENTURY MAKERS – SUTCLIFFE (LEFT) AND HAMMOND

Photo]

[*Central Press*

FIRST TEST MATCH – G. O. ALLEN STRUCK BY A BALL FROM NAGEL.
OLDFIELD GOES TO HIS AID

FIRST TEST MATCH – SUTCLIFFE, IN SCORING 194, HAD A SLICE OF LUCK AT 43. A BALL TRICKLED FROM BAT TO WICKET WITHOUT DISLODGING THE BAILS. MCCABE (FACING THE CAMERA) BETRAYS HIS FEELINGS

FIRST TEST MATCH – THE NAWAB OF PATAUDI, AFTER SCORING A CENTURY IN HIS FIRST INNINGS AGAINST AUSTRALIA, IS BOWLED BY NAGEL

FIRST TEST MATCH – ENGLAND NEEDED TO SCORE ONE RUN FOR VICTORY IN THE LAST INNINGS. SUTCLIFFE RIGHTLY HAD THE HONOUR OF MAKING THE WINNING STROKE

PLANS ON THE FIELD – AN ENGLISH GROUP AT THE FALL OF AN AUSTRALIAN WICKET

SECOND TEST MATCH – BRADMAN BOWLED FIRST BALL BY BOWES

SECOND TEST MATCH – RICHARDSON TRIES TO CATCH SUTCLIFFE

Only when Sutcliffe was in the 90s was there an anxious moment. A misunderstanding between the batsmen might have caused a run-out if Ponsford had been a little quicker in gathering and returning the ball.

At the close of play these two were still together – 252 for one – with Sutcliffe's score at 116. Sutcliffe had resisted all temptation to "have a go" after reaching his eighth Test Match century against Australia.

THE THIRD DAY

I feel sure that the Australian bowlers had been grateful for their Sunday's rest, while we, in our turn, were thankful that the rain which had been prophesied and seemed probable had held off.

It was clearly our policy to leave ourselves as few runs as possible to get in the fourth innings by piling on the agony in the first. Time and again, England teams, accustomed to time-limited cricket[4], have frittered away an advantage that has been hard won by the spade-work of the early batsmen.

I like to think that we had at least as accurate an appreciation of the requirements of Test Matches played to a finish as any side which has done battle for St. George and the Dragon in the past.

It is a curious coincidence that the only three Indian batsmen who have played for England all made a century in their first Test Match against Australia. Pataudi was following in the footsteps of the great K. S. Ranjitsinhji and his nephew, K. S. Duleepsinhji, who should have been with us.

The day's play turned our score from 252 for one to 479 for six. Hammond was out first – unluckily caught at cover point off Nagel. The handle of his bat – the rubber grip of which had worked loose – slipped round in his hand and deprived the stroke of its accuracy.

Sutcliffe's innings ended for 194 after seven and a quarter hours of batting. He was leg before wicket to Wall off a ball which kept unexpectedly low.

---

[4] The Ashes Tests in 1932–3 were played to a finish, irrespective of the time taken.

Pataudi was blamed in some quarters for the slowness of his play. Again, criticism seemed scarcely generous. A young player who makes a hundred in his first Test Match is entitled to little but praise, and it was up to Leyland and myself, who followed in the batting order, to push the score along, seeing that one end was so firmly held by Pataudi, who at close of play was not out 80.

THE FOURTH DAY

Next morning, Pataudi, clothed on his way to the ground in the same garments he had worn the previous day, even to such details as collar, tie, and handkerchief, achieved his ambition by completing his century. His clothing was "just so" to satisfy a cricketing superstition.

The remaining batsmen, however, failed rather ignominiously, though Leyland was unfortunate in the manner of his dismissal.

Throughout our innings, which closed for 524, Grimmett and O'Reilly had worked like Trojans. Between them they bowled 131 overs, 54 of which were maidens. Neither Wall, Nagel, nor McCabe was in his best form, though Wall's three wickets for 104 was no mean performance for a fast bowler, on a Sydney wicket, in an innings of over 500 runs.

The beginning of Australia's second innings was almost a repetition of her first. With only 2 runs on the board, Larwood clean bowled Woodfull with a very fast in-swinging yorker.

At this stage of the Tour, as I have said, Woodfull was neither in full practice nor in first-class health. This seemed to make him unusually slow and ponderous in his movements, but the ball which our Nottingham Express provided for his undoing might have dismissed any batsman, particularly when it is remembered that the ball swerves little enough at any time in Australia, and that Larwood's usual tendency is to swerve away from rather than into the batsman.

With the score at 10, and Fingleton shaping well, Ponsford was clean bowled round his legs by what appeared to be a very simple half-volley from Voce.

McCabe was given a wonderful reception when he came in to bat. Two of their best batsmen gone, and Australia still 150 behind. McCabe had been sent in instead of Kippax and scored a single off his first ball.

In Larwood's next over, Fingleton survived a confident appeal for leg before wicket. For some reason best known to himself, he ducked at a ball which did not rise half-stump high. Had the verdict been against him, he would have looked supremely ridiculous.

McCabe hit Voce for a magnificent 6, which momentarily put the crowd on the best of terms with themselves and their new champion. The score mounted steadily to 60 for two.

I had brought Hammond on to bowl just before this. I said to him, as I had said to Allen in the first innings, that now or never was the time. I felt that in the short time left us that day it should be possible to keep up the pressure until the close of play, but that in order to do so I should give Larwood a really good rest. Then, if all went well, I proposed, for once in a way, to bowl him right out.

Seldom can a bowler have made a better response. Hammond took 2 wickets for 2 runs. A well-disguised slow ball had McCabe all at sea and palpably leg before wicket, and off the very next ball Voce caught Richardson at first slip. The manner of his dismissal was a trifle unlucky, as the ball glanced off the wicket-keeper's pad straight into Voce's hands. For a moment Richardson was unsighted, and, not knowing what had happened, stood looking at the umpire. I had visions of another "Kippax incident", but we were spared that.

Larwood had his rest, and returning like a giant refreshed took the wickets of Kippax, Oldfield, Fingleton, and Grimmett in rapid succession.

We were left with about twenty minutes to get the last pair out, but Nagel and Wall put up an unexpectedly stout resistance. Larwood, though very tired, still looked like taking a wicket at any time, but for all that I think he was kept on too long.

Off the last ball but one of the day Verity should have got his first Test Match wicket against Australia, but Ames made his only blunder and missed a chance of stumping Nagel. The next ball yielded one run, thereby robbing England of an innings victory.

THE FIFTH DAY

The end came quietly next morning, with no addition to the score. Allen bowled a maiden over, and it was left to Voce, with the third ball of his first over, to spreadeagle O'Reilly's stumps.

Though the gates had been thrown open to the public free, the "Hill", usually packed to its full capacity during a Test Match, boasted but one solitary spectator, who, in the words of the song, had "brought his dog", though he did not propose to mow a meadow. He was the centre of far greater interest than were the cricketers. One of the English side succeeded in smuggling a camera on to the field to snapshot the "lone watcher", who, feeling the burden of Australian barracking honours sitting heavily upon his shoulders, did once venture the opinion that we should "never get them out".

Only one ball was necessary to give England a 10-wickets victory. The full scores follow.

AUSTRALIA – FIRST INNINGS

W. M. Woodfull, c Ames, b Voce	7
W. H. Ponsford, b Larwood	32
J. H. Fingleton, c Allen, b Larwood	26
A. F. Kippax, lbw, b Larwood	8
S. J. McCabe, not out	187
V. Y. Richardson, c Hammond, b Voce	49
W. A. Oldfield, c Ames, b Larwood	4
C. V. Grimmett, c Ames, b Voce	19
L. Nagel, b Larwood	0
W. J. O'Reilly, b Voce	4
T. W. Wall, c Allen, b Hammond	4
Extras	20
Total	360

FALL OF THE WICKETS – FIRST INNINGS

1	2	3	4	5	6	7	8	9	10
22	65	82	87	216	231	299	300	305	360

BOWLING ANALYSIS – FIRST INNINGS

	O.	M.	R.	W.
Larwood	31	5	96	5
Voce	29	4	110	4
Allen	15	1	65	0
Hammond	14.2	0	34	1
Verity	13	4	35	0

Voce bowled 3 no-balls and Larwood 1.

ENGLAND – FIRST INNINGS

H. Sutcliffe, lbw, b Wall	194
R. E. S. Wyatt, lbw, b Grimmett	38
W. R. Hammond, c Grimmett, b Nagel	112
Nawab of Pataudi, b Nagel	102
M. Leyland, c Oldfield, b Wall	0
D. R. Jardine, c Oldfield, b McCabe	27
H. Verity, lbw, b Wall	2
G. O. Allen, c and b O'Reilly	19
L. Ames, c McCabe, b O'Reilly	0
H. Larwood, lbw, b O'Reilly	0
W. Voce, not out	0
Extras	30
Total	524

FALL OF THE WICKETS – FIRST INNINGS

1	2	3	4	5	6	7	8	9	10
112	300	423	423	470	479	518	522	522	524

BOWLING ANALYSIS – FIRST INNINGS

	O.	M.	R.	W.
Wall	38	4	104	3
Nagel	43.4	9	110	2
O'Reilly	67	32	117	3
McCabe	15	2	42	1
Grimmett	64	21	118	1
Kippax	2	1	3	0

Wall and O'Reilly each bowled 3 no-balls.

AUSTRALIA – SECOND INNINGS

W. M. Woodfull, b Larwood	0
W. H. Ponsford, b Voce	2
J. H. Fingleton, c Voce, b Larwood	40
S. J. McCabe, lbw, b Hammond	32
V. Y. Richardson, c Voce, b Hammond	0
A. F. Kippax, b Larwood	19
W. A. Oldfield, c Leyland, b Larwood	1
C. V. Grimmett, c Allen, b Larwood	5
L. Nagel, not out	21
T. W. Wall, c Ames, b Allen	20
W. J. O'Reilly, b Voce	7
Extras	17
Total	164

FALL OF THE WICKETS – SECOND INNINGS

1	*2*	*3*	*4*	*5*	*6*	*7*	*8*	*9*	*10*
2	10	61	61	100	104	105	113	151	164

BOWLING ANALYSIS – SECOND INNINGS

	O.	*M.*	*R.*	*W.*
Larwood	18	4	28	5
Voce	17.3	5	54	2
Allen	9	5	13	1
Hammond	15	6	37	2
Verity	4	1	15	0

Voce 1 no-ball; Allen 1 no-ball and 1 wide.

ENGLAND – SECOND INNINGS

H. Sutcliffe, not out	1
R. E. S. Wyatt, not out	0
Total (no wkt.)	1

Bowling: McCabe 0–1.

9

The Second Test Match

(At Melbourne, December 30 – January 3. Australia won by 111 runs)

There had been a rather long interval between the First and Second Test Matches. Four years before, there had been no such interval, with the result that the Australian Selectors were placed in a difficult position in that they lacked both time and opportunity to reorganize a side which had been overwhelmingly defeated in the First Test.

On this occasion the Selectors were afforded plenty of time, and though from their point of view the result ultimately proved satisfactory, the preliminaries can have given satisfaction to no one. The fact that until the morning of the second match the Australian captain did not know whether he was to lead the side, or indeed whether he was to play at all, would appear to indicate considerable divergence of opinion, which savoured unpleasantly of panic.

To those of us who knew Woodfull's record as an International cricketer[1], such hesitation seemed well-nigh incredible. I do not think that the Board of Control would have survived, at least in its existing form, had its Selection Committee been ungenerous enough to drop Woodfull, either as captain or player. That feelings were running high may be gathered from the following paragraph from *The Australasian*, headed "An Undercurrent of Feeling":

The Board, whose members are unknown when cricket is the subject

---

[1] W.M. Woodfull (1897–1965) captained Australia in 25 of the 35 Test Matches in which he played, averaging 46.00 with the bat. Known as 'The Great Unbowlable', he once played two full seasons without permitting the ball to hit his wicket.

under discussion, are no doubt doing their best for the game according to their lights, yet there is no affinity between them and the players, and it is no good for the game.

As an instance one little act will be sufficient to show the Board's hostility to the players. It is reported that the Board recently decided upon giving a dinner at which the English team were to be invited, invitations not being sent to the Australian team. It seems scarcely credible; and yet it has never been contradicted, to my knowledge. One would like to know the reason for such discrimination. To save the situation, Canon Hughes (President of the Victorian Cricket Association) came to the rescue, the result being that both teams were entertained to dinner on the night of the second day of the match. The Board might have little confidence in the players, but it can be stated without fear of contradiction that the players have less confidence in the Management.

Many people expressed doubt whether Bradman would accept the Board of Control's ruling against the player-journalist.[2] Personally, I could not see that Bradman had any alternative but to abide by this rule. The rule seems eminently sound, from whatever angle it may be regarded. A player cannot do full justice either to his side or himself in such strenuous circumstances, if he is at the same time to give of his best as a writer.

Even Bradman's most ardent worshippers would have found it hardly possible to defend their idol, had he preferred to court success with the pen rather than the bat at such a time. Throughout the series, two, and sometimes three, of the Australian team were in the habit of broadcasting a description of the match at the close of each day's play. I may be old-fashioned, but I fail to see what useful purpose can be served by such performances.

The side which ultimately took the field for Australia included O'Brien, Ironmonger, and Bradman, who took the places of the three players dropped from the side so decisively beaten at Sydney, namely, Ponsford, Kippax, and Nagel.

That the changes were sound and the selections judicious admits

---

[2] The Australian team, like the English, were forbidden to work for the Press, although Bradman did broadcast a daily report over the airwaves after play had ceased.

of no argument; Australia's batting and bowling were strengthened alike, while her fielding was not materially weakened.

The Melbourne wicket has attained a worldwide notoriety for the life and vagaries which it displays up to lunch-time on the first morning of a match. Fast and fast-medium bowlers have always revelled here for the first one and a half hour's play. It was here, during the M.C.C.'s 1911–12 tour in Australia, that S. F. Barnes, until he was barracked, is said to have bowled better at the start of a match than anyone has ever bowled before or since in the history of cricket.[3]

In view, then, of our knowledge of the Melbourne Ground, which between us extended back exactly thirty years, and of the fact that it had not belied its reputation on the previous occasions upon which we had played there during our tour, we decided to make one change from the side successful at Sydney, Bowes being preferred to Verity. This entailed our playing a full battery of fast bowlers, Larwood, Voce, Allen, and Bowes, with Hammond to help if necessary.

It is easy to be wise after the event, but after taking all the circumstances into consideration, it will be found that it was not our bowling which let us down. Indeed, to dismiss Australia twice for such trifling totals was, to my mind, the greatest of the many triumphs enjoyed by our bowlers, with the exception of a wonderful performance on the second day's cricket in the Brisbane Test Match.

THE FIRST DAY

Although the day was a Friday the world's record for the attendance at a cricket match was broken, 63,973 persons passing the turnstiles.[4] For the second time Woodfull beat me in the toss. Larwood, with the wind and slope to help him, opened our bowling with

[3] By lunch on 30th December 1911, the 38-year-old Barnes had taken the first four Australian wickets for three runs. The Wisden match report makes no mention of barracking.

[4] 63,973 people were at the ground. The M.C.G. still holds the world record for attendance at a Test match: 90,800 on the second day of the Australia vs. West Indies Test in 1961.

Voce. Woodfull took Fingleton in with him in place of Ponsford, and instead of taking the first ball, as was his custom, he deputed this duty to his colleague from New South Wales.

During the first two overs, although both our bowlers appeared to be bowling as fast as usual, I was surprised at the apparent total absence of life in the wicket. In his second over, Larwood changed to leg-theory (as he was to do at Adelaide in the Third Test Match). In the third over we had to bowl with a ball which had already gone at the seam.

With considerable difficulty the Board of Control had been induced to accept as a playing condition that in the event of a ball having to be replaced, one as similar as possible should be substituted. Match balls with which only two overs have been bowled are not easy to find, and the umpires accordingly offered us a new ball. For their own protection I suggested that they should obtain the sanction of the Authorities. After one of the umpires had left the field for that purpose, Woodfull remarked that he did not consider it fair that we should have a brand-new ball. In point of fact, the question had obviously passed out of either his hands or mine, but it would, I think, have been open to me to suggest that the waste of nine minutes' play before lunch on the Melbourne wicket was more than compensation for the substitution of a new ball.

However, to avoid possible unpleasantness or sense of grievance, I waived the point and allowed him to knock the new ball about. The necessary "pat-ball" to achieve this object caused considerable merriment among the spectators.

I hoped that with the advent of the fresh ball the expected "life", which we had so confidently anticipated from an ordinary Melbourne wicket, would be duly forthcoming. In this we were disappointed, and Larwood completed his first spell of bowling without taking a wicket. It was thus left to Allen to effect a separation. This he did, with the total at 29, by clean bowling Woodfull.

After lunch, taken at 42 for one, O'Brien, who had been restraining himself with difficulty, underestimated Pataudi's ability as a fieldsman, and a smart piece of work on the latter's part resulted in O'Brien being run out.

Bradman appeared to have entirely recovered from his indisposition, though the continuance of the Press controversy with regard to player-writers can scarcely have contributed to his mental ease. When he came in, he had to face Bowes. Off the very first ball he attempted what can only be described as a very daring shot for any batsman, whatever his class. The ball was by no means a bad length ball, but Bradman, who certainly could not have accustomed himself to the light or the pace of the wicket, attempted a full-blooded hook and had the mortification of seeing his wicket well and truly shattered.

At this unexpected disaster a yell went up all round the ground, to be followed by something suspiciously like silence. Just about this time Fingleton completed his fifty. The spirit of Woodfull, with an added dourness of his own, seemed to have descended upon Fingleton, who had played so well against us in the New South Wales match.

The leg-theory presented little or no difficulty to him, and doubtless he was justified in leaving the chance of scoring runs at a good rate to forcing batsmen such as Bradman, McCabe, and Richardson; but though I am sure that Fingleton has made a good many runs against slow bowling, whenever he was in I could not help wishing for the services of a slow leg-break bowler.

The wicket, which had been lifeless enough in all conscience before lunch, was now absolutely dead, and we were at another disadvantage in that we had been deprived of the services of Larwood, whose boots were giving him much trouble. The crowd jubilantly seized upon the opportunity to jeer at his discomfiture.

Test Matches have been won and lost by lack of attention to such details. No cricketer, and particularly a fast bowler, can be too careful in this respect. There is no substitute for personal attention. Suffice it to say that many interesting stories and suggestions as to what actually had happened to Larwood's boots were current at the time.[5]

---

[5] Larwood had to go off the field twice, each time for a considerable period, on the first day of the match. DRJ was not impressed.

McCabe, sound batsman that he is, was a shadow of the McCabe we had seen in the first innings at Sydney. He appeared to have developed a slight weakness outside the off stump, which we were not slow to try to exploit. After nearly an hour he obliged us by pushing a ball into the hands of the fieldsman in the gully. Soon after five o'clock Fingleton's long innings came to a close, when Allen clean bowled him. Though his 83 included only three fours, he was the Australians' outstanding batsman, for without him their total would have been modest indeed.

With five men out for 156, we had good cause to be satisfied, particularly in view of the known weakness of the Australian tail.

Oldfield, who had joined Richardson, played exceedingly correct cricket, and after a long and hot day in the field our bowling was beginning to show signs of tiring, though the courageous way in which Allen, Voce, and Bowes had sustained our attack was a splendid example of determination and stamina in face of considerable difficulties.

Just before the close of play Richardson edged one from Voce into Hammond's safe hands at backward square leg. Hammond, I should add, had been bowling an unimpeachable length during this last trying hour, and so enabled me to use our fast bowlers in short spells from the other end. Grimmett had barely time to come in, but in the brief space left for play, Voce claimed him as another victim, Sutcliffe taking a good catch. Play closed with the score at 194 for seven wickets.

THE SECOND DAY

Just as the first day had been a triumph for the English bowlers, so the second day was to prove a triumph for their opposite numbers on the Australian side. Where all were deserving of the highest praise, it is invidious to discriminate. It was this match which set the seal upon O'Reilly's fast-rising reputation. The rising of a new star is often the occasion for the disappearance of another below the horizon. The setting star was Grimmett's. Personally, I am inclined to doubt whether the South Australian rightly deserved the declination which was to be his, for though Wall and O'Reilly shared eight wickets between them, Grimmett played an important part in their success, bowling 14 overs at a cost of 18 runs for one wicket.

With only three wickets in hand the Australian total was increased to 228, Oldfield, after playing as well as anyone on the side, being left not out at 27.

However highly one may praise the Australian bowling for its guile and accuracy, no sufficient excuse can be found to account for the feebleness of our batting. With the exception of Sutcliffe, and in a less degree Leyland and Allen, the less said about our efforts the better. With the total at 30, Wyatt, to his surprise, fell a victim to the bowler's appeal for a ball at which he made no stroke, merely covering his wickets with his pads; and the roar which greeted Hammond's dismissal with the score at 43 was a clear tribute to the wholesome respect in which this batsman is held by an Australian crowd. The ball with which Wall bowled him appeared to keep a little low and hasten off the pitch.

Elated by this early success, the Australian fieldsmen crowded round the bat. In the circumstances it is not easy to blame the batsmen for allowing the fielding side to get on top.

Sutcliffe was never very comfortable, and, though he attempted to open out on one or two occasions, the results could not have encouraged him or, for that matter, anyone else to take liberties with some accurate bowling. McCabe should have caught him when in the thirties, in the slips off Grimmett. But, uncomfortable as he was, Sutcliffe was slowly obtaining the upper hand in his most determined manner.

Pataudi, though playing perfectly correctly, seemed unable to get going, and soon had the misfortune to drag a ball from a long way outside the off stump on to his wicket. With the idea of helping Sutcliffe with a forcing batsman at the other end, I sent in Leyland instead of myself, hoping at the same time that a left-hander might embarrass the accuracy of the Australian attack.

This alteration very nearly proved successful, but after making 22 runs in really convincing style Leyland lashed at O'Reilly, missed the ball and was clean bowled.

I followed, but it was not to be my lucky day, for after I had made only one run Oldfield held a brilliant catch wide on the leg side off a leg glide, which in the ordinary way would have scored a run or even two. Ames was the next victim, falling to a shot which, for so good a batsman, can only be described as wild. Indeed, it very closely resembled the stroke which had cost Bradman his wicket in the first innings.

Allen was playing as well as anyone, and, though Larwood was clean bowled by O'Reilly's fast ball, there always seemed a possibility that a stand might be made at any moment. But it was not to be, and with Voce's dismissal play closed, with the score at 161 for 9 wickets.

Though every allowance be made for the fact that the wicket was tricky, and that it was even receptive of spin – a characteristic that had never been associated with a Melbourne wicket on the second day – there can be no excuse for our very feeble batting performances.

THE THIRD DAY

The third day's play was again witnessed by a record crowd, 68,188 spectators being present, and this large number may be attributed to the Australians' somewhat unexpected success on the Saturday, when the attendance amounted to only 37,000.

Our first innings soon closed, with the addition of only 8 runs, Allen being out for a well played 30. He had rightly done his best to hit the bowling, and gamely lost his wicket in the attempt.

Perhaps this match was, in its way, the most remarkable instance of a Test Match seesawing, first in favour of one side and then in favour of the other, until the very last ball had been bowled. This Monday was, emphatically, England's day. Not only did we dismiss Australia for 191, but we made 43 of the runs that were necessary to give us victory without the loss of a wicket before the close of play – and yet, at the end of the second day, we were 67 runs behind, with only 1 wicket in hand.

Immediately after the opening of Australia's second innings we met with success. After noticing how Fingleton had shaped to Allen in the first innings, I decided to make an experiment by putting Allen on against the wind and slope, to open the attack. This move proved effective, for, after scoring a single, Fingleton nibbled at the ball, as he had done more than once in the first innings, and was caught at the wicket.

With the total at only 27, O'Brien was clean bowled by Larwood. Bradman then came in to play what proved to be by far his best and most worthy innings of the series. With the ball hardly rising more than stump high, he was always at ease with the fast bowlers. Moreover, he adopted more orthodox methods. Why he ever deserted such methods will always remain a mystery to me, for, relying on them on this occasion, he obtained the complete mastery which so many Australians associate with his batting. He was at the top of his form, and played a great innings for his side. With the score at 81, Woodfull, who from all appearances was as solid as Fingleton had been in the first innings, played a ball straight into Allen's hands at forward short leg.

At this stage the Australians seemed to have more than discounted the lead of 59 runs they had obtained on the first innings.

Then followed the most dangerous stand of the innings, for, after Allen had caused McCabe to play on, Richardson and Bradman raised the total from 81 to 135.

It was a hot day, and what we should have done without Hammond I really do not know, for none of our fast bowlers really cared to face the double burden of slope and wind. I had put on Bowes at this end with two objects, firstly that he might repeat his first inning's success against Bradman, and secondly that with the adverse wind he might tend to run the ball away from the bat. He was very nearly successful, as he induced Bradman to make his one error, when he played at a ball which just missed both bat and wicket by a fraction of an inch. With this exception Bowes was not very convincing. He never seemed to get the same pace out of the wicket as he can and does in England. Curiously enough, the wicket in this match played better on the third day than at any other period.

With Ironmonger, the last man, to come in, Bradman was within two runs of his century. Ironmonger had two balls to play before the over ended. The first one shaved his off stump, the second his leg stump. In the next over from Voce, Bradman duly completed a great hundred. Immediately afterwards Ironmonger was run out. It almost looked as if he meant to get out, for there was undoubtedly a run in the stroke. Bradman carried his bat, and had a magnificent and well-deserved reception on his return to the pavilion.

I cannot praise our bowling too highly, and while the fast bowlers again bore the lion's share of the work, they would be the first to admit how much they owed to Hammond, whose efforts, like their own, so thoroughly deserved to be ranked as match-winning.

Again Fortune seemed to be smiling upon us, for we were to start our second innings with the knowledge that we required only 251 runs to win the match. How fickle was the Goddess remains to be seen.

We opened our innings, and the wicket, now at its best, enabled Sutcliffe to play as good an innings in the time at his disposal as one could wish to see.

Whatever may have been said about his batting in the first innings, there can be no two opinions about the 32 runs he made before the close of play. They bore the stamp and hallmark of a master-batsman. I had again altered the batting order, sending in Leyland with Sutcliffe, and our two Yorkshiremen remained undefeated at the close of play, with the total reading 43.

We needed but 208 runs to win, with all our wickets in hand!

FOURTH AND LAST DAY

The fourth and last day opened with ideal weather for the batting side – great heat and a bright light.

The task of getting the 250 runs necessary to give us victory should have been well within our power, particularly with our excellent start overnight to help us. But half the charm of cricket, whatever its class, is its uncertainty.

Had the Melbourne wicket played anything like it had played the previous night, I feel confident that we should not only have accomplished our task, but accomplished it easily. This was the general opinion, which no doubt accounted for the small attendance – the smallest of any day of the match.

Australia met with an early success, O'Reilly producing a splendid ball which bowled Sutcliffe before he could increase his overnight score. The ball pitched on the middle and leg stump, and, turning just enough to beat the bat, flicked the off bail.

Thus early, the wicket, which had played so well overnight, appeared to be treacherous. Before this, Leyland had added 9 runs to his score and seemed to be batting as well as Sutcliffe had overnight.

Without any addition to the total, Leyland fell a victim to a cruel piece of bad luck. He swung his bat vigorously at a long hop well outside his legs, and the ball, keeping low, hit his pads and rebounded on to the stumps.

Pataudi and Hammond were now together, and, though Hammond seemed perfectly at ease, Pataudi appeared the reverse of comfortable. After making five rather uncertain runs, he played a half-hearted shot to Ironmonger. It was clear from the way in which both batsmen were shaping that both O'Reilly and Ironmonger were turning the ball very considerably. I was therefore prepared for trouble when I went in.

Though I received only three balls, these were quite sufficient to prove, to my satisfaction at least, that those correspondents who gave it as their considered opinion that there was nothing wrong with the wicket must either have had their attention diverted to some direction other than where the game was taking place, or must have temporarily lost their powers of observation and judgment.

Owing to my height, I succeeded in smothering the first ball before it had time to turn more than four or five inches from leg. The second ball turned approximately a foot and a half, and I left it alone. The third ball, off which I was caught at slip, turned rather quickly about half the distance of the last. Ninety-nine times out of a hundred I should have missed it completely.

Four wickets down for the addition of only 27 runs was a shattering start, but we had still plenty of talent to come, and, best of all, Hammond, whom the Australians have such good reason to fear, was still not out.

Ames, when only 7 more had been added to the score, was

brilliantly caught by Fingleton, furnishing O'Reilly with his third victim.

At this moment of crisis, Wyatt came in, and played really steady and convincing cricket.

In the circumstances, with more than usual depending on him, Hammond decided that aggression was the best policy, and, accordingly, made a determined attempt to hit the bowlers off their length. Hammond has been blamed for this – erroneously in my opinion.

In similar circumstances I hope he will adopt precisely similar tactics, and that those tactics will be crowned with success, for desperate situations call for desperate remedies.

Hammond was the next victim, falling to a well-judged catch in the deep by O'Brien off O'Reilly's bowling.

For a short time Wyatt and Allen played their best game, and this is saying a great deal. They were helped by a sudden improvement of this amazing wicket; at any rate, the ball ceased to turn in the alarming manner it had been doing until then.

That, in the absence of rain, a ball should turn at all appreciably on a Melbourne wicket on the fourth day of a match may surprise many who, like myself, saw this wicket play beautifully on the eighth day of a match only four years before.

Well as Wyatt and Allen played, one could not help feeling that it was a forlorn hope. The bat never attained ascendancy over the ball, and after Wyatt had been given out lbw, for the second time in the match to O'Reilly, the end was not long delayed.

The seventh wicket had fallen at 135, and the whole side was out for 139, Allen being beautifully stumped by Oldfield off Ironmonger, when rightly having a hit. Both O'Reilly and Ironmonger had bowled magnificently, exploiting the wicket for all it was worth, and without giving away any unnecessary runs.

Their analyses (O'Reilly: 24 overs for 66 runs and 5 wickets; Ironmonger: 19 overs for 26 runs and 4 wickets) make good reading for Australian eyes.

After the drubbing which Australia received in the First Test Match, her comeback in the Second cannot be too highly praised.

Throughout the match, Woodfull handled and captained his side magnificently.

At the close, thousands of people rushed across the ground to carry the Australian players shoulder-high to the pavilion. The Victorian Cricket Association held an informal reception, and the crowd would not disperse until Woodfull and I had made short speeches.[6]

When English teams land in Western Australia they are welcomed and entertained by one of the most charming and delightful of men whom it has ever been my fortune to meet: the Hon. George Miles. Though Mr. Miles has taken an active interest in Australian cricket for more than forty years, this was the first occasion upon which, owing to the vast distances of the Australian Continent, it had been possible for him to see a Test Match. After the match, he said to me: "To think that I have been missing this sort of thing for forty years!"

I did my best to assure him that normally Test Matches such as the one he had just seen could not be expected to take place more than once in a decade or so, but I am afraid that my words failed to convince him. He insisted on seeing every one of the remaining games, in the hope that another as dramatic would take place before it was due under the law of averages.

The full scores follow:

AUSTRALIA – FIRST INNINGS

J. H. Fingleton, b Allen	83
W. M. Woodfull, b Allen	10
L. P. O'Brien, run out	10
D. G. Bradman, b Bowes	0
S. J. McCabe, c Jardine, b Voce	32
V. Y. Richardson, c Hammond, b Voce	34
W. A. Oldfield, not out	27
C. V. Grimmett, c Sutcliffe, b Voce	2
T. Wall, run out	1
W. J. O'Reilly, b Larwood	15
H. Ironmonger, b Larwood	4
Extras	10
Total	228

[6] The crowd, magnanimous in victory, gave DRJ a rousing cheer on this occasion.

FALL OF THE WICKETS – FIRST INNINGS

1	2	3	4	5	6	7	8	9	10
29	67	67	131	156	188	194	200	222	228

BOWLING ANALYSIS – FIRST INNINGS

	O.	M.	R.	W.
Larwood	20.3	1	52	2
Voce	20	3	54	3
Allen	17	3	41	2
Hammond	10	3	21	0
Bowes	19	2	50	1

Larwood 2 no-balls; Allen 2 wides

ENGLAND – FIRST INNINGS

H. Sutcliffe, c Richardson, b Wall	52
R. E. S. Wyatt, lbw, b O'Reilly	13
W. R. Hammond, b Wall	8
Nawab of Pataudi, b O'Reilly	15
M. Leyland, b O'Reilly	22
D. R. Jardine, c Oldfield, b Wall	1
L. Ames, b Wall	4
G. O. Allen, c Richardson, b O'Reilly	30
H. Larwood, b O'Reilly	9
W. Voce, c McCabe, b Grimmett	6
W. Bowes, not out	4
Extras	5
Total	169

FALL OF THE WICKETS – FIRST INNINGS

1	2	3	4	5	6	7	8	9	10
30	43	83	98	104	110	122	138	161	169

BOWLING ANALYSIS – FIRST INNINGS

	O.	M.	R.	W.
Wall	21	4	52	4
O'Reilly	34.3	17	63	5
Grimmett	16	4	21	1
Ironmonger	14	4	28	0

Wall 2 no-balls

AUSTRALIA – SECOND INNINGS

J. H. Fingleton, c Ames, b Allen	1
W. M. Woodfull, c Allen, b Larwood	26
L. P. O'Brien, b Larwood	11
D. G. Bradman, not out	103
S. J. McCabe, b Allen	0
V. Y. Richardson, lbw, b Hammond	32
W. A. Oldfield, b Voce	6
C. V. Grimmett, b Voce	0
T. Wall, lbw, b Hammond	3
W. J. O'Reilly, c Ames, b Hammond	0
H. Ironmonger, run out	0
Extras	9
Total	191

FALL OF THE WICKETS – SECOND INNINGS

1	2	3	4	5	6	7	8	9	10
1	27	78	81	135	150	156	184	186	191

BOWLING ANALYSIS – SECOND INNINGS

	O.	M.	R.	W.
Larwood	15	2	50	2
Allen	12	1	44	2
Bowes	4	0	20	0
Voce	15	2	47	2
Hammond	10.5	2	21	3

Allen 4 wides; Voce 1 no-ball

ENGLAND – SECOND INNINGS

H. Sutcliffe, b O'Reilly	33
M. Leyland, b Wall	19
Nawab of Pataudi, c Fingleton, b Ironmonger	5
W. R. Hammond, c O'Brien, b O'Reilly	23
D. R. Jardine, c McCabe, b Ironmonger	0
L. Ames, c Fingleton, b O'Reilly	2
R. E. S. Wyatt, lbw, b O'Reilly	25
G. O. Allen, st Oldfield, b Ironmonger	23
H. Larwood, c Wall, b Ironmonger	4
W. Voce, c O'Brien, b O'Reilly	0
W. Bowes, not out	0
Extras	5
Total	**139**

FALL OF THE WICKETS – SECOND INNINGS

1	2	3	4	5	6	7	8	9	10
53	53	70	70	77	85	135	137	138	139

BOWLING ANALYSIS – SECOND INNINGS

	O.	M.	R.	W.
Wall	8	2	23	1
O'Reilly	24	5	66	5
Ironmonger	19.1	8	26	4
Grimmett	4	0	19	0

Wall 1 no-ball

10
The Third Test Match[1]

(At Adelaide, January 13–19. England won by 338 runs)

There is, probably, very little difference between Australian crowds in the three capital cities. Before the Third Test Match started in Adelaide, however, there were obvious signs and portents that the Adelaide crowd was in a mood to make itself felt. Two days before the Test Match, both sides were at the Adelaide Oval practising. The ground authorities had thrown open the ground without any charge for admittance, so that, in the circumstances, it is, perhaps, unfair to suggest that the four or five thousand spectators present were truly representative of the best elements in an Adelaide crowd.

It seemed a pity that, throughout our tour in Australia, advantage was not taken of the opportunity to collect a little money for charitable or relief funds on such occasions. An admission charge of 3d. or even 6d. would not have been excessive. But the mere fact that no charge for admission was made should have placed such spectators as attended under a more than ordinary obligation to behave themselves. Suffice it to say they seized the opportunity to exhibit such a display of hooliganism as to make practice a farce. On the day immediately preceding the Test Match the ground was consequently closed to the public while practice was in progress.

---

[1] The row over English tactics really got underway after the 3rd Test, in which both Woodfull and Oldfield received serious blows at Larwood's hands. The first telegram was despatched to London during the match (see Appendix p. 173).

To return to the match – the selection for two, if not three, places in the English team afforded the Selectors considerable food for thought. In the first place I insisted that the Selection Committee should consider the advisability of dropping myself. In order that they should be free to decide without embarrassment I retired from the room, only to be met on my return with a flat *non possumus*.

In the next place, the ascendancy which the spin bowling of O'Reilly and Ironmonger had obtained over our batting in the second Test Match was a fresh obstacle for us to surmount. With this in view it seemed that there were two lines open to us; first, to try a change of batting tactics, making aggression our policy, and the second to introduce another left-hander into the side. Fortunately we happened to have the ideal combination of both these characteristics in Paynter. The next question to decide was who among the batsmen should stand down to make room for him. The choice lay between Wyatt and Pataudi. It was a difficult decision to take, but in spite of his fine score in the First Test Match, the Nawab of Pataudi would, I feel sure, have been the first to admit that his batting, for some little time previously, had not been up to the very high standard which he sets for himself and which everybody has been led to expect of him.[2] Moreover – and it is a fact of equal importance – he seemed to have lost some of that aggressiveness which comes with perfect timing. He it was, therefore, that made way for Paynter, and Wyatt remained. And now that I look back on the two great-hearted performances which he gave us with the bat in the course of this all-important match, I cannot help feeling that we were not only fortunate, but fully justified in our choice.

Adelaide has the reputation of being a notoriously unsympathetic wicket for fast bowlers. Bowes had found it so on the occasion of our first visit to the Adelaide Oval. At this early stage in the Australian season, the wicket, according to the groundsman, was by no means up to its high standard, though to us it seemed a batsman's paradise. By the time we returned to Adelaide for the Test, however, the cooch

[2] Christopher Douglas, in *Douglas Jardine: Spartan Cricketer*, questions DRJ's given reason for dropping Pataudi, and suggests that the Nawab's refusal to field close in to the bat, as well as his predilection for fraternising with the enemy off the pitch, may have influenced the decision.

grass had come into its own, and we were promised a wicket even more perfect than usual. This promise was carried out to the letter. With the exception of the first hour, when the ball is apt to leave a dark mark on the spot upon which it pitches, and the wicket to display a little of the life which used to be associated with the Melbourne wicket before the Second Test Match, the Adelaide wicket proved as good as, if not better than, any wicket upon which we played throughout the tour.

Indeed, the state of the ground reflected the highest possible credit upon Albert Wright, its able and genial curator.

Four years before, Sutcliffe, Hammond and myself had seen J. C. White win the Fourth Test Match for England on this ground with slow left-hand bowling.[3] We had, therefore, no hesitation in restoring Verity to the place which he had in the First Test Match. Here again our selection proved particularly fortunate, for, apart from doing all that was asked of him with the ball, Verity played two innings with the bat to which he may well look back for the rest of his life with pleasure and pride.

The English team, then, was made up as follows: D. R. Jardine, R. E. S. Wyatt, G. O. Allen, H. Sutcliffe, W. R. Hammond, L. Ames, H. Larwood, M. Leyland, W. Voce, E. Paynter, H. Verity, with F. R. Brown as twelfth man.

The only change in the Australian team which had been successful at Melbourne was the substitution of Ponsford for O'Brien, a right-handed for a left-handed batsman. The Australians were represented by: Woodfull, Bradman, McCabe, Ponsford, Richardson, Oldfield, Grimznett, Wall, Fingleton, O'Reilly and Ironmonger, with O'Brien as twelfth man.

I may mention incidentally that two of our team made the journey from Melbourne to Adelaide by car. I was informed of their intention at the last moment after all arrangements had been made. Long train journeys, which are so inseparably associated with the

---

[3] White took 13 for 256 in a marathon encounter, which England won by 12 runs on the 7th day. Jardine typically refrains from mentioning his own part in the victory: his 3rd wicket stand of 262 with Hammond in the second innings, of which he scored 98, was a record against Australia.

Australian tour, are certainly irksome, but the journey by motor, interesting as it may be, cannot be recommended as a good preparation for a Test Match. I speak from experience, as on our return from Adelaide I travelled by car myself.

THE FIRST DAY

With the help of a miniature black cat, lent to me for the occasion by Leyland, I succeeded in winning the toss for the first time in the Test series. I was so delighted that, when Clem Hill remarked to me that he thought it ought to be a close game, I chaffingly inquired how it was that he had not heard who had won the toss.

When England had lost four wickets for 30 runs, this remark of mine bid fair to recoil upon my head. On the combined advice of Sutcliffe and Hammond, I decided to open the innings myself, in partnership with the former. Sutcliffe and I had been opening batsmen more than once on our previous tour, with satisfactory results, but our initial effort on the present occasion was far from gratifying to either of us.

At the start, the wicket played with considerable life, and against some accurate bowling by Wall and O'Reilly, neither Sutcliffe nor I could make much headway. One of the fast bowler's deliveries, which kicked awkwardly, struck Sutcliffe on the shoulder, to the huge delight of the crowd, which applauded vociferously. Indeed, it was frequently noticeable throughout the tour that a blow from the ball, so long as the victim was an Englishman, was the signal for a demonstration of public approval, while if an Australian happened to be the victim, the English bowler was as often as not booed and "counted out".

With only four runs on the board after some twenty minutes' play, I stepped too far across in trying to turn Wall to leg, only to see my wicket broken after the ball had hit my pads. A cross wind was blowing at the time, and I cannot help thinking that for once in a way the ball must have swerved with the bowler's arm to an unusual degree, for the ball by then was by no means new.

Misfortunes followed in rapid succession. Hammond came in

next and had an uncomfortable over from Wall, two balls rising head high. In the next over from the fast bowler, Hammond played his famous forcing stroke off the back leg, but mistimed the ball, which appeared to keep a little low and to hasten off the pitch. Oldfield, standing a long way back, brought off a magnificent catch in his inimitable way.

With the first ball of his seventh over O'Reilly, who had been bowling very accurately and varying his pace skilfully, induced Sutcliffe to play a rather diffident shot for so great a batsman. The ball appeared to lift a little off the bat, and Wall, standing very close in at forward square leg, brought off an excellent snap catch.

Nor is this the full tale of our opening disasters, for Ames, who had been at the wicket for twenty minutes without scoring, fell a victim for 3 to Ironmonger's quicker ball, which had him in two minds at the very moment when we were thinking he had got over his anxious period. Four wickets for 30 runs was sensation enough, and the crowd were naturally in a frenzy of delight.

Australia, however, was destined not to get another wicket until the score had been raised to 186, thanks to a stand by Wyatt and Leyland which started with half-an-hour still remaining for play before lunch. This fine partnership, quite apart from the excellence of the batting, was a great example of our capacity of fighting back under adverse circumstances.

Personally I have never seen Wyatt play so well or with such freedom. His final score of 78 contained no fewer than three sixes, and while one is accustomed to see a succession of powerful hooks and cuts from Wyatt's bat, on this occasion his driving, straight and through the covers, was the outstanding feature of a truly excellent display at a critical time.

Leyland has made a succession of big scores on the Adelaide ground. Indeed, up to date I believe that this was the first and only match at Adelaide in which he has played without making a hundred runs in one innings. But, if I may say so, not one of the centuries which he has made at Adelaide was a better or more valuable contribution than the 83 runs he scored on this occasion. From the start he refused to be put on the defensive, or to be affected in any way by the disasters which occurred before he went in to bat.

Woodfull worked through the complete list of his bowlers twice without avail. A well-baited leg trap proved equally fruitless, and it was not until after tea that O'Reilly succeeded in breaking the fifth wicket stand. The partnership had produced 156 badly needed runs, when Leyland shaped for a stroke on the offside, and was unlucky enough to drag the ball into his wicket. There were thirteen fours in Leyland's score, and, apart from a possible chance of stumping off Grimmett when he was in the thirties, no praise can be too high for this exceedingly fine effort.

Wyatt did not long survive his fighting partner. He was caught by Richardson off Grimmett from a half-hearted drive. Wyatt, be it said, was the first to declare that the ball should have given four runs to the batting side instead of a wicket to our opponents. Wyatt's innings, like Leyland's, cannot be too highly praised.

On the fall of Leyland's wicket, Paynter followed. From the start of his innings Paynter was aggressive, dancing down the wicket to Grimmett and never appearing in the least difficulty with either O'Reilly or Ironmonger.

Throughout the day Wall had bowled with splendid stamina, and gave the appearance from the ringside of being the best of the bowlers. But by this time he was a very tired man. Wall takes a longer run than Larwood. All his efforts to cut this down have proved unavailing. As a result he takes, I think, longer to bowl an over than any other bowler I have ever encountered.

Like an American lawn tennis player nursing his strength, Wall walks back from the wicket at a snail's pace, with head bowed as though deep in thought. Indeed he is thinking, no doubt, how best he may bring confusion to the batsman at the other end. I do not believe that an Australian crowd would permit him to walk back quite so slowly, were he a visitor.

Paynter and Allen safely survived the new ball, but with the return of Grimmett, with the score at 228, Allen was given out lbw to the second ball of his first over.

I was blamed for changing the batting order and sending Verity in to bat instead of Larwood. It was suggested that, in view of the fact that there were only eighteen minutes left for play and the Australian bowlers were tired, Larwood might well have been responsible for twenty or thirty valuable runs.

This might well have been so. Personally, however, I rate Larwood's batting capabilities so highly that I felt confident that if he was to get runs, the fact that the bowling might or might not be tired was of very little importance. That the confidence I placed in Verity was justified by the results is neither here nor there. Few of us could have imagined that the partnership which he and Paynter began that evening would remain unbroken until after lunch next day.

The score of 236 for seven wickets at the close of play, though by no stretch of imagination can it be called good, was at least considerably better than looked probable or even possible at one period. Let me add that throughout the day the Australian fielding left little to be desired.

THE SECOND DAY

The grip which Australia had obtained early in the match, though loosened by Wyatt's and Leyland's great stand, was finally severed by the partnership of Paynter and Verity before lunch on the second morning. These two batsmen carried the score from 228 to 324. Towards the end of his innings Verity made some delightful cuts and drives on the off side. With the exception of one snick, which went head high through the slips, no fault could be found with his innings.

Paynter has well earned his reputation as a good man at a crisis, and until he was well caught by Fingleton off Wall, he had made no semblance of a mistake.

Unfortunately for us, the innings closed at five minutes past three. Had I not thought that Voce and Larwood would add 40 or 50 runs to our total, I should have urged them to have a hit and get out. I might even have declared our innings closed before 3 o'clock, for under the conditions of play ruling in Test Matches in Australia, when an innings closes after three o'clock a tea interval is taken between the innings. We were thus faced with two and three quarter hours in the field without a break – an unpleasantly long outing in Australia, and especially so, as we were relying very largely on fast bowling to get our wickets. The truth of this was forcibly brought home to us, for though we got four wickets for 51 runs we had shot our bolt as an attacking force by 5:15. In the last hour of the day Ponsford and Richardson raised the score from 51 to 109.

It has never fallen to my lot to see better bowling and out-cricket than were displayed at the start of the Australian innings. While Fingleton, Richardson and McCabe, in their different styles, were showing an increasing mastery over leg-theory, all three from time to time were inclined to nibble at the ball outside the off stump.

No fast bowler likes to start bowling against the wind, and there is nearly always a breeze blowing in Australia. Allen had been successful in getting Fingleton to nibble at the ball in Melbourne, and with this in mind, and in spite of having to bowl Allen against the wind, we tried again with gratifying results, for before he had scored Fingleton just touched a ball at which he was compelled to play and Ames was given a simple catch. Bradman, on coming in to bat, received a great ovation. He started with tremendous confidence, but after hooking Allen twice off good length balls, he offered an easy chance off Larwood to Allen, who was standing close in at forward square leg. It was gratefully accepted.

Both our bowlers had thus met with an early success, and every cricketer knows how much this means to the fielding side at the start of a Test Match.

Owing to the long outing with which we were faced, I took Allen off, well as he was bowling, after he had bowled three overs against the wind. I intended giving him a short rest before he took Larwood's place down wind. Larwood, however, before he went off, induced McCabe to give a simple catch to backward square leg, the batsman mistiming the ball, hitting it on the splice.

In the meantime Woodfull had been playing with his customary solidity. For the sake of continuity I have described the play up to the fall of the third wicket as if nothing much had happened.

As was our invariable custom, for the first two or three overs Larwood had opened the bowling downwind with three slips and a gully. In his second over he made one ball turn back enough to beat the bat. As I was standing in the gully, I was able to observe this from the batsman's shot and it was duly confirmed by a signal from Ames. With the last ball of his second over Larwood again brought the ball back and Woodfull, stepping outside his off-stump, failed to connect with his bat and received a nasty crack on his left side.[4]

Pandemonium instantaneously broke out. After sympathizing with Woodfull and bidding him take his time, I walked down the pitch to Larwood, where I found Hammond encouraging him to take no notice of the signs and sounds of trouble that were brewing at the ringside. I added my own words of encouragement, and asked him if he was able to run the ball away at all, to which he replied that, far from making it go away, he was turning the ball back.

I was, accordingly, not surprised when, at the start of his next over, Larwood made a sign to me that he wanted a leg-side field.[5] Had either he or I realized the misrepresentation to which we were to be subjected, neither of us would have set that particular field for that particular over.

Woodfull is an old hand, and had he been "grey and groggy", as the majority of the Australian Press suggested, he knew perfectly well that he had only to ask me for leave to discontinue his innings for his request to be instantly and readily granted.

I do not imagine that Woodfull himself would claim that he was either grey or groggy.

After play had been resumed, and just when Woodfull was looking thoroughly set, Allen came on for his third spell and, bowling very fast down wind, caused Woodfull to play a defensive shot fractionally late and drag the ball into his wicket.

That was the extent of our success for the day. Ponsford, who was

---

[4] Most accounts describe the point of impact as having been 'over the heart'. In the dressing-room later, Woodfull, speaking to Sir Pelham Warner, the English manager, remarked famously that 'Of two teams out there, one is playing cricket, the other is making no effort to play the game of cricket.'

[5] Larwood's account differs from DRJ's here: he claims that the decision was taken by his captain.

dropped off Allen with his score at two, may be counted as lucky, for the catch went to Hammond, who is just about the last person in whose direction one would select to hit a catch. Richardson, playing restrained cricket, remained undefeated with Ponsford at the close of play, but he too had some narrow escapes, playing at several balls from Allen which appeared to shave his stumps. With luck on our side, and everything going right, we might well have had eight instead of only four wickets down that night.

THE THIRD DAY

Starting the day with six wickets in hand, but 232 runs behind our total, Australia was now depending almost entirely upon Ponsford and Richardson. These two were the last of the recognized batsmen on the Australian side, and for us it was a pleasant thought that we had only to get one of them out to be in that comfortable situation known in cricketing language as having "one end open".

Voce's ankle, which had been a source of trouble throughout the Tour, was giving him considerable pain, and this handicap, needless to say, gave me many an anxious moment. In the circumstances it seemed best to bowl Voce as sparingly as possible, in the expectation that a weekend's rest would go far towards getting him fit for Australia's second innings. Accordingly, we opened again with Larwood and Allen, in the hope of getting a quick wicket.

Ponsford started brilliantly, square-cutting Larwood to the boundary twice in one over. But at 131 Allen got us the wicket for which we were striving so hard by causing Richardson to play on. Oldfield, who came in next, is not now rated very highly as a batsman, but from time to time he can play an absolutely first-class innings. He certainly did so on this occasion, playing all our bowling as well as anyone on the Australian side, though Verity was able to keep him very quiet.

The Ponsford–Oldfield partnership, which had realized 50 runs in just under the hour, remained undefeated at the luncheon interval, Ponsford having scored 80 and Oldfield 26.

The first over after lunch might have resulted in Oldfield's dismissal, when Ames missed a difficult catch on the leg-side off Hammond. In view of the score, I was nursing Larwood for the new ball at 200. Voce, who had started the bowling with Hammond in spite of his injured ankle, had both batsmen in difficulties.

Ponsford, after being applauded for making the best score until then, stepped across too far, in the manner which had become almost a habit with him, and had his middle stump knocked backward in Voce's third over.

With the new ball we returned to the Larwood and Allen combination. Grimmett soon fell a victim to the latter. With Wall as partner, Oldfield, who had been playing very well, seemed on the point of opening out with the idea of getting runs as quickly as possible. In attempting an attacking, but rather cheeky, shot off one of Larwood's deliveries, which by no stretch of imagination could be described as having been pitched short, Oldfield seemed to lose sight of the ball half-way through his shot, and received the ball on the right side of his head.[6]

He is not a tall man, and he had stooped in an attempt to mow the ball round to mid-wicket. Whether he just touched the ball with his bat or not, I do not know, but the fact that he was hit on the right side of the head is evidence of the fact that he had gone right through with the shot.

Needless to say, we were all extremely upset, and even Oldfield's immediate assurance that it was his own fault for losing sight of the ball increased our regret for the accident to this splendid cricketer.

Oldfield was prevailed upon not to continue his innings, and the end came with Australia's total standing at 222, the time being 3.30. In spite, therefore, of our first long spell in the field, Australia had only managed to keep us there for little more than a day.

Sutcliffe and I again opened the innings, but with seven runs on the board Sutcliffe once again fell a victim to the leg trap, which the Australians have set for him from time to time ever since 1924. On this occasion he hit a short ball from Wall in the middle of his bat, only to have the mortification of seeing O'Brien, who

---

[6] The knock resulted in a minor fracture, causing Oldfield to miss the Brisbane Test.

had come out as substitute, bring off a grand catch at deep square leg.

Richardson was keeping wicket in place of Oldfield. Truly he is a versatile cricketer, though it would, of course, be an exaggeration to say that, as a wicket-keeper, he was in the same class as Oldfield. Yet I will venture to say that on this occasion Richardson gave an exhibition of wicket-keeping which would have done credit to many a wicket-keeper of international reputation.

Having won the toss, it was our policy to proceed slowly. Time was on our side, and the longer we could remain at the wicket the greater was the chance of the wicket breaking up enough to assist our bowling in the last innings. Wyatt, promoted to first wicket down, joined me, and we remained together till the close of play, with the score standing at 85, Wyatt having made 47 and myself only 24.

On the occasion of drinks being brought out into the field an Australian barracker made one of the few humorous remarks which we were privileged to hear on this tour. Seeing the Australian captain about to offer me a drink, he shouted: "Don't give him a drink! Let the—[not batsman!] die of thirst!"

THE FOURTH DAY

Starting the fourth day with a lead of 204 and nine wickets in hand was a cheerful prospect indeed, and one which few could have imagined at all likely after the deplorable start of our first innings. But the day throughout was marked by exceedingly accurate bowling, only 211 runs being scored between 12 o'clock and the close of play. If the day was dull for the spectators, the change from the incidents of the previous days was at least a relief for the cricketers.

Right at the start of the day Wyatt fell a victim to the wiles of O'Reilly; and Allen, who followed him, was for the second time out to Grimmett, for the same score as he made in the first innings, just when he looked set for great things.

With the total at 154 I misjudged a straight ball from Ironmonger, and, although Hammond and Leyland batted excellently and with every confidence, the accuracy of the bowling kept both these aggressive batsmen very largely on the defensive. Indeed, the first time Leyland had ventured a rather daring pull drive, he was well caught off a skier by Wall for a well-played 42.

Hammond's dismissal came as an anticlimax, for in the last over of the day, and with Bradman bowling, Hammond appeared to hit a little too hard at a full pitch, and snicked the ball onto his wicket. From the confident way he had been playing, it looked as if nothing but a mischance would stop him from making yet another century.

THE FIFTH DAY

Two light showers in the early morning had little or no effect on the wicket. If anything, the rain had made it easier, and Ames and Verity, aided by a little fortune, proceeded to add 98 runs to our total. It was indeed pleasant to see Ames in form with the bat at last, as, for so great a player, he had been quite out of luck in the representative matches until then. When he is well set, there are few better hitters of a cricket ball. Verity's second innings was a replica of his previous invaluable effort.

We missed the services of Paynter very badly. He had sprained his ankle in the field. Another left-hander after Leyland's dismissal would have been invaluable. As it was, Paynter could barely hobble to the wicket. Again the close of our innings was badly timed, for we left ourselves the prospect of two and a half hours in the field without a break.

Australia, however, was faced with 531 runs to make in the last innings. Up to the present time no side has proved victorious after being set 400 or more runs to make in the last innings of a Test Match.

Australia's last innings was almost a replica of her first, if Bradman's score is substituted for Ponsford's. At the close of play four wickets had fallen for 120 runs, though it may be observed that the rate of scoring was considerably higher than in the first innings, as bad light had put a stop to play at 5.30. Once again we obtained a flying start, for with the third ball of his second over Larwood scattered Fingleton's stumps. Fingleton qualified himself for a place amongst the distinguished unfortunates who have made a "pair" in a Test Match. Ponsford, promoted to No. 3 on the batting list, hit a ball from Larwood's original spell of off-theory hard and straight into gully's hands. Two wickets were down for 12 runs.

The next wicket added 88 runs in sparkling style, of which Bradman, with Woodfull as a running partner, accounted for 66, bringing to bear all his battery of powerful and delightful strokes. Whether he played the ideal game for his side in the circumstances is hard to say. He was severely criticized by many of the old brigade in Australia.

In the middle of his innings he made the pace so hot that somehow one felt that it simply could not last. Larwood, Allen, Voce and Hammond all had a go at him, and although Hammond subdued him for a couple of overs, it was left to Verity to restrict the rate of scoring in a manner worthy of Wilfred Rhodes at his best. The field was spreadeagled to save fours. At first Verity was not over successful, but after hitting him to mid-wicket for six, Bradman attempted to carry mid-off, who, meanwhile, had been dropped back some twenty or thirty yards. The result was a sharp chance of "caught and bowled", which Verity did well to accept. This occurred just after the advent of the hundred on the board had been vociferously applauded by the crowd. With the exception of Larwood, Verity throughout the Tour struck me as more likely to get Bradman out than any other of our bowlers.

All this time Woodfull had been as solid as a rock. Leg-theory presented no difficulties to him, and though his scoring was the reverse of brisk he was obviously playing the right game for his side.

McCabe, after staying twenty minutes at the wicket, was out in exactly the same manner as Sutcliffe had been in the second innings. He swung a ball from Allen high up to long leg, where Leyland, covering the ground in fine style, safely held a difficult catch.

Play closed with the Australians needing 411 runs for victory, with only six wickets in hand.

THE SIXTH DAY

As long as Woodfull and Richardson stayed together there was always a prospect of Australia putting up a reasonable score, but with Richardson's dismissal, after the partnership had raised the score from 116 to 171, the end loomed in sight. Oldfield was unable to bat, and the remaining wickets added only 22 runs. Woodfull remained undefeated at the close with 73, having batted throughout the whole innings in a Test Match for the second time in his career.

Larwood's and Allen's figures – 19 overs for 71 runs and 4 wickets, and 17.2 overs for 50 runs and 4 wickets respectively – speak for themselves. But Verity, with 20 overs, twelve of which were maidens, and one wicket for 26 runs, was almost as valuable to the side.

The full scores follow:

ENGLAND – FIRST INNINGS

H. Sutcliffe, c Wall, b O'Reilly	9
D. R. Jardine, b Wall	3
W. R. Hammond, c Oldfield, b Wall	2
L. Ames, b Ironmonger	3
M. Leyland, b O'Reilly	83
R. E. S. Wyatt, c Richardson, b Grimmett	78
E. Paynter, c Fingleton, b Wall	77
G. O. Allen, lbw, b Grimmett	15
H. Verity, c Richardson, b Wall	45
W. Voce, b Wall	8
H. Larwood, not out	3
Extras	15
Total	341

FALL OF THE WICKETS – FIRST INNINGS

1	*2*	*3*	*4*	*5*	*6*	*7*	*8*	*9*	*10*
4	16	16	30	186	196	228	324	336	341

BOWLING ANALYSIS – FIRST INNINGS

	O.	M.	R.	W.
Wall	34.1	10	72	5
O'Reilly	50	19	82	2
Ironmonger	20	6	50	1
Grimmett	28	6	94	2
McCabe	14	3	28	0

Wall 3 and O'Reilly 4 no-balls

AUSTRALIA – FIRST INNINGS

W. M. Woodfull, b Allen	22
J. S. Fingleton, c Ames, b Allen	0
D. G. Bradman, c Allen, b Larwood	8
S. McCabe, c Jardine, b Larwood	8
W. H. Ponsford, b Voce	85
V. Y. Richardson, b Allen	28
W. A. Oldfield, retired hurt	41
C. V. Grimmett, c Voce, b Allen	10
T. W. Wall, b Hammond	6
W. J. O'Reilly, b Larwood	0
H. Ironmonger, not out	0
Extras	14
Total	222

FALL OF THE WICKETS – FIRST INNINGS

1	2	3	4	5	6	7	8	9
1	18	34	51	131	194	212	222	222

BOWLING ANALYSIS – FIRST INNINGS

	O.	M.	R.	W.
Larwood	25	6	55	3
Allen	23	4	71	4
Hammond	17.4	4	30	1
Voce	14	5	21	1
Verity	16	7	31	0

Voce 1 no-ball

ENGLAND – SECOND INNINGS

D. R. Jardine, lbw, b Ironmonger	56
H. Sutcliffe, c O'Brien (sub), b Wall	7
R. E. S. Wyatt, c Wall, b O'Reilly	49
G. O. Allen, lbw, b Grimmett	15
W. R. Hammond, b Bradman	85
M. Leyland, c Wall, b Ironmonger	42
L. Ames, b O'Reilly	69
H. Verity, lbw, b O'Reilly	40
H. Larwood, c Bradman, b Ironmonger	8
E. Paynter, not out	1
W. Voce, b O'Reilly	8
Extras	32
Total	412

FALL OF THE WICKETS – SECOND INNINGS

1	2	3	4	5	6	7	8	9	10
7	91	123	154	245	296	394	395	403	412

BOWLING ANALYSIS – SECOND INNINGS

	O.	M.	R.	W.
Wall	29	6	75	1
O'Reilly	50.3	21	79	4
Ironmonger	57	21	87	3
Grimmett	35	9	74	1
McCabe	16	0	42	0
Bradman	4	0	23	1

Wall 2 no-balls; O'Reilly and McCabe each 1

AUSTRALIA – SECOND INNINGS

W. M. Woodfull, not out	73
J. H. Fingleton, b Larwood	0
W. H. Ponsford, c Jardine, b Larwood	3
D. G. Bradman, c and b Verity	66
S. McCabe, c Leyland, b Allen	7
V. Y. Richardson, c Allen, b Larwood	21
C. V. Grimmett, b Allen	6
T. W. Wall, b Allen	0
W. J. O'Reilly, b Larwood	5
H. Ironmonger, b Allen	0
W. A. Oldfield, absent, hurt	0
Extras	12
Total	**193**

FALL OF THE WICKETS – SECOND INNINGS

1	2	3	4	5	6	7	8	9
3	12	100	116	171	183	183	192	193

BOWLING ANALYSIS – SECOND INNINGS

	O.	M.	R.	W.
Larwood	19	3	71	4
Allen	17.2	5	50	4
Voce	4	1	7	0
Hammond	9	3	27	0
Verity	20	12	26	1

Larwood 2, Allen 2, and Verity 1, no-balls; Allen 1 wide

11
Actions and Reactions

The period between the Third and Fourth Test matches was, needless to say, an anxious time for the touring team, but for none was it more trying than for myself.

This was, perhaps, the first occasion upon which the public at home had an opportunity of learning of the heartening support which it was my fortune to receive from every member of the side throughout the whole tour.

During the course of the Third Test match an Adelaide newspaper had seen fit to publish an article which, alike from the misrepresentations, inaccuracies and the innuendoes it contained, had raised the temperature of the team from simmering to boiling point. I do not propose to waste the reader's time by quoting the article, since its only importance lay in the rejoinder which it drew from our men.

Apart, however, from my personal gratification at this rejoinder, I really think that our policy of silence had been overdone – not that it would have mattered one way or the other to the Australian public, since comparatively few of the Australian papers considered it necessary to publish the team's resolution.

Since returning to England, however, I have gathered that a vast number of people at home genuinely felt that they had been left in the dark to a degree which exceeded the bounds of common justice.

Every playing member of the touring team had agreed to refrain from giving interviews or writing articles for the duration of the tour.

A manager is technically entitled to give an interview, and in a limited degree the captain may exercise his discretion where interviews are concerned. That this rule, on general principles, is absolutely sound, there can be no possible doubt.

For my own part, I had no desire to enter the controversial arena, nor did I see what good I, as an active participant in the play, could have done by so doing, since nearly all the critics had adopted preconceived and prejudiced views one way or the other on the various controversies which had arisen. I did not flatter myself that any words of mine at that stage would have caused a single critic in Australia to alter or modify any judgment with which he had previously associated himself, unless perhaps it had been in the direction of less moderation.

The action of the Australian Board of Control, in wiring to the Marylebone Cricket Club in London in the middle of a Test match, had, for the time being at any rate, taken the matter out of our hands.

Personally, I was quite content to let it rest at that, though I had been at pains on more than one occasion to let it be known in certain quarters that in the event of there being any desire for a friendly conference, whether formal or informal, the managers of the team and its captain would be only too willing to co-operate.

In these days there cannot be many people who are sufficiently optimistic as to imagine that good, or even tangible results are likely to spring from conferences of any sort. In the circumstances, however, I, for my part, cannot help feeling that such a meeting could have done no harm, and that the Australian authorities would have been well advised to attempt to bring about some *rapprochement* on the spot before acting as they did.

After the behaviour of the crowd at Adelaide, and in view of the tone of a large section of the Australian Press, I deemed it wise that the whole side should have an opportunity of meeting and discussing leg-theory. In order, further, that they should do so with complete freedom, I made it clear that I did not propose to attend the meeting myself.

My reason for this was that there is a limit to the criticism and hostility which can be borne by any individual or collection of individuals. I felt exceedingly strongly that unless the team was whole-heartedly convinced of its own rectitude and sportsmanship, the enjoyment of the tour (which is a very vital factor in efficiency) would have been so seriously impaired that, solely for the sake of that efficiency, I should have been prepared to consider the abandonment of leg-theory.

The team, however, not only signified its unanimous approval of leg-theory, but met me and the managers, who were not present at the meeting, with the following resolution:

> The members of the M.C.C. England team have no desire to enter into public controversy, for they deplore the introduction of any personal feeling into the records of a great game. In view, however, of certain published statements to the effect that there is, or has been, dissension or disloyalty in their team, they desire to deny this definitely and absolutely, while assuring the public of England and Australia that they are, and always have been, utterly loyal to their captain, under whose leadership they hope to achieve an honourable victory.

The resolution speaks for itself, and I need hardly say that I was as much touched as I was delighted with this generous (and, if I may say so, typical) gesture from such a combination of good men and true.

After this we could afford a cynical and pitying smile when a certain Australian newspaper, by way of "doing its bit", placarded Brisbane, preparatory to the Fourth Test Match, with a poster entitled: "Jardine's Disrupted Team".

I cannot help wondering whether the editorial genius who evolved this startling "fact" had sufficient sense of humour to consider the reverse side of the picture presented. What must his judgment have been on an Australian team which, even after winning the toss in torrid Brisbane, was defeated by this band of "disrupted units"?

The Australian Board of Control, however, having taken the matter up with the M.C.C., even if they did not wish to enter into any conversations with those of us who were on the spot, in both senses of that term, might have created a very different atmosphere in Australia itself.

An announcement by the Board of Control, made a week after their first cable, to the effect that, having taken the matter up with the Marylebone Cricket Club, and in view of the fact that leg-theory had already been discussed up hill and down dale, any further questions connected therewith might safely be left to the M.C.C. and themselves to deal with as they thought fit, would have been a helpful and statesmanlike gesture from such a responsible body.

But, just as influential Australians appeared to be curiously disinclined to come into the open and denounce any Australian act, such as unfair barracking, however much they personally disapproved of it, so the Australian Board of Control seemed unwilling to raise a finger to check recriminations on a question which, since it was to be the subject of adjudication, might well have ceased to be a matter of public controversy.

For my part, though I was naturally displeased at the prospect of the notorious excitability of Australian crowds being further and continuously stirred by speeches, interviews, and articles, I was not inclined to attach too much importance to this.

The chief factors weighing in my mind in attempting to form a dispassionate judgment after an impartial survey of the facts, were that after the First Test match, which Australia lost in spite of McCabe's great innings, there had been very little talk about leg-theory, and, again, that after the Second Test match, which Australia won with Bradman giving every evidence of an impressive return to form, there had been nothing but jubilation.

The general impression to be formed after the Second Test match was that there was nothing wrong with leg-theory *provided it was mastered,* and that since two of Australia's champions had already mastered it, while others seemed to be well on the same road, everything in the garden was lovely. Had it been otherwise, surely that was the time for the Board of Control to approach us or the M.C.C. with their views on leg-theory, instead of waiting until the Third Test match had turned in our favour.

I had long since ceased to care what the Australian Press said about me, nor did I pay any heed to what individuals frequently said behind my back. I had, however, made up my mind quite definitely on one point, and that was that no Australian body, however august, should, as far as I was concerned, be at liberty to stigmatize the M.C.C. team as "unsportsmanlike" and be allowed to escape from retracting that amazing charge.

As has been said before in this book, there is a great deal of talk in Australia about good "sports" and good sportsmanship. It must have been clear to the Board of Control that it was as unthinkable as it was impossible that an English team should take the field with such an accusation hanging unretracted over them. The meanest intelligence can see how insidiously this latent form of incitement might have worked upon the feelings of a demonstrative crowd.

Whether the team played another Test match or not did not rest with me, but after considering every point of view I was firmly determined that I should not lead them on to the field of play in another Test match, unless and until that charge had been withdrawn. I made no secret of this.

Frankly, I did not flatter myself that I should have been a loss to the side – quite the reverse, for I was ready and willing to stand down on account of my own lack of form with the bat.

It has been said that public bodies do not find it easy or palatable to retract or withdraw. I do not profess to understand the reason for this, since the individuals who form those bodies are ordinarily quite ready and willing to do so in private life.

I knew that many members of the Board did not approve of the original telegram sent to the M.C.C.[1], and I deemed it only fair they should not be in any doubt as to the position which I should take up with regard to that one particular word.

---

[1] The majority of the A.B.C.'s members were not in Adelaide at the time and had not even seen a draft of the telegram before it was wired, although they had been asked by cable to give their general approval to a formal protest. The N.S.W. and Queensland delegates were opposed to the measure from the start.

Meanwhile, we continued to play cricket on the assumption that the tour in Australia would continue.

A preliminary overture, in the form of a formula embodying hopes for future good relations, as pious as they were admirable, was put forward with the suggestion that it should be signed by the Australian captain, the President of the Board of Control, the English captain, and the managers of the English team.

Whether this was primarily the work of politicians I really do not know. It was so rumoured at the time.

Personally, I considered the introduction of politics into cricket as deplorable as it was farcical, but I should have gladly signed this formula if it had contemplated the retraction of the word "unsportsmanlike" – but it did not.

Ultimately the offending word was withdrawn, and we heard no more of the formula.

Whether the formula was put forward as a tentative "feeler" or face-saver to minimize any loss of dignity which the Board of Control might have imagined that it would suffer upon retraction, I cannot attempt to say.

Personally, I was quite content to have the Board's retraction in good time instead of being left with a half-hearted apology on the morning of the match, when one might have been left in con-siderable doubt whether it should be accepted or not.[2]

---

[2] The cable arrived on 2nd February, eight days before the start of the 4th Test.

12

The Fourth Test Match

(At Brisbane, February 10–16. England won by 6 wickets)

After all, there was to be a fourth Test Match.

Brisbane in February can hardly be regarded as the ideal setting for any Test Match, but the scene of the match which decides the Rubber must stand out in a way peculiarly its own to those fortunate enough to be on the winning side.

Most people have heard the story of the newly bereaved widow of Brisbane who attended a *séance* in the hope of getting into communication with her late lamented. When, in due course, she was fortunate enough to succeed, she considered it her wifely duty to inquire whether there was any want she could supply.

The husband, who with commendable veracity had made no secret of his whereabouts, is said to have replied that, after Brisbane, even the Nether Regions struck him as cool and that he could do with an extra blanket at night.

That the Australian Selectors took many chances is scarcely open to argument. They gambled, not only on winning the toss, but they gambled also on rain, which may be generally expected at this time of the year in Brisbane. Finally, they gambled on the breaking up of the wicket, upon which they hoped to bat first – and to such a degree as would supply a replica of the Melbourne wicket on the fourth day of the Second Test Match, in which event of course rain would be superfluous.

Australia accordingly took the field with only three "class" bowlers, and, be it noted, one of these was a fast bowler, who, under such tropical conditions, could not be expected to last through long consecutive spells.

It is true that we played one of our spin-bowlers, Mitchell, but had Voce been fit it is a moot point whether he would not have been preferred to Mitchell. As it turned out, Mitchell more than justified his choice, both as bowler and fieldsman.

For some time we had been meditating a change in our tactics. The idea we had in mind was that, owing to a prevailing and consistent fear that our batting might break down, some of our batsmen were not playing their natural game with their accustomed freedom. I was reluctantly convinced of the truth of our suspicions, and the change was decided upon.

I admit that I was not altogether happy at the prospect of giving two of our batsmen *carte blanche* leave to try to hit the bowlers off their length, but most of my fears vanished with the selection of only three bowlers for the Australian Team.

Our scheme, as it happens, was not entirely successful, but I do not think it follows that it was any the less sound in conception on that account.

For the task of hitting off O'Reilly or Ironmonger we deputed Hammond and Leyland. In theory I do not think we could have made a better choice, however curious the ultimate result may have proved. Again I lost the toss, and it was with a sinking heart that I returned to the pavilion, for, like Mr. A. P. F. Chapman, I thought that tossing for Innings in Brisbane in February was like tossing for the Match, and I still believe that under normal circumstances, and in the majority of cases, the luck of the spin will be the determining factor.

THE FIRST DAY

The honours of the first day were undoubtedly with the Australians, their score at the close of play reading 251 for 3 wickets.

For the only time in the whole series of Test Matches, we did not get a quick wicket at the start to encourage us, for a new combination, Richardson opening with Woodfull, was to result in the highest first-wicket partnership of the series.

The day was grillingly hot, and what little wind there was proved extremely variable, so that it soon became necessary for Larwood to change ends in order to get what little assistance it afforded.

Early on, Richardson made one streaky shot, which did not quite carry to the slips, and Woodfull survived an appeal for a catch at the wicket on the leg side – there was a lot of noise going on at the time.

Between the twenties and thirties, Richardson made a cut which skimmed past my head, as I was fielding close in the gully. I had barely time to move one hand, but, undoubtedly, it was a possible chance.

A little later the same batsman, again playing to Larwood, lifted one to deep square leg, where Sutcliffe, who was a little slow in sighting the ball, just failed to reach the catch. But these were minor blemishes in an otherwise excellent innings.

Woodfull batted until ten minutes past five. He had been at the wicket for more than four hours – a length of time which entailed great physical strain under the trying weather conditions.

Though he scored very slowly, it was a great captain's innings, and in view of the accuracy of the bowling and the heavy responsibility resting upon his shoulders, there can be no doubt that he played precisely the right game for his side.[1]

Richardson's dismissal was due to an excellent piece of combination between Hammond and Ames. Early in his innings, just as he was running into double figures, Richardson had gone a long way out of his ground to a ball from Hammond outside his leg stump, but Ames had failed to gather the ball cleanly. Though it would be quite unfair to blame the wicket-keeper, this was a possible chance of stumping missed.

After lunch, however, the experiment was tried again, and this time Ames made no mistake. Richardson paid the penalty as the result of a first-class example of mutual understanding between bowler and wicket-keeper, combined with good observation and execution.

---

[1] Woodfull's innings was a display of stubbornness of the kind for which Jardine himself was famed.

Throughout the day Verity was to play an heroic part in maintaining one end. Verity is one of the most interesting bowlers whom I have had the privilege of observing at close quarters, for I would frequently stand at mid-off when he was bowling, offering him encouragement and advice. I believe that Verity prefers to bowl without advice, but he certainly accepted it with very good grace. Once or twice we registered a doubly satisfying success, though in all probability he would have done as well, if not better, had I been fielding in the deep!

I think he realized that a captain does often get to know his bowlers in this way, and I shall always look back on our occasional collaboration as a liberal education for myself.

At the fall of the first wicket Bradman came in. At the start, in spite of some pretty tired bowling, he was scarcely himself. He did not seem to sight the ball as quickly as usual, and his ordinarily splendid footwork seemed to be affected thereby. Though I do not think he gave an actual chance, he looked in danger of losing his wicket twice an over, and this was nothing like the Bradman whom we knew.

Of course, much depended on his innings, and this sense of responsibility may have weighed on his mind, after the criticism to which he had been subjected for his last innings in the Third Test Match. In spite of all the publicity which Bradman receives, he is, I think, inclined to be oversensitive to adverse criticism.[2]

Mitchell obtained his first Test Match wicket when he caused Woodfull to play over one of his leg breaks. Had the ball not hit the stumps Woodfull would have been stumped by a yard, for he had gone right down the wicket with the intention of getting to the pitch of the ball.

Though we had not been getting wickets throughout the day, I had been a little nervous of using Mitchell, for fear of increasing the

---

[2] It is perhaps true to say that Bradman, while blithely indifferent in the face of adulation, was touchy when criticized. Certainly his attempt to absolve himself of the charge of cowardice, grounded on his repeated hops towards leg when Larwood was bowling, brought forth a contradictory set of arguments: he simultaneously claimed that the tactic, in serving the purpose of his own self-preservation, was in the best interests of his team, and that it did not reduce the probability of his being hit.

rate of scoring. Immediately before Woodfull was out, the 200 had just been hoisted, and I remember mentally tossing up whether to give Mitchell another over or bring on the fast bowlers with the new ball. My decision to give Mitchell just that extra over must be reckoned fortunate. Mitchell was certainly bowling with great accuracy, but I confess that I thought he was more likely to dislodge Bradman, whom he had bowled neck and crop in a recent State match, than Woodfull, who usually plays this type of bowling so surely.

Shortly before the close of play, the new ball gained us another wicket, for McCabe, who had been shaping confidently in spite of one or two streaky shots through the slips, snicked one to the gully off Allen, who was bowling with wonderful power at the end of this hot and tiring day. The catch may be accounted one of those lucky snap-catches which stick, for the fieldsman freely admitted that he hardly saw the ball till it was lodged in his left hand.[3]

A word of praise is due to Ames, who throughout the day had only one extra against his name, and that a leg-bye.

Ponsford and Bradman were left not out with 8 and 71 respectively. Undoubtedly, it was Australia's day.

THE SECOND DAY

I make no secret of claiming that this, the second day of the Fourth Test Match, is the greatest day which English cricket has known for twenty years.

In spite of the boiling heat and the gruelling and disheartening experience we had had on the previous day, to get the seven outstanding Australian wickets for a paltry 89 runs, and to reply with just short of a hundred without the loss of a wicket, was, I maintain, a wonderful example of the indomitable fighting spirit with which our team was imbued – a contrast, if I may say so without offence, to some of the past teams which have represented England on the cricket-field.

---

[3] The coyness here is due to the fact that fieldsman in question was DRJ.

One of the difficulties little appreciated at home is that in Australia most English fast bowlers find it difficult to eat anything for lunch; the idea of food does not attract them, and, if they cannot manage to swallow something, there is a very noticeable falling off in stamina.

In the circumstances, we were indebted to our manager, Mr. R. C. N. Palairet, for a very good suggestion.[4] He did not often say much, but what he said was always as helpful as it was sound. On this occasion, in view of the terrific heat, he suggested that our bowlers should be given half a dozen sips of champagne.[5] All of us, I think, are agreed that the less use made of stimulants in all sport the better, but on this exceptional occasion the champagne proved an unqualified success. That we were not extravagant in its use will be appreciated when I say that three-quarters of a bottle sufficed for four individuals to have three drinks each. Further, it made it possible for some of them to eat a little lunch.

The wicket appeared rather faster than on the opening day, when Larwood, though bowling well enough, had not captured a single wicket. I called on him for a big effort, and this great-hearted cricketer made a typically magnificent response. But again I would stress the fact that the four wickets which Larwood took for 31 runs on this day were due in some measure to Verity's extraordinarily accurate bowling at the other end. In all, during this innings, Verity bowled 27 overs for 39 runs, and though he did not get a wicket, no batsman played him with confidence.

Ponsford had placed Larwood's first ball to leg for 4, but the rest of the over showed that there was more pace in the wicket than there had been on the previous day.

As an Australian paper described it: "There was a sharp duel between Bradman and Larwood, and the fast bowler won. Bradman was edging away from his wicket, and, when he stood back and tried

---

[4] The team was jointly managed by Sir Pelham Warner and R.C.N. Palairet. Palairet's main responsibility was for the financial side of the Tour.

[5] According to Christopher Douglas in *Douglas Jardine: Spartan Cricketer*, this tradition dated back to the days when the amateur touring captains received a limitless allowance of champagne.

to cut a ball on his leg stump, was bowled. It was a bad stroke made with a cross bat and deserved to fail."

With the addition of only three runs, Larwood clean bowled Ponsford. Again I quote from the same Australian newspaper: "The bowler's aim with Ponsford was to drive him in front of his wicket, not away from it as in Bradman's case, and he succeeded, for after Ponsford had hit Allen, fielding close in on the leg, he sped across to the next, and, not attempting to play it and not covering his wicket, looked on as it bowled his leg stump."

The opponents of leg-theory had to place their telescopes to their blind eye upon this and many similar occasions.

This was indeed an auspicious start.

Darling and Bromley both played extremely well in this, their first International encounter. Darling, however, appeared to have a weakness for nibbling at the off ball. The slips were accordingly strengthened. This move had the desired effect, for after he had collected 17 runs he made a somewhat injudicious dab at one of Allen's deliveries, offering Ames an easy catch at the wicket.

Meanwhile, Bromley appeared to be comfortably settled, but with Darling's dismissal he realized all too well that one end was now open for the bowling side.

It requires great strength of mind for a youth, new to first-class cricket, let alone International cricket, to make a courageous decision, and, having made it, to stick to it. In the very next over from Larwood, Bromley went for the bowling and was rewarded with no less than 12 runs, but in the course of the following over he made a weak shot which gave Verity the opportunity to hold a first-class catch, diving at full-length as he did so.

Just before lunch, Mitchell came on to bowl, and was rewarded by deceiving Love and having him adjudged leg before wicket. The remainder of the Australian innings was only notable for Ironmonger's highest score in Test Match cricket against England.

Sutcliffe and myself opened the English innings. Owing to the scarcity of bowling on the Australian side, O'Reilly, upon whose shoulders fell most of this burden, opened with Wall.

At the start, with the bowlers striving for a quick wicket, runs came at a fair pace, but meeting with no success the Australians seemed content to sit back and wait for us to make a mistake with the off-theory, with which they kept plugging away.

As I have already said, we had deputed two batsmen to hit one of their stock bowlers off his length. Neither Sutcliffe nor I was one of those selected for the duty, and it seemed to me that the two and a quarter hours left to us was hardly sufficient to give this experiment a fair trial. We had the whole of Monday before us, when we might be afforded a far better opportunity. Sutcliffe and I therefore concentrated on keeping our wickets intact for the last three-quarters of an hour.

A quarter of an hour before the official close of play the light became very bad, and, though we were well set, each of us made a stroke which convinced the other that an appeal against the light was advisable! The appeal was disallowed, but when the Australian captain brought on his fast bowler for the last two overs I appealed again, after seeing very little of the two balls which he delivered, and this time the appeal was successful.

Play accordingly ceased with the score at 99 for no wicket, and the seesaw, which after the first day had appeared to lean decidedly in Australia's favour, was now almost level again.

A great day for English cricket.

THE THIRD DAY

Over the weekend many an anxious eye was fixed on the sky, but the storm clouds, which had at one time threatened trouble, passed away without breaking. Monday, though hot enough in all con-science, was rendered more bearable for players and spectators alike by a cool breeze.

Some idea of the accuracy of the bowling before lunch may be gathered from O'Reilly's analysis, for in the first hour he bowled 9 overs unchanged, of which 6 were maidens. This will give the reader some idea of the length of time which it takes Wall to bowl an over. Ordinarily one reckons at least twenty overs to the hour, with normal scoring, but when two-thirds of the overs bowled from one end are maidens, the number of overs bowled in an hour should be considerably higher.

During the course of the day only 172 runs were scored for the loss of eight wickets. Apart from the accuracy of the bowling, this slow rate of scoring may be attributed to two other causes. In the first place, the bowlers soon had recourse to an off field, relying for wickets very largely upon the batsman getting himself out rather than being got out.

In the second place – and there is no reason to disguise the fact – upon three separate occasions, just as our batsmen had every appearance of getting set, we experienced decisions which, with the best will in the world, we could not consider as otherwise than unsatisfactory.[6] There is nothing to be gained by labouring the point, and I only mention it here as the decisions, which I shall not refer to in detail, were the subject of considerable discussion at the time. Suffice it to say that for the remainder of the tour we had no further cause for complaint.

The reader will remember how we had planned that Hammond and Leyland should attack the bowling as vigorously as possible. Further evidence of the accuracy of the bowling may be gathered from the fact that Hammond, determined as he was to carry out the idea of going for the bowling, remained at the wickets for ninety minutes, during which time he compiled only 20 runs, including one hit for six. Leyland, in his turn, was not much more successful, and on the second occasion upon which he lashed out fell a victim to an excellent catch at deep square leg off O'Reilly.

Putting it colloquially, if neither Hammond nor Leyland could "deliver the goods", it was unlikely that anyone else on our side would fare any better.

Now that the reader is conversant with our general plan of action, he may perhaps be amused to read the following extract from an article by Mr. J. Worrall in *The Australasian*:

"Englishmen as a class are imbued with the idea that the only style of batting that pays in a match to a finish is the cautious one – the

---

[6] The two umpires, who stood throughout the series, were G.Hele and G.E. Borwick.

bowling must be worn down – and Jardine is about the High Priest of the cult. The principle is wrong, of course . . .

Evidently the writer was content to assume that because we were unable to score fast, we must deliberately have intended to "go slow" – a curious application of the principles of logic!

Sutcliffe's invaluable innings of 86 was scarcely up to the very high standard which he has set for himself. At this period he was suffering from rather a bad patch, but the mere fact that he was out of form – a fact, needless to say, of which he was well aware – makes his performance appear to me the more admirable. Any cricketer in form and in luck can make plenty of runs, but it takes a rare combination of ability and determination to triumph when things are not going just right.

At the close of play on Saturday, Paynter had retired to hospital with a severe attack of tonsilitis, and I was informed that there was not the least chance of his being able to play on Monday. Good sometimes comes out of ill, and though Paynter should certainly have reported to me that he was not fit – for he was feeling far from well before the commencement of play – it is hard to blame over-keenness at any time, and quite impossible on this occasion in view of his subsequent memorable performance.

When I called at the hospital to see him on Sunday he was looking much better, and was the first to agree with me that if he had to break "bounds" and bat on crutches he would do so, were it humanly possible, and without a thought for consequences.

With the steady fall of wickets, Paynter, though weak and far from comfortable, came to our rescue, and after Hammond, Wyatt, Leyland, and Ames had departed at fairly regular intervals, he kept an end going for ninety minutes at the end of the day, in which time he scored 24 runs.

Just before the close of play, Larwood had begun to look really dangerous with the bat, hitting one 6, but within a few minutes of the drawing of stumps McCabe yorked him, and Verity was left to play out time.

THE FOURTH DAY

The partnership between Paynter and Verity was destined to be another turning-point in a game which was beginning to look unpleasantly like the Second Test Match at Melbourne with all its ups and downs. In all, Paynter and Verity remained together for nearly 2 hours and 40 minutes, raising the score by 92 runs. Had Paynter been stronger, he would in all probability have added considerably to this number, but he was still a sick man on Tuesday, and the weather was as tropical as ever.

Once again Verity played an innings the full value of which cannot be measured by the number of runs opposite his name in the scoring-sheet. Fairly early in his innings he mishit a half-hook, which lobbed into the air and fell safely to the ground between Bromley and Ponsford. Both fieldsmen made as though to catch the ball, and then, as so often happens, each left it to the other.

Slowly our score crept up to the Australian total. Had the match depended upon one innings, the position would have been full of drama as well as excitement, seeing that everything depended upon a sick man, but with the total at 356, Paynter, realizing that he had little, if any, physical energy left, jumped out to drive Ironmonger and skied the ball into Richardson's safe hands. Without further addition to the score, Mitchell provided O'Reilly with his fourth victim.

During the course of our innings, O'Reilly had bowled no fewer than 67 overs at the cost of under two runs an over – a wonderful performance of stamina and steadiness. Though not called upon to do so much work, Ironmonger was just as accurate.

Australia were left with 2 hours and 20 minutes batting. Woodfull and Richardson again opened the innings.

In spite of the great heat, I hoped to be able to maintain constant pressure, at one end at least, until the close of play. Accordingly, I was careful not to give any of our bowlers, with the exception of Verity, even a normal spell of bowling.

Before the score had reached 30, Larwood might have had Richardson's wicket. Richardson was playing with every show of confidence, but had Leyland sighted the ball a shade sooner he should have been able to catch Richardson off a full-blooded hook. As it was, Richardson made four runs from the stroke.

Richardson was the first to go, with the total at 46, falling to a catch at deep mid-off while trying to straight-drive Verity.

Woodfull could make very little progress, though he never looked like getting out, and Bradman opened his innings in an unusually cautious manner. When Allen had started to bowl, it was obvious that something was wrong, and I was much concerned to learn that his side was troubling him and causing pain, but Allen is a great-hearted cricketer, and, after the first unsuccessful spell, he agreed with me that the only course was to get thoroughly loose by continuous bowling, in the hope that the pain would disappear. This treatment ultimately proved successful. But it naturally became far more difficult to continue our policy of rapid changes, for once Allen was taken off, his side stiffened up again very quickly.

Bradman's start, though quiet, was far more convincing than the opening of his first innings. Suddenly he opened out to Larwood, carving the ball brilliantly through the gap between forward cover and third man. This was a repetition of the tactics which lost him his wicket in the first innings.

I noticed that, well as he played this daring shot, he could not keep it along the ground. Accordingly, I strengthened the off-side field by bringing over a wide mid-off and stationing Mitchell at square cover or backward point. Fortune favoured this rearrangement, for in the next over Bradman put the ball straight into Mitchell's hands.

After one more over at the incoming batsman (Ponsford), Larwood, who had bowled quite long enough, was rested, and Allen brought on in his place. Almost everything depended now on Ponsford and Woodfull.

Then came another of the many dramatic moments in a dramatic match. Allen was bowling to Ponsford with his square leg so far behind the wicket that I do not know whether he would not be more accurately described as leg slip. Before he had scored, Ponsford glanced a ball perfectly in this direction. Ninety-nine times out of a hundred this shot would be worth anything from one to four runs. This was the hundredth time. Larwood, though he must have been feeling thoroughly fatigued by his last spell of bowling, made a grab with his left hand in a manner worthy of an acrobat or a flying angel, and held perhaps the most remarkable catch which it has been my fortune to see.

For us it was a moment of triumph, but the measure of Woodfull's disappointment may perhaps be gathered from the fact that he dropped his bat.

I felt bound to admit to the delighted bowler that, the very next ball, I had intended to suggest that Larwood should be moved three or four yards squarer – another example of good luck.

Three wickets had now fallen for 81 runs.

Ponsford's dismissal seemed, however, to have affected Woodfull's play, which was not to have been expected of this placid and great-hearted cricketer. With only ten runs added to the score, he again fell a victim to Mitchell, playing what, for him, must be described as an unworthy shot, lobbing the ball into Hammond's safe hands at first slip.

McCabe and Darling played out time safely without further incident.

THE FIFTH DAY

With only McCabe, Darling, and Bromley left, it seemed unlikely that we should be faced with a large total in our last innings, but the haunting fear of rain was continually with us.[7]

In all, McCabe and Darling added 44 runs, weathering the first onrush of our attack on the morning of the fifth day. Then Verity brought about a separation when McCabe, trying to hook a ball which came with the left-hander's arm, did not cover his wicket with his legs, and, hitting over the ball, which appeared to creep, was

---

[7] Before the laws of cricket were overhauled in 1947, pitches could not be covered during a match. After 1947, covers were allowed to be used at each end of the pitch, but they could only extend for 3′ 6″ in front of the batting crease.

clean bowled. Bromley on this occasion did not give us much anxiety. He had become infected with Darling's tendency to nibble at the off ball, and duly fell a victim to this error.

I have described elsewhere how Darling was run out when looking well set. This misunderstanding was, in effect, the death-knell to Australia's last hope. The match could not be saved unless a deluge of rain came to the rescue. The remaining wickets fell in rapid succession to Larwood and Allen, both of whom had creditable figures, particularly Allen, who, with a damaged rib, was again bowling under difficulties.

With victory in our grasp it behoved us to take no chances, but that we were to be made to pay as dearly as possible for our win was obvious from the first ball bowled in our last innings. With only 5 runs on the board, Sutcliffe was out to a fine catch at cover by Darling off Wall. As the ball left the bat I thought the stroke was worth four runs, but on this occasion Sutcliffe's luck was out.

As frequently happened throughout the tour, I changed the batting order – in this instance with the idea of getting runs at one end at least, while worrying the stock Australian bowlers, who did not seem to like bowling to our left-handers. I accordingly promoted Leyland to No. 3 in the batting order, with the happiest results. But again I cannot restrain a smile at the failure of our scheme for hitting the bowlers off their length, for when Leyland's great innings closed for 86 runs, though making every attempt to score when possible, he had been at the wicket for no less than 3 hours and 40 minutes, while Hammond in 40 minutes scored only 14!

For my own part, after getting one or two runs at the start of the innings, I could make no progress at all, and I can only say in excuse for a very drab performance that at the time, Leyland was scoring quite freely, and that in view of Sutcliffe's early dismissal I did not feel justified in taking risks for the time being. However, had the wicket shown any real signs of breaking up, I should not have hesitated for a moment to get on or get out.

THE SIXTH DAY

As it was, it was not until the next morning, when we were within 30 runs of the necessary total, that the ball began to play any serious tricks.

Leyland's great innings was closed by a ball which lifted viciously, and a worse batsman might well have missed it. Leyland unfortunately was good enough to get out off it.

Appropriately, it was left to our invalid hero to make the winning hit just as the rain, which was to last for two whole days, came down in earnest.

The feelings of a captain of a side lucky enough to win the coveted Ashes might make a fit subject for a pen far abler than mine. The players, who in the representative matches had done and borne so much, were not alone in being affected with the thrill which can come so seldom in a lifetime. It was one of these who drew attention to what he described as "a most peculiar light in the Skipper's eyes", which he insisted on photographing then and there. The result, I am glad to say, was uninterestingly normal and generally voted a wasted negative.

When all was over, I remember, in spite of the excitement, looking forward to a good night's sleep, for I confess that the night before, as often as the wind shook the trees outside my bedroom window, I raised the mosquito curtains to see whether rain, the enemy we all feared, had not come at the last moment to snatch victory from our grasp.

The Australian team crowded into our dressing-room, where at my behest, and thanks to the hasty last-minute efforts of our good friend, Willie Pyke, of Sydney, we were able to offer our opponents a drink worthy of the occasion.

This unofficial ceremony was later followed by an official gathering arranged by Messrs. Hutchinson and Hartigan, of the Queensland Cricket Association, at which His Excellency, the Governor of Queensland (Sir Leslie Orme Wilson), and W. M. Woodfull made appropriately suitable speeches, to which I did my inadequate best to respond on behalf of sixteen of the best fellows with whom I can ever hope to be associated.

I cannot conclude my account of this match without reference to the death of Archie Jackson, which occurred during its progress and in the very city where it was being played.[8] All the twenty-two cricketers engaged felt that a shadow had been cast over the game which, had not Fate decreed otherwise, Jackson would have adorned with his batsmanship and his personality.

The full scores are: —

AUSTRALIA – FIRST INNINGS

V. Y. Richardson, st Ames, b Hammond	83
W. M. Woodfull, b Mitchell	67
D. G. Bradman, b Larwood	76
S. J. McCabe, c Jardine, b Allen	20
W. H. Ponsford, b Larwood	19
L. Darling, c Ames, b Allen	17
E. H. Bromley, c Verity, b Larwood	26
H. S. Love, lbw, b Mitchell	5
T. Wall, not out	6
W. J. O'Reilly, c Hammond, b Larwood	6
H. Ironmonger, st Ames, b Hammond	8
Extras	7
Total	340

FALL OF THE WICKETS – FIRST INNINGS

1	2	3	4	5	6	7	8	9	10
133	200	233	264	267	292	315	317	329	340

BOWLING ANALYSIS – FIRST INNINGS

	O.	M.	R.	W.
Larwood	31	7	101	4
Allen	24	4	83	2
Hammond	23	5	61	2
Mitchell	16	5	49	2
Verity	27	12	39	0

Larwood 1 no-ball

[8] See note on p. 49.

ENGLAND – FIRST INNINGS

D. R. Jardine, c Love, b O'Reilly	46
H. Sutcliffe, lbw, b O'Reilly	86
W. R. Hammond, b McCabe	20
R. E. S. Wyatt, c Love, b Ironmonger	12
M. Leyland, c Bradman, b O'Reilly	12
L. Ames, c Darling, b Ironmonger	17
G. O. Allen, c Love, b Wall	13
E. Paynter, c Richardson, b Ironmonger	83
H. Larwood, b McCabe	23
H. Verity, not out	23
T. B. Mitchell, lbw, b O'Reilly	0
Extras	21
Total	**356**

FALL OF THE WICKETS – FIRST INNINGS

1	2	3	4	5	6	7	8	9	10
114	157	165	188	198	216	225	264	356	356

BOWLING ANALYSIS – FIRST INNINGS

	O.	M.	R.	W.
Wall	33	6	66	1
O'Reilly	67.4	26	120	4
Ironmonger	43	19	69	3
McCabe	23	7	40	2
Bromley	10	4	19	0
Bradman	7	1	17	0
Darling	2	0	4	0

Wall 2 no-balls; O'Reilly 1

AUSTRALIA – SECOND INNINGS

W. M. Woodfull, c Hammond, b Mitchell	19
V. Y. Richardson, c Jardine, b Verity	32
D. G. Bradman, c Mitchell, b Larwood	24
W. H. Ponsford, c Larwood, b Allen	0
S. J. McCabe, b Verity	22
L. Darling, run out	39
E. H. Bromley, c Hammond, b Allen	7
H. S. Love, lbw, b Larwood	3
T. Wall, c Jardine, b Allen	2
W. J. O'Reilly, b Larwood	4
H. Ironmonger, not out	0
Extras	23
Total	175

FALL OF THE WICKETS – SECOND INNINGS

1	2	3	4	5	6	7	8	9	10
46	79	81	91	136	163	169	169	171	175

BOWLING ANALYSIS – SECOND INNINGS

	O.	M.	R.	W.
Larwood	17.3	3	49	3
Allen	17	3	44	3
Hammond	10	4	18	0
Verity	19	6	30	2
Mitchell	5	0	11	1

Larwood 1 no-ball

ENGLAND – SECOND INNINGS

D. R. Jardine, lbw, b Ironmonger	24
H. Sutcliffe, c Darling, b Wall	2
M. Leyland, c McCabe, b O'Reilly	86
W. R. Hammond, c Bromley, b Ironmonger	14
L. Ames, not out	14
E. Paynter, not out	14
Extras	8
Total (4 wkts.)	162

FALL OF THE WICKETS – SECOND INNINGS

1	*2*	*3*	*4*
5	78	118	138

BOWLING ANALYSIS – SECOND INNINGS

	O.	*M.*	*R.*	*W.*
Wall	7	1	17	1
O'Reilly	30	11	65	1
Ironmonger	35	13	47	2
McCabe	7.4	2	25	0

13
The Fifth Test Match

(At Sydney, February 23–28. England won by 8 wickets)

The Rubber had, of course, been decided at Brisbane, but the arrangements of the tour left us little or no chance of recovering from the strain and torrid heat of the deciding Fourth Test Match.

In order to do ourselves justice in the last Test Match, I had deemed it imperative to rest as many of the representative side as possible. Several of us, in any case, were in no condition to play cricket at all. We were fortunate enough to get berths on a ship from Brisbane to Sydney, and the voyage, with the weather favouring us, gave us a splendid rest and a comparatively cool time, while those on land were sweltering in the heat.

Tired as we were, we thus managed to turn out for the last Test in better fettle than might have been expected.

This resting of players also gave Newcastle, where the remainder of the team was playing, an opportunity of putting itself on the map as one of the few places in the world which have no desire to see Messrs. Hobbs and Warner play cricket![1]

Voce had now recovered, and in consequence he returned to the team which had tacitly come to be regarded as the eleven repre-

---

[1] Of the side who had played in the Brisbane Test, only Wyatt, Leyland and Mitchell made the train journey to Newcastle, in the Northern Districts of N.S.W., for the 3-day fixture. The other six members of the touring squad joined them, with Hobbs, still playing first-class cricket, and Warner, who at 59 had not played a first-class match for more than ten years, making up numbers. Feelings and wallets were both hurt, and the local Cricket Association asked the A.B.C. to claim compensation from the M.C.C. for loss of takings.

senting our full strength. This entailed Mitchell's standing down.

Some past touring teams, I believe, as soon as the Rubber has been decided, have followed the practice of playing all those who have not until then participated in a Test Match.

This may have been perfectly sound with an eye on the future, but, with the growth of International cricket today, it seems to me a mistaken policy to experiment in matches against Australia, a view with which the Selection Committee agreed. Australia made four changes in the team which took the field at Brisbane: O'Brien, Oldfield, Lee, and Alexander taking the places of Ponsford, Bromley, Love, and Wall respectively. Wall was suffering from a bruised heel. Lee and Oldfield undoubtedly strengthened the side. Many good judges, however, were sorry to see Bromley relegated to twelfth man, after his good showing at Brisbane.

The Australian Selection Committee would, of course, have been asking for trouble had they repeated their experiment of entering the field with only three bowlers.

THE FIRST DAY

For the fourth time, Woodfull won the toss and Australia had first use of a typical Sydney wicket.

The main features of the Australian innings were the brisk rate of scoring throughout and the lamentable failure of the English team to hold catches. The fact that the Rubber had been won may have made a difference, but this can hardly be urged as an explanation for dropping, at a moderate estimate, twelve catches. It is an experience which happens to every team at some time. There is no explaining it. One had just to put up with it, for I have never yet heard of a cricketer who did not mind dropping a catch. In contrast to our efforts when the ball was in the air, our ground fielding throughout was good and could scarcely have been bettered.

We made an auspicious start, Richardson being caught in the gully off Larwood before a run had been scored. Bradman, on his home pitch, came in first wicket down, and started right away to give a display of fireworks, edging away from his wicket in order to puncture the off-side when leg-theory was being bowled, and, when off-theory was in force, stepping across and hooking the ball to the vacated on-side.

Here, again, the pace seemed at times a little too hot to last. In his second spell, Larwood once again proved Bradman's master, clean bowling him when he was attempting an unorthodox shot[2], which, when successful, is dazzling to a degree, but when, as in this case, it results in a broken wicket, looks unworthy of a great batsman.

Woodfull had contented himself with playing the role of running partner to Bradman, and the manner of his dismissal was a trifle unlucky, for though he played a ball from Larwood in the middle of the bat, he played it down straight on to his wicket. The ball before he was dismissed struck me as the fastest ball that I had ever seen. It pitched a length, but then seemed to soar, passing over and outside the off stump. Larwood, in the course of two spells before lunch, had the remarkable figures of 3 wickets for 14 runs; this on as good a wicket as any batsman could ask for. That was the extent of our success for a long time.

O'Brien followed Bradman, and though he had his fair share of luck, being dropped no fewer than three times – twice in the slips and once at the wicket, all off Larwood – he played a fine aggressive innings. McCabe at the other end, though severe on Voce, contented himself with rather restrained cricket. Between them, these two had added 99 runs when O'Brien entirely mistimed a long hop from Voce and put it gently into Larwood's hands at square leg.

Darling, who came next, was dropped twice, shortly after running into double figures, Hammond and Allen being the unfortunate bowlers, though Allen dropped the catch off his own bowling. However easy a "caught and bowled" may look, it is seldom so in practice – least of all when the bowler is a fast bowler, and for that reason less able to recover his balance quickly after delivering the ball.

Allen's side was still troubling him. Before playing him we had debated the desirability of doing so with considerable anxiety. However, though Allen did not have a good match with the ball, he

---

[2] Bradman was attempting a leg-glance, presumably having moved to the off.

played an exceedingly valuable innings with the bat, and it is no exaggeration to say that he was not favoured with the best of luck when bowling.

After tea, Verity, who had been bowling very satisfactorily, got us a much needed wicket when McCabe's sound innings ended by his chopping a ball rather tamely to Hammond at first slip.

Oldfield, coming in unexpectedly before Lee, played soundly, and at the close of play Australia were left in the enviable position of having scored nearly 300 runs for the loss of 5 wickets.

THE SECOND DAY

Next morning, after scoring 15 or 16 more runs, Oldfield began to bear a charmed life. He was dropped no fewer than three times, Larwood on each occasion again being the unlucky bowler.

I am anticipating, however, for before Oldfield was dismissed, Darling, after playing some streaky shots through the slips, was finally clean bowled by a well-disguised fast yorker from Verity. Lee came in to use the long handle, and, after an uncertain start against Larrwood, proceeded to hit with great vigour. It was a fine effort for a newcomer in a Test Match against England; he soon caught up Oldfield, who was still batting steadily. Lee, who should have been caught in the deep, eventually fell to extra cover off a skier.

Shortly after lunch, Oldfield was run out by a grand return from Paynter. Paynter must certainly rank among the first twenty fieldsmen. On this occasion he excelled even the very high standard he sets himself.

It was pleasant to see Oldfield entirely recovered from his Adelaide injury and playing excellently.[3]

The eighth wicket fell at 414, and though O'Reilly was given a couple of lives, both off Allen, the Australian innings closed for 435, easily their best total for this series.

Before the close of play, England replied with 159 for 2. Opening

---

[3] According to Laurence Le Quesne in *The Bodyline Controversy*, Larwood 'was at pains to bowl a full length' at Oldfield.

the innings with Sutcliffe, I was soon given a life in the slips, but after making 18, with the total at 31, I was caught at the wicket on the leg side, for the third time in this series – a brilliant piece of work by Oldfield, who during the match proved conclusively that he was in his best form with the gloves, as with the bat.

Hammond once again proved his liking for the Sydney ground, and though he did not start any too confidently, soon gave all the bowlers little ground for hope. Sutcliffe was playing like the tired man he was. Sometimes I feel inclined to think that Sutcliffe rather enjoys appearing to be in difficulties: he so rarely fails to surmount them.

Shortly before the close of play, he fell to a good catch by Richardson off O'Reilly. On this occasion I made what turned out to be a truly fortunate decision. With very few minutes left for play, I sent in Larwood to bat.

Quite apart from Larwood's undoubted abilities as a batsman, I was very largely guided in my decision by his brilliant bowling in the first innings. Great as were his triumphs throughout this tour, to my mind he had never stood out quite so far above his colleagues as he did in the last match of the series of Test Matches. It seemed to me imperative that if he was to give of his best in the second innings as a bowler, he should be given every chance of a good rest.

THE THIRD DAY

Saturday morning (the Test had started on a Thursday) saw Larwood and Hammond raise the total from 153 (159 overnight) to 245. Orthodox purists of the old school of off-side play might have fancied themselves back with the giants of old. I do not imagine that R. H. Spooner, R. E. Foster, Trumper, or Duff[4] can have hit the ball harder or more cleanly and accurately on the off-side than

[4] R.H. Spooner (1881–1961), English opening batsman of sublime elegance, had a special propensity for driving fast bowlers on the off side; the Worcestershire and England batsman R.E. Foster (1878–1914) was one of the few who, according to Wisden, 'did not lose his brilliancy on the off-side' when facing modern 'swerve' bowlers; for note on V.T. Trumper (1877–1915) see p. 27; R.A.Duff (1878–1911) played in his first Test at Melbourne in 1902 against England, scoring 104 in the second innings, and driving the ball with 'splendid power'.

Hammond and Larwood did that morning. Better cricket of that type I do not expect to see again. The only innings in my experience which could honestly be placed higher was Archie Jackson's century four years before in his first Test Match at Adelaide.

All good things must come to an end, and immediately after passing the century mark Hammond was out lbw to Lee – a useful first wicket for a bowler to take when playing in his first Test Match against England!

We all hoped that Larwood would crown his wonderful bowling feats with a Test century, but after lunch, with his score at 98, he mishit a ball from Lee and had the mortification of seeing Ironmonger make a lot of ground and hold a good catch at mid-on. It was a grand innings in every way and many Australians – in spite of what they had said and written – were, I think, genuinely disappointed that Larwood failed to get those last two runs.[5]

Hammond and Larwood had seen us safely over the anxious period which often comes with the new ball at 200, but it was too much to expect Leyland and Wyatt to keep up the pace which their forerunners had set. With Larwood's departure, the bowling seemed to gather new life, Ironmonger in particular having a very accurate spell. Just when these two might have settled down and produced a really match-winning total, Leyland was the victim of a mis-understanding, being run out by yards. It was most unfortunate for us, but it was the first occasion in Test Matches upon which we had lost a wicket in this annoying manner – a fact which speaks well for our running and calling throughout the rest of the tour.

Ames, who might have pressed our advantage home, also ran himself out. It is said that the camera cannot lie. There certainly appeared in the paper next day a picture showing that Ames's bat had passed the crease just before Oldfield had gathered the ball. I have been unable to procure a copy of this print; the substitute published was taken a fraction of a second later. I can, however, imagine the uproar and correspondence there would have been, had such a picture been produced of Bradman in similar circumstances.

---

[5] Larwood received a thundering ovation as he returned to the pavilion.

As it was, Ames on his return to the pavilion gave us a laugh when asked, as he was taking off his pads, whether there was anything we could get him. Instead of replying "Lemonade" or "Ginger-ale", he answered: "Yes, a pistol to shoot myself with."

The play closed with the total at 418 for 8, Allen being not out for a well-played 25. It looked as if the match, after an innings apiece, would be very open, though much depended on how the wicket wore.

In this connection, I should say that four years before, Alexander, on the occasion of a State match, had caused us considerable anxiety by the way in which he cut the wicket up after delivering the ball. When he played against us earlier on this tour, he did exactly the same thing: though on that occasion, against every rule of cricket, the groundsman had seen fit to repair his havoc over the week-end, as well as to cover the wicket.

Needless to say, beyond drawing attention to these incidents, we did not consider it worthwhile to make any official protest. Apart from the fact that the protest would have been futile, it seemed to me that there had already been too much of that sort of thing on the tour. Early in our first innings, however, Sutcliffe had drawn the umpire's attention to Alexander's habit and was well booed by the crowd for his pains. The spot which Alexander made was on the leg stump, and the right length for Ironmonger to exploit from the other end. This gave rise to the regrettable scene during our second innings – to which I am referring elsewhere.[6]

THE FOURTH DAY

On Monday morning, Verity and Voce remained long enough with Allen for him to raise his score from 25 to 48 by excellent cricket,

---

[6] Sutcliffe had complained about Alexander's follow-through in the first innings; DRJ reiterated the complaint at the start of the second, provoking a raucous reaction from the crowd. The umpires apparently accepted his point and spoke to Woodfull, the Australian captain. Alexander reacted with a succession of short balls, one of which struck DRJ painfully on the hip, but he refused assistance and continued to bat, with blood trickling down his leg, until he was dismissed.

and our innings closed for 454; a bare lead of 19 runs.

Once again Australia was to fail remarkably in the second innings. Richardson joined the band of unfortunate cricketers who have made a pair of spectacles in a Test Match, for in Larwood's first over he was out to a good catch at square leg by Allen.

One wicket for no runs. There followed the only stand of the innings (between Woodfull and Bradman), which raised the score to 115. Bradman started in much the same manner as in his first innings: stepping away from his wicket and carving Larwood to the off side. It was midway through his innings that Bradman was hit, for the first and only time in all the innings which he played against us in Australia. He was struck on the arm by a ball about six inches outside the leg stump which he was endeavouring to play in the direction of cover-point. It was not a serious blow and had no effect on his batting.

Larwood was now obviously going lame. His foot was causing him great pain, and with his retirement to the pavilion, we were faced with an anxious period. Bradman continued to monopolize the scoring, with Woodfull quietly holding the other end, collecting ones and twos.

Our two left-handers, however, came to our rescue right nobly. Bradman had taken to moving away from his wicket when playing Verity as well as Larwood, but then started running down the wicket to our slow bowler. After he had made some runs in a manner similar to his innings at Adelaide, Verity had him beaten with a ball which Bradman made into a yorker, after being completely deceived by the pace.

With the score at 115 for one wicket and the day nearly half-gone, it never entered my head that we should be called upon to bat before the close of play.

With Bradman's dismissal, however, a landslide in the Australian batting took place. Woodfull could find no one to stay with him, and Voce, feeling perhaps that the mantle of his disabled county colleague had fallen on his shoulders, dismissed O'Brien and McCabe for 9 runs.

Though Verity had dismissed Bradman from the pavilion end, I changed him over in order to give our fast bowling what little assistance could be gained from the light breeze. Bowling to the pavilion end, Verity exploited the spot made by Alexander to such good purpose that none of the Australian batsmen, with the exception of Woodfull, could withstand him.

In his last spell from this end, Verity took four wickets for less than 20 runs, his total figures being 5 for 33 in 19 overs, 9 of which were maidens.

Lee made 15 runs so quickly that his partnership with Woodfull could not be dignified by the name of a stand. Both fell victims to Allen. O'Brien, McCabe, Darling, O'Reilly, and Alexander walked in and out in rapid succession. The Australian innings closed, leaving England with a quarter of an hour's batting before the close of play.

Australia's fifth failure to score 200 runs in the second innings, after making 115 for one wicket, did not strike me as quite so satisfactory for us as the figures might indicate. I felt that what Verity could do on the damaged spot, Ironmonger might do equally well. In view of the short time remaining for play, I did not care to jeopardize Sutcliffe's valuable wicket, and on that account took Wyatt to open the innings with me. I felt that Sutcliffe should be cast for the part of the sword of Damocles, so that, even if a wicket or two fell quickly next morning, the Australians would find they had still to cope with Sutcliffe and Hammond. No wicket fell overnight, 11 runs being scored without loss.

THE FIFTH DAY

Next morning Ironmonger started bowling towards the damaged end, several balls lifting and turning unpleasantly. Ironmonger is, of course, one of the most accurate bowlers in the world, and I felt that the longer he went on planting the ball on and about the spot on the wicket, the worse it was likely to get. Accordingly I decided to take the first possible opportunity of trying to hit him into the empty out-field. However good the intention may have been, the result was wretched, for at the very first attempt I just failed to get the pitch of the ball, which turned and lifted. An easy slip-catch was the result.

Leyland followed, but after enduring two very accurate overs from Ironmonger who, naturally, did not fancy bowling to a left-hander, played back at a ball which turned very sharply, hit him on the pads, and rebounded on to the wicket. That, however, was the extent of Australian success, for Wyatt and Hammond, by faultless cricket, raised the score from 43, at which both the first and second wickets had fallen, to 168, so leaving us victors by the big margin of 8 wickets.

For the second time, the winning hit was a six, Hammond hitting Lee over mid-off. It was a hit with the force of a brassy shot which might well have raised envy in the breast of an open golf champion.

Perhaps Hammond was unlucky not to have had the chance of making a second century, but nearly as much credit is due to Wyatt, who, though never scoring slowly, assumed the part of junior partner and played as well and steadily as he can ever have done.

I am sure that we all heaved a sigh of relief as the match was won. Besides giving us the decisive margin of four to one, this our latest win made the tally between England and Australia in finished Test Matches equal at 51 wins apiece.[7]

The full scores of the match follow:

---

[7] The tally now stands at 126 victories to Australia, 94 to England.

AUSTRALIA – FIRST INNINGS

V. Y. Richardson, c Jardine, b Larwood	0
W. M. Woodfull, b Larwood	14
D. G. Bradman, b Larwood	48
L. P. O'Brien, c Larwood, b Voce	61
S. J. McCabe, c Hammond, b Verity	73
L. Darling, b Verity	85
W. A. Oldfield, run out	52
P. K. Lee, c Jardine, b Verity	42
W. J. O'Reilly, b Allen	19
H. H. Alexander, not out	17
H. Ironmonger, b Larwood	1
Extras	23
Total	435

FALL OF THE WICKETS – FIRST INNINGS

1	2	3	4	5	6	7	8	9	10
0	59	64	163	244	328	385	414	430	435

BOWLING ANALYSIS – FIRST INNINGS

	O.	*M.*	*R.*	*W.*
Larwood	32.2	10	98	4
Voce	24	4	80	1
Allen	25	1	128	1
Verity	17	3	62	3
Hammond	8	0	32	0
Wyatt	2	0	12	0

Voce 1 wide

ENGLAND – FIRST INNINGS

H. Sutcliffe, c Richardson, b O'Reilly	56
D. R. Jardine, c Oldfield, b O'Reilly	18
W. R. Hammond, lbw, b Lee	101
H. Larwood, c Ironmonger, b Lee	98
M. Leyland, run out	42
R. E. S. Wyatt, c Ironmonger, b O'Reilly	51
L. Ames, run out	4
E. Paynter, b Lee	9
G. O. Allen, c Bradman, b Lee	48
H. Verity, c Oldfield, b Alexander	4
W. Voce, not out	7
Extras	16
Total	454

FALL OF THE WICKETS – FIRST INNINGS

1	*2*	*3*	*4*	*5*	*6*	*7*	*8*	*9*	*10*
31	153	245	310	330	349	374	418	434	454

BOWLING ANALYSIS – FIRST INNINGS

	O.	*M.*	*R.*	*W.*
Alexander	35	1	129	1
McCabe	12	1	27	0
O'Reilly	45	7	100	3
Ironmonger	31	13	64	0
Lee	40.2	11	111	4
Darling	7	5	3	0
Bradman	1	0	4	0

AUSTRALIA – SECOND INNINGS

V. Y. Richardson, c Allen, b Larwood	0
W. M. Woodfull, b Allen	67
D. G. Bradman, b Verity	71
L. P. O'Brien, c Verity, b Voce	5
S. J. McCabe, c Jardine, b Voce	4
L. Darling, c Wyatt, b Verity	7
W. A. Oldfield, c Wyatt, b Verity	5
P. K. Lee, b Allen	15
W. J. O'Reilly, b Verity	1
H. H. Alexander, lbw, b Verity	0
H. Ironmonger, not out	0
Extras	7
Total	182

FALL OF THE WICKETS – SECOND INNINGS

1	2	3	4	5	6	7	8	9	10
0	115	135	139	148	161	177	178	178	182

BOWLING ANALYSIS – SECOND INNINGS

	O.	M.	R.	W.
Larwood	11	0	44	1
Allen	11.4	2	54	2
Hammond	3	0	10	0
Voce	10	0	34	2
Verity	19	9	33	5

Allen 3 no-balls

ENGLAND – SECOND INNINGS

D. R. Jardine, c Richardson, b Ironmonger	24
R. E. S. Wyatt, not out	61
M. Leyland, b Ironmonger	0
W. R. Hammond, not out	75
Extras	8
Total (2 wkts.)	168

FALL OF THE WICKETS – SECOND INNINGS

1	2
43	43

BOWLING ANALYSIS – SECOND INNINGS

	O.	M.	R.	W.
Alexander	11	2	25	0
O'Reilly	15	5	32	0
Ironmonger	26	12	34	2
Lee	12.2	3	52	0
McCabe	5	2	10	0
Darling	2	0	7	0

O'Reilly 1 no-ball

14
Australian Crowds

No book on any M.C.C. tour would be complete without some reference to the crowds which flock to see the matches. For the sake of continuity I have made little reference to the crowds or their behaviour in the chapters devoted to the Test Matches. Let it be said at once that one cannot but admire the enthusiasm which prompts tens of thousands of spectators to sit or stand, for six or seven hours on an Australian summer's day, in order to watch every ball bowled.

A well-known Australian sporting writer has said that the habit of barracking has made Australian crowds a byword the world over. That Australians themselves are extraordinarily sensitive to criticism is a fact which any visitor to their country will have discovered for himself. I find it, therefore, the harder to understand why no effort has been made by cricketing authorities to moderate or suppress a line of conduct which, though universally condemned, has frequently produced just the type of criticism one would expect Australians, resenting it as they do, to do their utmost to prevent.

Unlike most Englishmen, the Australian, while impatient of criticism from without, is not given to criticizing either himself or his country. He reserves his criticisms for direction against other countries and their inhabitants. His general attitude is too frequently that of the Irishman who said, "My mother, right or wrong; my wife, drunk or sober." Australia can do no wrong in his eyes.

I will not go so far as to suggest that there are not circumstances which might occasionally justify such an attitude. Australians, however, would do well to remember sometimes that there are other standards of behaviour besides their own, and that it is possible that there is much to be said in favour of those other standards.

Of the several members of the M.C.C. team, many had played cricket in South Africa, India, West Indies, New Zealand, Canada, and the United States. The behaviour of crowds in these countries, in our estimation, was very different from that which was frequently experienced from Australian crowds.

To take the most charitable view of the position, the behaviour of Australian crowds at its best, when judged by the standards accepted by the rest of the world, is not naturally good.

The Marylebone Cricket Club has seen fit to draw attention to the behaviour of spectators at Test Matches in Australia. We may rest assured that before the Premier Club would consider so much as a reference to the matter, the facts must have been fairly and exhaustively discussed in the light of first-hand evidence, and from the evidence of eye- (and, I might almost add, ear-) witnesses.

That many Australians would resent reproof was, as I have indicated, inevitable. It is, however, interesting to observe the manner in which it has been sought to sidetrack the M.C.C.'s protest. Roughly, two lines appear to have been adopted. First, there was the rather unworthy suggestion that the M.C.C. had merely attempted to sidetrack the question of leg-theory. I do not propose to deal with this suggestion at any length, since it is only necessary for the reader to refer to the telegrams which have passed between the M.C.C. and the Board of Control to convince himself of its pettiness.

The second line of defence, however, we will consider in some detail, since it goes to the root of the whole matter. It is high time, moreover, that full publicity were given to the evils of barracking. A policy of reticence has been given a very fair trial, the only result of which has been that barracking has grown steadily and progressively worse. That this has been the general experience of English sides, since the War, there can be no doubt.

The second line of defence is that it is impossible to control 50,000 people who make up their minds to protest against a certain type of bowling.

Let us avoid any misunderstanding. The protest against the

behaviour, or misbehaviour, of Australian crowds goes far deeper than the apologists of the second line would have us believe.

The protest, I imagine, is not in any way confined to the behaviour of the crowds in their attempt to settle the question of leg-theory by mob-law. It goes far deep than that. In point of fact, it reaches back to the far-off days of 1879, more than twenty years before leg-theory was even thought of.

Probably the two most disgraceful scenes which ever marred Australian cricket grounds were due, not to any theory or practice of bowling, but to the decisions of Australian umpires against Australian batsmen. Let us not mince words. Whatever views may be held on the barracking of players – whether in favour or against – no sane sportsman can suggest that it is anything but dastardly to barrack an umpire, whatever the circumstances may be.

The following is a description of the first incident, quoted from the *Daily Telegraph of* March 29, 1932:

A remarkable battle on an Australian cricket ground, with an angry crowd swarming over the field to attack the umpire, who was strenuously defended by naval officers, is recalled by the death of Lord Harris.

The *Daily Telegraph* is today able to publish extracts from a contemporary description of the episode – a letter now in possession of the Rev. Gordon Tidy, Rector of Stanton St. Quintin, Wiltshire.

Mr. Tidy stated yesterday that the author of the letter, his cousin, Mr. Charles Gordon Spring, was at the time a Midshipman serving in Australian waters. He added that when Lord Harris was shown the letter some time ago he approved it, but denied that he had knocked anyone down.

The "disgraceful scene", as it was later described by a cricket historian, occurred at Sydney in 1879, when an eleven taken out by Lord Harris was playing New South Wales. Before the match it was expected that the Australians would be easy winners.

Much money was in the balance, and the onlookers were wildly excited. The letter, after describing how in the first innings the English team unexpectedly made 267, and the Australians were all out for 177, continues as follows:

"Our joy was unspeakable; the Australians (under the rules then existing) had to follow their innings, so they commenced, and had got about eighteen runs when H. Murdoch, their great bat, was run out.

"The betting men in the pavilion, who saw their money disappearing before their eyes, raised a cry of 'Unfair!' and declared the umpire's decision wrong. The umpire was a Melbourne man.

"There is not, I think, the smallest doubt that Murdoch was two feet out of his ground when his wicket was put down.

"No sooner did those who ought to have known better begin making a row than the roughs took the matter up and rushed on to the ground in large numbers. There were only about three or four policemen and about ten thousand spectators.

"One of the roughs rushed up and collared the umpire. Lord Harris immediately knocked him head over heels.

"Another fellow then struck Lord Harris with a stick. At this, Hornby (who had played football for England) went at the fellow like a flash of lightning and had him by the throat. Then the crowd rushed in to the rescue.

"Directly Lord Harris was seen letting out, all the naval officers present, about twenty of us, and a few other gentlemen, jumped over the palings and rushed to the assistance of the English team. However, we were not much wanted.

"There was only one fellow who wanted rescuing, and he was the man Hornby had hold of. They passed close to me in the crowd. The wretched man was as helpless as a child, and in vain did the roughs try to rescue him.

"Hornby took his prisoner through the pavilion and pitched him right through the Committee-room window. When Hornby appeared again, with his shirt all torn, he was loudly cheered, even by the roughs themselves."

The crowd, it would appear, was fairly good-tempered but demanded another umpire. This, Lord Harris, who refused to leave the ground, was determined they should not have. The Governor, who was present, sent for policemen, but each time the umpire reappeared the people rushed on to the ground again.

"Lord Harris behaved awfully well, leaning up against the paling, with all the roughs crushing round him, smoking a cigarette. He waited till 6 o'clock announced the time for drawing the stumps, when the team formed a ring round the umpire and marched him out through the crowd.

"This was on Saturday. On the Monday morning it rained hard, and now what I call poetic justice was done. Had the match been allowed to proceed on Saturday, the Australians must have got a lot of runs, and the English team would have had the bad wicket. Instead of which the Australians had to go in. The Englishmen got them all out for 49 runs, thus winning the match in one innings and 41 runs."

The second scene occurred during P. F. Warner's first Test Match tour in Australia in 1903–4. Here is his description of the incident, which occurred after Hill[1] had been given run out by the Umpire Crockett[2]:

When Crockett told Hill he was out he showed by his manner that he was greatly surprised at the decision. Hill *did not say a word in protest* to Crockett, but the way in which he walked back to the pavilion could not possibly have left anyone in doubt as to what he himself thought of Crockett's ruling. Immediately after Hill had reached the pavilion a perfect storm of groans and hisses came *from the members in the pavilion,* and this chorus of disapproval was immediately taken up by the "rinkers".

A minute or two later I walked to the pavilion, with the intention of asking the members to desist; but instead of them listening to me, the "booing" became louder than ever. At this moment, Noble[3], who was next in, came from the pavilion, and we walked together to the pitch. We both sat down for a few minutes, waiting for the disturbance to subside.

During these moments Noble and I were talking the matter over, and I told him that we should be compelled to leave the field if the demonstration against Crockett did not cease. After a while the noise abated somewhat, and Noble advised me to go on with the game. The moment we started play, the noise became, if possible, greater than ever, and shouts of "How much did you pay Crockett, Warner?", "Have you got your coffin ready, Crockett?", and "Which gate are you leaving by, Crockett?" rent the air.

[1] Clem Hill (1877–1945). See note on p. 45.
[2] Wisden notes that the long-serving Australian umpire Robert W. Crockett (1853–1935) was universally respected for the impartial accuracy of his decisions.
[3] M. A. Noble (1873–1940). See note on p. 27.

It was a most difficult situation but I think that, on the whole, I acted wisely in not withdrawing the team from the field. People in England, however, can have no conception of the yelling and hissing that went on that afternoon right up to the drawing of stumps; even such hardened Test Match players as Hirst and Rhodes were quite upset.

I myself was fielding deep mid-on to Braund when Hill was given out, so was not in a position to say whether the decision was correct or not; but Foster, who was standing at short-leg, and Hayward, who was at deep-point, declare that Hill was out by a foot. But this is really beside the point; Crockett was there to decide such questions, and from his ruling there could be no appeal. There was absolutely no excuse for this demonstration, which was as disgraceful as it was unwarranted. It was started, as I have said, in the members' pavilion, from which point it was impossible to see what had occurred.

As the players returned from the field, Crockett, who eventually left the ground under the care of two detectives, was "hooted" at more fiercely than ever by many of the members in the pavilion, though it is only fair to add that a large section applauded him loudly, and one member, I was informed, was so disgusted with the behaviour of his fellows that he forthwith resigned his membership. Noble and the Australian Eleven generally were as much upset as we were, and next morning I received scores of letters condoling with us on the bad treatment we had received. The whole business was an insult to the game of cricket.

Mr. F. A. Iredale[4], in a letter to the *Daily Mail*, stated that my walking to the pavilion was the cause of the trouble. In answer to Mr. Iredale I would like to point out that the row had already begun before I started on my fruitless journey to the pavilion. All I intended to do was to appeal to the better feelings of the members, and if they had allowed me to do so I feel sure I would have succeeded in persuading them to stop the demonstration against Crockett.

Even in those distant days, an old International cricketer such as Mr. Iredale was not immune from the disease of seeing things with only one eye.

---

[4] F.A. Iredale (1867–1926) played Test cricket for Australia between 1896 and 1900, averaging 36.68 with the bat.

During the course of the tour we were afforded similar examples, including one which caused us more mirth than annoyance. An old and well-known Australian International had decided, from a distance of some one thousand odd miles, that the wicket at Hobart was quite fit for play! I cannot say that I ever participated in an incident in any way comparable with these two historic scenes. The nearest approach to it occurred not in a Test Match, but in a match against Victoria in 1929, when Mr. Chapman had to take the English team off the field. This intolerable situation was firmly handled by Ryder, the Victorian captain, who declared his State's innings closed.

The reason of this outburst of irrational hooliganism was almost unbelievably childish. Victoria had scored a great many runs. In fact, a new ball was requisitioned with the total near 600.[5] One batsman (Woodfull) had already made well over 200 runs, while the other (Ironmonger) had just come in at the fall of the ninth wicket.

It might have been expected that the spectators, in view of the size of their side's total, would be in a good humour, or at least would not have objected to a side which had fielded out for 600 runs taking the advantage which a new ball confers on the fielding side. But no. It was considered unsporting of the English team to take a new ball, and to put on a bowler who ordinarily used the new ball, against a tail-end batsman such as Ironmonger. The incident, it may be said, was attributed to a lack of humour on the part of the English team. One can only suppose that the Australians arrived at this startling conclusion by conveniently forgetting that a bowler and a new ball are used as much against one batsman as another; and that, apart from the natural desire of a fielding side to get batsmen out as quickly and cheaply as possible, a side which has fielded out for 600 runs is as anxious to return to the comparative rest and quiet of the dressing-room, as an Australian crowd to see its further discomfiture.

So far as the behaviour of crowds is concerned, cricket cannot be

---

[5] The previous new ball had been taken at a total of approximately 370 owing to the condition of the old ball.

compared with baseball or football, for in these two games a confused medley of sound and shouting means little or nothing to the players, who have not the time to pay attention to it, or the ability to distinguish one single word, save perhaps on the occasion of a kick at goal being taken. In this respect cricket has more in common with lawn tennis or golf. In both these games Australian crowds conform to the standard of behaviour that is accepted the world over.

If it is seriously suggested that the authorities who are responsible for maintaining order on Australian grounds are justified in pleading their inability to control their crowds, it might well be suggested that the sooner they consider the advisability of making way for those who can, the better it will be for all.

If, on the other hand, it is maintained that the behaviour of Australian crowds is perfectly fair and unobjectionable, and that it is in the best interests of cricket that the greatest of all cricket matches, England versus Australia, should be played in the atmosphere such as I have described, it will be known, once and for all, whether the Australian authorities are, or are not, in favour of the continuance of such behaviour.

It is no use blinding oneself to the fact that a total absence of any attempt on the part of the authorities to control their crowds and demonstrations must give rise to a feeling that these performances, even if they have not the active support of the authorities, at least have their tacit approval.

Although we were fortunate in not being concerned in a scene on the grand scale, we were constantly subjected to the annoyance of minor episodes, the cumulative effect of which was far more distressing. Possibly we owe our avoidance of a general action to a rumour that, in the event of the English side leaving the field on account of the treatment they were receiving, it was possible that they would refuse to return. The authorities, finding themselves in a dilemma, would then be forced to decide whether they should claim the match against a side refusing to play, thereby publishing the circumstances to the world at large, or face a demonstration of their own supporters when no further play was forthcoming, for that day at least.

The Australian, whether he be the man in the street or the mayor of a town "way back", by force of habit is constantly at pains to emphasize the good nature and fairness of the Australian barracker. Towards the end of our tour there was a noticeable weakening of this conviction. But there is no doubt that a combination of constant repetition and the wish to believe in its truth is responsible for its general acceptance. This childlike faith, and its twin – "that barracking is so amusing and the remarks so clever and entertaining" – is an excellent example of auto-suggestion or Couéism. No one who knew the members of the last two English teams in Australia would accuse them of lacking a sense of humour.

But I dare swear that during the course of the two tours not a score of really funny remarks emanated from outside the pickets, and the constant repetition of such threadbare "humour" became so pointless as to become a weariness of the flesh. Perhaps the man who makes one reasonably amusing remark early in the day collects a little following which regards him as a hero. He has to play up to his admirers for the rest of the day, or lose his public. I have often wondered how the spectators in the neighbourhood of a loud-mouthed barracker could tolerate so intolerable a nuisance. The majority of them must be keen in the first place to be there at all. One would expect that any genuine enthusiast would be tempted to tell the owner of an empty head and a pair of brazen lungs that he was spoiling the enjoyment of others round about him by going off at minute intervals like a raucous maroon.[6] But I understand that this does not happen.

On the field of play, of course, one necessarily hears far more than those who sit aloft and far removed, whether in the Press Box or in the rooms and offices of the various cricketing associations. Many of the gentlemen who occupied seats in those quarters would, I feel sure, object to their wives and children spending a day with the main crowd and hearing words, not often used in the presence of women and children, freely bandied about from twelve o'clock to the close of play.

---

[6] A type of firework.

For my part, I have played in only ten Test Matches, but I have never yet heard an Australian batsman or bowler barracked by a crowd in a Test Match in Australia. The nearest approach to the barracking of an Australian took the form of a little mild and sarcastic clapping when Ironmonger fielded a ball: Ironmonger in the opinion of Australian crowds being a slow and clumsy fieldsman.

On the other hand, I have seen nearly every member of the visiting side treated to a strong dose of the crowd's disapproval. Ask any cricketer who has played cricket for England in Australia during the last twenty years, and he will tell you that boasts concerning the impartiality of an Australian crowd are so vain as to be almost pathetic.

I am not suggesting that an Australian crowd should always be expected to be impartial: I am only pointing out how utterly unfounded is the claim to impartiality.

The following incident occurred in the last innings of the last Test Match, and was described in an Australian paper as follows:

There was a demonstration by a section of the big crowd which witnessed the play in the Fifth Test Match at the Sydney Cricket Ground yesterday, when the English captain, D. R. Jardine, complained to Umpire Borwick about the fast bowler, Alexander, running on the wicket.

The crowd jeered and "counted out" Jardine, and barracking broke out afresh when he patted the spots on the wicket. . . . There was a regrettable scene in Alexander's fourth over. The fast bowler was still bowling over the wicket, and one ball rose sharply and struck Jardine a sickening blow on the left side. Immediately there was a roar from the crowd, and then, while some of the fieldsmen approached Jardine, many of the spectators joined in sustained applause. Such conduct was unpardonable.

I need only add that a former Australian captain agreed with me that the wearing of the wicket, against which I was protesting, should never have been permitted.

At Brisbane, on two occasions, the ball bounded queerly and disabled an English fieldsman. On both occasions the crowd jeered and cheered. Are these to be taken as examples of impartial criticism?

I could refer to many similar incidents. I will refrain, however, for I have already indicated sufficiently clearly the kind of treatment which has been so frequently meted out to English sides in the past. There is, however, one example of a breach of manners which I shall mention, if it is only to express our regret that such rudeness should have occurred.

On the occasion of a certain State match, a high dignitary honoured the proceedings with his presence. As is the usual custom on these occasions, both sides lined up on the grass outside the pavilion gate to have the honour and privilege of being introduced to him. While this short ceremony was being performed, I distinguished the well-known sounds of a "counting out".

I was at a loss to account for the cause. At that time, for reasons which I need not specify, I was temporarily the object of what may be described as a mild form of "popularity" campaign. I accordingly offered to bet an even penny with the opposing captain on whether it was he or I who was receiving this latest mark of the crowd's favour and attention. To my surprise, I was informed that the bet was off, since it was neither of us, but the dignitary, who was receiving this token of the crowd's loyalty and esteem, and for no better reason (for he was extremely popular) than that his presence resulted in a postponement of the game for three minutes.

I am sure I can speak for the Australian as well as the M.C.C. team when I say that we were deeply sensible of the honour done us by this visit. Both teams, I know, resented this unfortunate and regret-table lapse of manners. Here was Democracy arrogating to itself the right to demand its full pound of flesh, for which it had paid the magnificent sum of a shilling or two at the gate, and refusing to concede three minutes of a whole day's cricket to a visit which should mean as much to the crowd as it does to the officials of the ground and the players concerned.

It is often suggested in Australia that any barracking that may occur is the fault of the players, never of the Australian public; and it is urged, in mitigation, that every freeborn Australian has an absolute and inalienable right to self-expression.

Whether one subscribes to this Article of Faith is not of much importance. My objection is limited to the hostility and lack of taste to which this self-assumed licence gives rise.

I cannot help thinking that a psychologist would find it extra-ordinarily interesting to experiment with an Australian barracker. Let him consider the following case, which, I hasten to add, is purely hypothetical. An Australian barracker has expressed his disapproval of a batsman's efforts for his side in his usual unmeasured terms, and has proceeded to satisfy any doubts which there may have been as to the batsman's ancestry and ultimate destination. The batsman then walks to the ringside and genially offers the larrikin his bat and pads, expressing the hope that he will take his place at the wickets and show how the game should really be played. There would be, I think, an essential difference between the Australian barracker and his mild English equivalent. I believe that the Australian barracker, after accepting the challenge and making a sorry exhibition of himself at the wickets, would suffer no confusion, since, if I am right, the crowd would acclaim him as "a good sport".

In similar circumstances I feel equally confident that an English barracker would pray that the ground might swallow him. He would certainly disappear through the crowd in record time.

It is not for me to suggest a remedy for unfair barracking, but I should like to see the following experiment tried:

Before the gates are opened for a match, let notices be posted over every turnstile, stating that no play is guaranteed. Inside the ground, let the crowd be faced with further notices to the effect that, in the event of any barracking or noisy demonstrations, play will auto-matically cease for the space of half an hour.

Supposing that the game was a New Year match between Victoria and New South Wales. On the first day of this experiment I do not imagine that there would be an hour's play. On the second and subsequent days I doubt if there would be half an hour's stoppage.

One objection to this procedure, however, would be that the home crowd would have the power to suspend play by means of a series of scenes and demonstrations and so force a draw when circumstances looked unfavourable for their side. For all that, I think the experiment might prove interesting and worth trying.

I have said that one does not expect an Australian crowd to be impartial. In size of population Australia is a small country compared with England, and I will go so far as to suggest that impartiality might even be construed as an unworthy sign in the less populated country, which, for that reason, feels "up against it", but I can assure the reader that any fear of over-impartiality may be summarily dismissed.

Much of the trouble arises, no doubt, from over-keenness on the part of spectators, and on that account one should not judge too harshly. An English team touring in Australia is for many Australians a symbol which gives them an opportunity of demonstrating their loyalty.

Now the cricketers who compose our touring teams are modest fellows, and when, on arrival at a town, they have a great reception, they would be the first to admit that the reception was very largely unconnected with their own merits, but simply a tribute to the Motherland, which, for the time being, it is their privilege to represent on a cricket field.

Unfortunately, however, one is sometimes left with the unpleasant feeling that demonstrations of hostility are not always solely directed against the players.

That some Australians felt this themselves I know only too well. After several occasions in which the crowds had excelled themselves, my mail-bag frequently contained half a dozen letters of sympathy, bidding me pay no attention to such exhibitions, which, in the writer's opinion, were only another example of Bolshevism, Southern Irish antipathy to the Motherland, or whatever was the particular writer's pet antipathy. While I appreciated the thought that inspired these letters, I am afraid such explanations, however ingenious or varied, could never bear impartial investigation.

The Australian Press could do much to help in this respect. I have grave doubts, however, whether, with the exception of one or two of the leading papers in Melbourne and Sydney (which, in all probability, are not read by the majority of barrackers), the Australian cricketing authorities can count on much help from this quarter.

One has only to criticize anything which exists in Australia to raise a hue and cry in its defence, irrespective of the merits of the case.

No doubt a lot of barracking is thoughtless, nor is it to be expected that Australia should appreciate the Imperial responsibilities of cricket as deeply as we do at home[7]; but a consideration of these responsibilities should prove a great incentive to action on the part of those who are determined that these painful exhibitions of hooliganism shall be suppressed.

It is only too seldom appreciated in England, let alone Australia, that there are millions of British citizens throughout the world who take their cue, so far as behaviour at cricket matches is concerned, from Test Matches between England and Australia – matches which have so much in their past history to appeal to all of us, irrespective of colour, creed, or race.

Already I am told that the accounts of last winter's cricket have scarcely conduced to the orderliness of spectators, even in this country, though I cannot say that I have noticed this myself. Rather let the responsible authorities everywhere deal firmly with what is rapidly becoming a menace to the enjoyment of the best of all summer games. As they do their work, may they have the satisfaction of seeing:

> "The hooting mob of yesterday in silent awe return
> To glean up the scattered ashes into history's golden urn."

---

[7] See Ric Sissons' and Brian Stoddart's book *Cricket and Empire* for an account of the tangled relations between the two.

15

A Digression –
On Fishing

Elsewhere I have touched on the importance of enjoying a tour to the full. While it is not possible for cricketers to drink too deeply of life and yet maintain the necessary fitness and stamina to weather a long and tiring tour, it would be neither natural nor healthy for them to think cricket, dream cricket, and play cricket all the time.

Between the inky but enthusiastic ages of eight to fourteen, unlimited play may seem the height of bliss. It did to me. Today, however, too much cricket is expected of most first-class cricketers.[1] A high pitch of enthusiasm is all very well for a time, but flesh and blood cannot escape the inevitable bugbear of staleness. With a touring side consisting of 17 players, the opportunities of standing down from a match are comparatively frequent. All players need a rest – the captain by no means least – and in affording me occasional relief the team showed every consideration. They realized that "the Skipper had a lot taken out of him during the course of a Test Match", and it was at their suggestion that it became almost a rule that the "Skipper" should always have a match off immediately after a Test.

It is possible to travel thousands of miles through Australia without gaining the least conception of the country and its prevailing conditions. The first time I visited Australia, for instance, I travelled

---

[1] During the 1932 English season DRJ played 39 innings in 29 first-class games.

from Perth to Brisbane. I saw five State capitals and not a single rabbit.

By missing an occasional match, I was afforded not only the opportunity of seeing something of the real Australia, but of enjoying another form of Australian hospitality.

Punch, with good reason, has commented on the absurd publicity given to cricketers' hobbies and peculiarities, even to the clothes they wore or should have worn. I had one hobby (if I may use the term to connote a passion for fishing) which stood me in good stead throughout this tour. There is no better way of seeing a country, or of forgetting the troubles of life, than to pursue the gentle art of Izaak Walton.

Had I not been able to rely upon so capable a vice-captain as R. E. S. Wyatt, I could not have deserted the side, as I did upon three separate occasions: once in Australia, once in Tasmania, and once in New Zealand.

Cricket and fishing seem to have something in common. My conversion to fishing was in some measure due to the late Andrew Lang.[2]

St. Andrews, that old grey city by the sea, which is the home and cradle of golf, always reckoned Mr. Lang "a bit of a character". Perhaps it was his incurable loyalty to cricket – in spite of his environment – that earned him this reputation in a town which was not lacking in "characters". Indeed, I think that Mr. Lang was living up to his reputation when he extended his friendship to a very small boy and heaped kindnesses upon his head.

Those early associations with Mr. Lang are treasured memories.

To my delight he treated me as a "grown-up". He would discourse to me at length on subjects as far apart as Cricket and Scottish History, and, if at that early age I was unable to appreciate his profound scholarship, I could certainly share his enthusiasm for the game.

---

[2] Andrew Lang (1844–1912) was an astoundingly prolific man of letters, who wrote on many subjects, including Spiritualism, old French Ballads, and indeed cricket: his brother T.W. Lang was the famous Oxford and Gloucestershire fast bowler. According to his obituary in The Times (22nd July 1912) there was in Lang's manner (as in DRJ's) a 'touch of superciliousness', but (as with DRJ) it 'did not go very deep nor prevent his being loved by his friends.'

SECOND TEST MATCH – WOODFULL BOWLED BY ALLEN FOR 10

THIRD TEST MATCH – WOODFULL LOSES HIS BAT IN PLAYING LARWOOD TO LEG

THIRD TEST MATCH – VOCE'S LEG FIELD WHEN BOWLING TO PONSFORD

Photo]   [*Central Press*

HAMMOND, MAGNIFICENT AS A SLIP FIELD, CAUGHT LITSTER, IN THE MATCH
AGAINST QUEENSLAND, BY HOLDING A BALL WHICH STRUCK HIS CHEST

FOURTH TEST MATCH – WOODFULL BOWLED BY MITCHELL, WHO TWICE HAD HIS WICKET IN THIS MATCH

FOURTH TEST MATCH – RICHARDSON FINELY STUMPED BY AMES OFF HAMMOND FOR 83

FOURTH TEST MATCH – BROMLEY, THE YOUNG LEFT-HANDER, CAUGHT BY VERITY OFF LARWOOD

FOURTH TEST MATCH – WOODFULL DUCKS TO A BALL FROM LARWOOD WHICH KEEPS LOW ENOUGH TO STRIKE HIM IN THE RIBS. HERE IS A FULL LEG FIELD. LEFT TO RIGHT: LEYLAND, ALLEN, AMES, JARDINE, VERITY, SUCLIFFE

FOURTH TEST MATCH – MCCABE CAUGHT BY JARDINE (ARM OUTSTRETCHED) OFF ALLEN FOR 20

FIFTH TEST MATCH – JARDINE CAUGHT AT SLIP BY RICHARDSON OFF IRONMONGER

FIFTH TEST MATCH – LARWOOD JUST MISSES HIS CENTURY. CAUGHT BY IRONMONGER OFF LEE FOR 98

FIFTH TEST MATCH – HAMMOND (101 AND 75 NOT OUT) – A STUDY IN FORCEFUL GRACE

FIFTH TEST MATCH – HAMMOND: A STUDY IN EXPRESSION AFTER A BALL FROM O'REILLY HAD PASSED HIM

FIFTH TEST MATCH – AMES RUN OUT FOR 4. A VERY MUCH-DEBATED VERDICT

FIFTH TEST MATCH – HAMMOND (LEFT) AND WYATT COMING IN AT THE END OF THE MATCH

CRICKETERS AT "CHAMPAGNE POOL", WAIRAKEI HOT SPRINGS, NEW ZEALAND. IN FOREGROUND ARE H. SUCLIFFE (EXTREME LEFT), R. E. S. WYATT (SIDEWAYS TO CAMERA), G. O. B. ALLEN (NEAREST CAMERA), P. F. WARNER (IN SHIRT SLEEVES), T. B. MITCHELL. (EXTREME RIGHT). THE MAORI GUIDE IS BEHIND MITCHELL

We were in complete agreement that the two "Cs" – Cricket and Classics – were the two most important things in the world.

One day Mr. Lang staggered me with the announcement that he felt we should add Fishing to the two "Cs", and I shall never forget the shock I suffered on listening to this unabashed declaration of heresy.

Even a present of the wherewithal to buy a rod hardly weakened my contempt for the "new religion".

I am bound to confess that today I rank that one-time heresy before both of the two "Cs"!

Practically no fishing in Australia is preserved, nor is there any restriction upon the manner in which fish may be caught.

Three good friends of mine were kind enough to take me to the only public fishing which, as far as I know, is reserved exclusively for fly fishermen. This entailed a journey of nearly 200 miles from Melbourne, which we accomplished with nothing worse to record than three burst tyres.

I shall not attempt to describe the joys of being again "where the bright waters meet"[3]; I leave this for abler pens than mine.

On our arrival we were greeted by Mr. Harold Herbert, whose pictures are well known to all art lovers. On this occasion, Mr. Herbert excelled himself. Giving his artistic temperament full play, he had decorated the hut assigned to me with a variety of trays, each bearing the inscription, "For the Ashes". Over my mirror he had dangled a fearsome notice forbidding cricketers to wade in pads, while over my bed hung the well-known cricketing picture, entitled "The Hope of his Side".

Subsequently, Mr. Herbert informed me that he had scoured the whole of the adjacent Bogong Valley to procure this priceless art treasure.

Fortunately, one of my hosts, Mr. Tom Luxton, was a fisherman of approximately the same class as myself. My two other hosts, Lytton and Carl Stephens, were classes above us and would rank as

---

[3] The quotation is from the title of Harry Plunkett Greene's classic evocation of chalk stream fishing, published in 1924.

masters in any part of the world.

I do not propose to try the patience of even the keenest fisherman by recounting our exploits in detail. Two incidents must suffice. The first has no connection with fishing, save that the charm of fishing is so often enhanced by the opportunities that are afforded to the student of Natural History. Two of my companions saw a kookaburra bird (familiarly known as the "laughing jackass") accidentally touch the water and drench its feathers. The unfortunate bird then perched himself on a post near the riverside to dry his feathers. This was too much for one of his companions, who swooped down from a tree and knocked him off. This sally was greeted with a volley of sarcastic chuckles from another kookaburra perched on an observation-point nearby.[4] No sooner had the wretched bird emulated "Brer Rabbit" by "gaddering himself tergedder" and resuming his perch than the whole business was repeated to the accompaniment of further sarcastic chuckles.

After the third performance my friend, deeming it prudent to intervene, placed the unfortunate kookaburra on a post screened by a branch. This acted as a protection from further assaults. After a quarter of an hour's industrious preening, the insulted bird flew away, pursued by nothing worse than more chuckles.

My friends were all high priests of the dry-fly cult. On the first evening, just before dusk, two of us came upon a large pool covered with irises. Undeterred by the carcass of a dead pig which was stranded on the bank, we started fishing. For the next thirty minutes we repeatedly changed our flies, but without the least response on the part of the fish.

> "Oh, never a fly contains a hook,
> Fish say, in the Eternal Brook."[5]

---

[4] It is tempting to interpret the 'kookaburra incident' allegorically with, perhaps, DRJ as the beleaguered victim, and the dastardly tormentors as Australian barrackers . . .

[5] This is from Rupert Brooke's poem *Heaven*, which continues: 'But more than mundane weeds are there, / And mud, celestially fair, / Fat caterpillars drift around, / And Paradisal grubs are found;'. Brooke possessed great cricketing as well as poetic talent: he topped the Rugby School bowling averages in 1906, with 19 wickets at an average of 14.05.

As far as we could discover, the fish were feeding on the surface upon a small black gnat about the size of a sturgeon's egg. There was no imitating this insect, and after an hour we abandoned the attempt in disgust.

Curiously enough, in my own limited experience, I have noticed this phenomenon four times in the Southern Hemisphere. For, in addition to the present occasion, I have met with it twice in Tasmania and once in New Zealand. For want of a better term, we called this behaviour on the part of the fish "smutting". The only occasion on which I have known the fisherman to win under these conditions was when I put my pride in my pocket, and risked the contempt of my brother anglers by offering two sunk flies. The reward was instantaneous. Each fly was quickly taken, and I had the satisfaction of landing both fish: one on a small Blue Charm, the other on a March Brown.

Most fishermen have heard of the wonderful sport that is to be enjoyed in the catching of monsters in New Zealand, while Norway, Iceland, Newfoundland and Labrador are famous the world over and have their several champions. Tasmania, however, seems to have escaped the notice of all but a very few of those who are devoted to the gentle art.

On the occasion of the M.C.C. tour in 1928–29, I had been fortunate enough to savour the delights of fishing in Tasmania's little-known interior. It is curious, especially in these days, to find comparatively wide areas of the large-scale map of Tasmania still marked as unexplored, and I have it on the authority of an amateur explorer that even in modern maps there are many sheets of water incorrectly marked, while others are not shown at all. Who knows what sport awaits an enterprising fisherman with the time and opportunity to trek off with half a dozen pack-horses to try his luck

On disembarking at Launceston I was delighted to find my host of four years ago waiting on the quayside. Almost before we had exchanged greetings, he was inquiring after my intentions with regard to fishing. To which I replied that they were as determined as they had been four years ago, but that I hoped they would be attended with better results.

It was not possible for us to depart immediately, as, while in

Melbourne, I had promised a friend to attend the prize-giving at his old school in Launceston, the oldest school in Australasia. Here, I may say, I was awarded a prize which I shall always treasure, the school authorities in their wisdom having diagnosed quite correctly that scholastic successes had come my way at very infrequent intervals.[6] My fisherman host had decided to take me to the same stretch of water we had visited four years previously. This is called the Penstock, and though it is situated roughly half-way between Launceston and Hobart, it lies considerably off the beaten track. Here the water for hydraulic power is collected. In its way it is probably the most remarkable piece of fishing water in the world. Its altitude is between three and four thousand feet above sea level. After the heat of Australia it is almost a pleasure to find it necessary to thaw one's waders, which have frozen stiff while hanging out to dry overnight. This, indeed, was our experience in 1929, when we had camped in tents. Since then my host had built with his own hands a delightful fishing hut, calling it by a most appropriate aboriginal name meaning "The Song of the Birds".

One side of the lagoon, over a stretch of about two miles, was for the most part only nine inches deep at a distance of twenty or thirty feet from the bank. Some idea of the size of the trout may be gathered when I say that on the occasion of our first visit we caught some nineteen fish averaging just over six pounds, anything under four pounds being returned. While it is not always easy to conceal one's own presence in such shallow water, it is not difficult to spot the moving fish. A large trout cruising just beneath the surface looks more like a shark, with its dorsal fin out of the water, than a harmless brownie.

In our camp it was the rule that no gaff or landing net should be used; any fish, whatever its size, must be beached. All the fishing is dry fly, and 2× or 3× casts are used. In spite of the lightness of the tackle and the genuine fighting powers of these large brown trout, it is extraordinary how "hard" one learns to be after fishing for any

---

[6] Perhaps so, but it should be remembered that DRJ pursued his academic career amidst formidable rivals, at Winchester and then Oxford.

length of time in these waters. I cannot help feeling that in our own country most fishermen who are lucky enough to hook a three- or four-pound trout treat him with far too much respect, largely due to the very natural fear of losing a big fish.

At the Penstock there is no such fear, and the fisherman who is new to the district soon finds himself prepared to try experiments which he would never dream of risking in similar circumstances at home.

Since my first visit, my friends had for the most part given up beaching their fish. They now carry in their breast pocket a stick about nine inches long, slightly weighted at one end. In four or five minutes they will bring a five-pound fish to their feet, tap him on the head with the stick while still in the water, and attach him to their belt. The carrying belt, it may be added, is by far the most convenient device for carrying several heavy fish at a time. The Penstock has a fascination all its own, and it is not always easy amid such surroundings to resist the temptation to spend much time in watching fish rather than fishing for them.

My host had a great theory that fish frequently sleep during the daytime. He told me that he had often seen fish come hurrying into the shallow water to secrete themselves beside or beneath protecting weeds, and that from the ease with which they could be surprised, and the futility of fishing a dry fly over them, he concluded that they had retreated there to sleep. On one occasion I remember putting my fly beside a single reed growing out of the water, which was on the regular run of a fish I had been watching for about five minutes.

While I was waiting for his return another fish came in from the deeper water at an angle which would have forced him to cross my line, lying as it was in water four or five inches deep. About nine feet away from my line he pulled up dead, pointing my line like a well-trained dog. After a few seconds he cruised a foot or two towards it. I should like to describe him in the words of Rupert Brooke, as "Rippling in dark ecstasy", but I fear I cannot truthfully do so.

If ever a fish registered quite clearly that "he knew all about that game", this fellow did, and turning, he made off for the deep water. Perhaps I should add that I was so intrigued with his manoeuvres that I missed the fish for which I was fishing. He had taken my fly just as I was bidding farewell to his inquisitive companion.

There were four of us in my host's hut, and my three companions, who were experts, did their best to teach me all they knew. They were then engaged in carrying out an exceedingly interesting experiment. Even during my four years' absence, the fish on the Penstock had shown very noticeable diminution in size, though not in number. A fair percentage of the fish caught (we returned them under 3lbs. on this occasion) could fairly have been described as "slabs", as their weight was far short of the standard one might have expected from their size.

My friends were taking samples of the backbones of healthy fish which were up to normal weight, and also of these "slabs", for the purpose of analysis in the laboratory. I believe that all over Tasmania difficulty has been encountered both with livestock and crops, owing to a curious lack of natural phosphates. It seems possible that this deficiency may also account for the falling off in size and the poorness of their condition.

If the laboratory tests prove that there is a marked deficiency of phosphates in the "slabs", the experiment is to be carried one stage further. Phosphates will be carted up to the Penstock and sprayed as regularly as possible over a small area on the bushes from which the flies, upon which the fish feed, hatch out. Any consistent improvement in the condition of the fish caught in this locality will then be noted over a period.

Where brown and rainbow trout are found together, the rainbow usually succeeds in ousting the brown. On the Penstock, however, there are very few rainbows, and the feed is so plentiful that there is more than enough for all.

The cold of the night and the cool of the morning are delightfully refreshing, but the days can be exceedingly hot, and the rays of the sun striking direct or reflected from the water rapidly transform one's face into a living advertisement for vintage port.

The scene changes to Lake Taupo, in the North Island of New Zealand. Here, after seeing the Geyser Valley and the fairy-like beauty of the land and riverside, one is prepared for anything: even for a fish as magnificent as those which decorate the walls of almost every hotel and rest-house.

Fish in Taupo vary considerably in size from year to year, but the average must be as high as anywhere in the world. Much stronger rods and tackle are ordinarily the fashion in New Zealand as compared with Tasmania. On Taupo, and the rivers out of the lake, dry fly fishing is little practised. To achieve success in the river mouths and further upstream, most fishermen, whatever their skill and previous experience, will find it advisable to go to school again.

The correct method is more like salmon fishing in low water in the autumn than anything else I know, except that a greased line is not used. Much, I believe, depends upon a curious twitching movement in carrying the slack into one's left hand in lengths of approximately three inches at a time. It is essential that the whole water should be covered more steadily than is usual in salmon fishing; but local knowledge of the river-bed and where the fish may be expected to lie, is, as elsewhere, half the battle.

Within a two-mile radius, the weary fisherman may find three different sorts of warm sulphur or iron baths to comfort him. These baths should cure an ordinary human being of any normal form of rheumatism: they certainly cured me. Their temperature varies considerably. They are extremely well-run and at a trifling cost; moreover, they have the sovereign advantage of rendering bathers immune from catching cold, however cool the night air may be in comparison with the temperature of the water.

The people of Taupo literally exude kindness and good fellow-ship: they cannot do enough for a stranger within their gates. Their genuine love and admiration for the Mother country is as patent as it is encouraging.

The Maoris, too, are friendliness personified, and though first-class fishermen themselves, are always ready to give both advice and the weirdest of flies to any brother angler. The flies they use must be seen to be believed, but there is no doubt that they catch the fish better than any other legitimate contrivance.

Taupo, in all its loveliness, should be one of the most popular playgrounds of the world.[7] I shall never forget my all too brief stay in this fisherman's paradise, nor the unbounded kindness showered upon me by Mr. Branson and his charming family; nor yet the kindness of my host, Johnny Sheehan.

[7] There is no longer any shortage of places to stay in Taupo: the area is now a major tourist destination.

Appendix

M.C.C. AND BOARD OF CONTROL

Below are given the cables exchanged between the M.C.C. and the Board of Control concerning leg-theory bowling, beginning with that sent by the Board during the third Test Match at Adelaide:

JANUARY 18. BOARD OF CONTROL TO M.C.C.

Body-line bowling has assumed such proportions as to menace the best interests of the game, making protection of the body by batsmen the main consideration and causing intensely bitter feeling between the players as well as injury. In our opinion it is unsportsmanlike. Unless stopped at once, it is likely to upset the friendly relations existing between Australia and England.

[Gratton once delivered a celebrated description of a speech by Lord Claire. Allowing for a hot day, hasty tempers, and a more than usually ill-behaved and demonstrative crowd, I think that Gratton's description of that speech rings all too true of the Board of Control's original communication to the Marylebone Cricket Club: "Great generosity of assertion, great thrift of argument, a turn to be offensive without the power to be severe – fury in the temper and famine in the phrase."]

JANUARY 23. M.C.C. TO BOARD OF CONTROL

We, the Marylebone Club, deplore your cable message and deprecate the opinion that there has been unsportsmanlike play.

We have the fullest confidence in the captain and team managers. We are convinced that they would do nothing that would infringe the laws of cricket or the spirit of the game and we have no evidence that our confidence is misplaced.

Much as we regret the accidents to Woodfull and Oldfield, we understand that in neither case was the bowler to blame.

If the Board wishes to propose a new law, or rule, the proposal shall receive our careful consideration in due course.

We hope that the situation is not now as serious as your cable message appears to indicate, but if it is such as would jeopardize the good relations between the English and Australian cricketers and if you consider it desirable to cancel the remainder of the programme, we would consent with great reluctance.

JANUARY 30. BOARD OF CONTROL TO M.C.C.

We, the Australian Board of Control, appreciate your difficulty in dealing with the matter raised in our cable without having seen the actual play. We unanimously regard body-line bowling, as adopted in some games of the present Tour, as being opposed to the spirit of cricket and unnecessarily dangerous to players. We are deeply concerned that the ideals of the game shall be protected and therefore appoint a sub-committee to report on action necessary to eliminate such bowling from all cricket in Australia from the beginning of next season. Will forward copy of committee's recommendation for your consideration and hope for your co-operation in application to all cricket. We do not consider it necessary to cancel remainder of programme.

FEBRUARY 2. M.C.C. TO BOARD OF CONTROL

We note with pleasure that you do not consider it necessary to cancel the remainder of the programme and that you are postponing the whole issue until the Tour is completed. May we accept this as a clear indication that the good sportsmanship of our team is not in question?

We are sure you appreciate how impossible it would be to play any Test in the spirit we all desire unless both sides are satisfied that there is no reflection on their sportsmanship. When your recommendation reaches us it shall receive our most careful consideration and will be submitted to an Imperial Cricket Conference.

FEBRUARY 9. BOARD OF CONTROL TO M.C.C.

We do not regard the sportsmanship of your team as being in question. Our position was fully considered at the recent meeting in Sydney and is as indicated in our cable message of January 30. It is the particular class of bowling referred to therein which we consider as not in the best interest of cricket, and in this view, we understand, we are supported by many eminent English cricketers. We join heartily with you in hoping that the remaining Tests will be played with the traditional good feeling.

On April 28, the Board of Control sent proposals to the M.C.C., suggesting the following addition to the Laws of Cricket:

> Any ball delivered which, in the opinion of the umpire at the bowler's end, is bowled with the intent of intimidating the batsman or injuring him, shall be considered unfair and "no ball" shall be called.
>
> The bowler shall be notified of the reason. If the offence be repeated by the same bowler in the same innings, he shall be instructed by the umpire to cease bowling, and the over shall be regarded as completed. The bowler shall not be permitted to bowl again during the innings.

JUNE 12. M.C.C. TO BOARD OF CONTROL

The committee presume that the class of bowling to which the proposed new law would apply is that referred to as "body-line bowling" in the Australian Board of Control's cable of January 18.

The committee consider that the term "body-line" bowling is misleading and improper. It has led to much inaccuracy of thought by confusing the short bumping ball, whether directed on the off, middle, or leg stump, with what is known as "leg-theory".

The term "body-line" would appear to imply a direct attack by the bowler on the batsman. The committee consider that such an implication applied to any English bowling in Australia is improper and incorrect.

Such action on the part of any bowler would be an offence against the spirit of the game, and would be immediately condemned. The practice of bowling on the leg stump, with a field placed on the leg side necessary for such bowling, is legitimate, and has been in force for many years.

It has generally been referred to as "leg-theory". The present habit of batsmen who move in front of their wicket with the object of gliding straight balls to leg tends to give the impression that the bowler is bowling at the batsman, especially in the case of a fast bowler when the batsman mistimes the ball and is hit.

The new law recommended by the Australian Board of Control does not appear to the committee to be practicable. Firstly, it would place an impossible task on the umpire, and secondly, it would place in the hands of the umpire a power over the game which would be more than dangerous, and which any umpire might well fear to exercise.

The committee have had no reason to give special attention to "leg-theory" as practised by fast bowlers. They will, however, watch carefully during the present season for anything which might be regarded as unfair or prejudicial to the best interests of the game.

They propose to invite opinions and suggestions from county clubs and captains at the end of the season, with a view to enabling them to express an opinion of this matter at a special meeting of the Imperial Cricket Conference.

With regard to the reports of the captain and managers, the committee, while deeply appreciative of the private and public hospitality shown to the English team, are much concerned with regard to the barracking, which is referred to in all the reports and against which there is unanimous deprecation.

Barracking has unfortunately always been indulged in by spectators in Australia to a degree quite unknown in this country. During the late tour, however, it would appear to have exceeded all previous experience, and on occasions to have become thoroughly objectionable.

There appears to have been little or no effort on the part of those responsible for the administration of the game in Australia to interfere, or to control this exhibition. This was naturally regarded by members of the team as a serious lack of consideration for them.

The committee are of opinion that cricket played under such conditions is robbed of much of its value as a game, and that unless barracking is stopped, or is greatly moderated, in Australia it is difficult to see how the continuance of representative matches can serve the best interests of the game.

The committee regret that these matters have to be dealt with by correspondence and not by personal conference. If at any time duly accredited representatives of Australian cricket would meet the committee in conference, such conference would be welcomed by M.C.C.

(Signed) W. Findlay, secretary, M.C.C.

A word or two upon the recommendation of the Sub-Committee appointed by the Board of Control may not be out of place. That Committee consisted of Messrs. M. A. Noble, R. J. Hartigan, W. M. Woodfull and V. Richardson.

The terms of reference given to the Sub-Committee on appointment can have left no shadow of doubt in their own or anyone else's minds that they were expected, even ordered, to produce some solution eliminating leg-theory. This was clear, apart from the tenor of the Board of Control's own cabled messages to M.C.C., which can have left no doubt in anyone's mind as to the only type of report which would be acceptable to them.

I think, in the circumstances, cricketers the world over will agree that the Sub-Committee were set an impossible task. Though loyally accepted in Australia, I do not imagine that their suggested solution will meet with much approval anywhere else. In any case, I cannot help feeling that, though one would not dream of cavilling at any of the names selected to serve on the Sub-Committee, the recommendations might have been happier, and would certainly have carried more weight had the personnel included one who was, or had been, solely a bowler.

Messrs. Hartigan, Woodfull and Richardson neither would, nor could, make any claim to any skill or experience with the ball; while Mr. Noble, though a great all-rounder, was just as likely to see things from the batsman's as from the bowler's point of view. Moreover, Noble is always supposed to have been responsible for inducing Armstrong to abandon leg-theory.

THE PLAY IN FIGURES

No book describing a cricket tour would be complete without its statistical section. To the student of cricket, detailed figures illuminate and enrich the story of the play.

Those which follow have been compiled by that very thorough statistician of cricket, Mr. W. Ferguson, official scorer to the M.C.C. team throughout the tour.

TEST BATSMEN AND BOWLERS

The following tables show how individual batsmen and bowlers fared against each other in each innings of the five Test Matches. The top line opposite the batsman's name shows first innings figures, and the bottom line those for the second innings.

ENGLAND 1ST TEST MATCH

Batsmen	Wall			Nagel			O'Reilly			Grimmett			McCabe			Kippax			Totals		
	B.	R.	W.	B.	R.	W.	B.	R.	W.	B.	R.	W.	B.	R.	W.	B.	R.	W.	Balls	Runs	How Out
Sutcliffe	73	41	1	74	36	–	159	53	–	155	40	–	31	21	–	4	3	–	496	194	L.B.W.
	–	–	–	–	–	–	–	–	–	–	–	–	1	1	–	–	–	–	1	1	Not out
Wyatt	24	13	–	27	8	–	27	14	–	13	3	1	1	1	–	–	–	–	91	38	L.B.W.
	–	–	–	–	–	–	–	–	–	–	–	–	–	–	–	–	–	–	–	–	Not out
Hammond	30	12	–	39	24	1	82	24	–	74	45	–	17	7	–	–	–	–	242	112	C.
	–	–	–	–	–	–	–	–	–	–	–	–	–	–	–	–	–	–	–	–	–
Pataudi	55	15	–	96	35	1	85	19	–	114	23	–	22	10	–	8	–	–	380	102	B.
	–	–	–	–	–	–	–	–	–	–	–	–	–	–	–	–	–	–	–	–	–
Leyland	1	–	1	–	–	–	–	–	–	–	–	–	–	–	–	–	–	–	1	0	C.
Jardine	26	9	–	18	7	–	11	3	–	11	4	–	16	4	1	–	–	–	82	27	C.
Verity	5	2	1	–	–	–	–	–	–	6	–	–	4	–	–	–	–	–	15	2	L.B.W.
Allen	20	11	–	10	–	–	25	4	1	11	4	–	–	–	–	–	–	–	66	19	C. & B
Ames	–	–	–	–	–	–	8	–	1	–	–	–	–	–	–	–	–	–	8	0	C.
Larwood	–	–	–	–	–	–	7	–	1	–	–	–	–	–	–	–	–	–	7	0	L.B.W.
Voce	–	–	–	–	–	–	1	–	–	–	–	–	–	–	–	–	–	–	1	0	Not out
G. Total	234	103	3	264	110	2	405	117	3	384	119	1	91	43	1	12	3	–	1390	495	–

In the second innings, it will be noted, only one run by England was needed to complete this match. Sutcliffe scored it off McCabe's bowling.

ENGLAND 2ND TEST MATCH

Batsmen	Wall B.	R.	W.	O'Reilly B.	R.	W.	Grimmett B.	R.	W.	Ironmonger B.	R.	W.	Totals Balls	Runs	How Out
Wyatt	10	6	–	41	7	1	–	–	–	–	–	–	51	13	L.B.W.
	–	–	–	23	19	1	6	2	–	21	4	–	50	25	L.B.W.
Sutcliffe	52	20	1	45	15	–	60	10	–	25	7	–	182	52	C.
	20	14	–	22	1	1	8	7	–	13	11	–	63	33	B.
Pataudi	5	2	–	32	1	1	18	6	–	23	6	–	78	15	B.
	15	4	–	16	1	–	–	–	–	5	–	1	36	5	C.
Hammond	6	8	1	1	–	–	–	–	–	–	–	–	7	8	B.
	7	3	–	32	16	1	–	–	–	4	4	–	43	23	C.
Leyland	19	6	–	37	16	1	–	–	–	6	–	–	62	22	B.
	7	–	1	23	13	–	4	4	–	17	2	–	51	19	B.
Larwood	–	–	–	7	7	1	–	–	–	4	2	–	11	9	B.
	–	–	–	6	4	–	–	–	–	1	–	1	7	4	C.
Voce	12	4	–	15	2	–	3	–	1	–	–	–	30	6	C.
	–	–	–	1	–	1	–	–	–	4	–	–	5	–	C.
Jardine	7	1	1	–	–	–	–	–	–	–	–	–	7	1	C.
	–	–	–	–	–	–	–	–	–	3	–	1	3	–	C.
Ames	10	4	1	–	–	–	–	–	–	–	–	–	10	4	B.
	–	–	–	2	–	1	–	–	–	8	2	–	10	2	C.
Allen	9	1	–	32	11	1	7	2	–	26	16	–	74	30	C.
	–	–	–	19	8	–	6	6	–	38	9	1	63	23	Stumped
Bowes	–	–	–	1	1	–	8	3	–	–	–	–	9	4	Not out
1st Inngs. Total	130	–	4	211	–	5	96	–	1	84	–	–	–	–	–
2nd ”	49	–	1	145	–	5	24	–	–	115	–	4	–	–	–
G. Total – –	179	73	5	356	122	10	120	40	1	199	63	4	854	298	–

ENGLAND 3RD TEST MATCH

Batsmen	Wall			O'Reilly			Ironmonger			Grimmett			McCabe			Bradman			Totals		
	B.	R.	W.	B.	R.	W.	B.	R.	W.	B.	R.	W.	B.	R.	W.	B.	R.	W.	Balls	Runs	How Out
Sutcliffe	15	6	—	28	3	1	—	—	—	—	—	—	—	—	—	—	—	—	43	9	C.
	1	—	1	10	7	—	—	—	—	—	—	—	—	—	—	—	—	—	11	7	B.
Jardine	15	2	1	3	1	—	—	—	—	—	—	—	—	—	—	—	—	—	18	3	B.
	56	12	—	59	8	—	70	13	1	56	14	—	19	7	—	6	2	—	266	56	L.B.W.
Hammond	9	2	1	6	—	—	—	—	—	—	—	—	—	—	—	—	—	—	15	2	C.
	40	23	—	68	21	—	75	19	—	31	8	—	32	14	—	1	—	1	247	85	B.
Ames	13	1	—	13	1	—	12	1	1	—	—	—	—	—	—	—	—	—	38	3	B.
	17	10	—	61	19	1	47	9	—	38	13	—	—	—	—	10	18	—	173	69	C.
Wyatt	26	18	1	52	21	—	34	12	—	32	20	—	32	7	—	—	—	—	176	78	C.
	30	15	—	36	8	1	35	7	—	22	16	—	15	3	—	—	—	—	138	49	C.
Allen	13	4	—	2	—	—	—	—	—	3	1	1	12	10	—	—	—	—	30	15	L.B.W.
	5	7	—	17	6	—	23	6	—	11	2	1	3	1	—	—	—	—	59	15	L.B.W.
Verity	24	7	—	67	14	1	21	14	—	29	8	—	6	2	—	—	—	—	147	45	C.
	17	10	—	28	8	1	49	8	—	24	7	—	6	4	—	7	3	—	131	40	L.B.W.
Leyland	28	11	—	65	24	—	38	23	—	43	22	1	16	3	—	—	—	—	190	83	B.
	12	5	—	6	—	—	25	10	1	28	14	—	22	13	—	—	—	—	93	42	C.
Paynter	53	13	1	69	15	—	15	4	—	61	39	—	18	6	—	—	—	—	216	77	C.
	—	—	—	14	15	—	1	1	—	—	—	—	—	—	—	—	—	—	15	1	Not out
Voce	13	8	1	—	—	—	—	—	—	—	—	—	—	—	—	—	—	—	13	8	B.
	—	—	—	3	2	1	7	6	—	—	—	—	—	—	—	—	—	—	10	8	B.
Larwood	1	—	—	3	3	—	—	—	—	—	—	—	—	—	—	—	—	—	4	3	Not out
	—	—	—	2	—	—	10	8	1	—	—	—	—	—	—	—	—	—	12	8	C.
1st Inngs. Total	210	—	5	308	—	2	120	—	1	168	—	2	84	—	—	—	—	—	—	—	—
2nd ,,	178	—	1	304	—	4	342	—	3	210	—	1	97	—	—	24	—	1	—	—	—
G. Total	388	147	6	612	161	6	462	141	4	378	164	3	181	70	—	24	23	1	2045	706	—

ENGLAND 4TH TEST MATCH

Batsmen	Wall B.	R.	W.	O'Reilly B.	R.	W.	McCabe B.	R.	W.	Ironmonger B.	R.	W.	Bromley B.	R.	W.	Bradman B.	R.	W.	Darling B.	R.	W.	Balls	Runs	How Out
Sutcliffe	55	26	—	102	32	1	12	5	—	57	18	—	15	3	—	3	2	—	—	—	—	244	86	L.B.W.
	6	2	1	5	—	—	—	—	—	—	—	—	—	—	—	—	—	—	—	—	—	11	2	B.
Wyatt	—	—	—	25	6	—	5	1	—	4	1	1	10	4	—	—	—	—	—	—	—	44	12	C.
	—	—	—	—	—	—	—	—	—	—	—	—	—	—	—	—	—	—	—	—	—	—	—	—
Jardine	42	9	—	69	17	1	32	4	—	37	11	—	11	5	—	—	—	—	—	—	—	191	46	C.
	16	10	—	19	9	—	12	1	—	65	4	1	—	—	—	—	—	—	—	—	—	112	24	B.
Hammond	18	5	—	23	8	—	13	2	1	26	1	—	10	2	—	3	2	—	—	—	—	93	20	B.
	—	—	—	26	5	—	6	3	—	43	6	1	—	—	—	—	—	—	—	—	—	75	14	C.
Leyland	20	5	—	17	1	1	17	7	—	8	4	—	6	—	—	—	—	—	—	—	—	48	12	C.
	18	4	—	102	43	1	26	12	—	87	26	—	—	—	—	—	—	—	—	—	—	235	86	C.
Ames	3	—	—	5	4	—	8	1	—	43	3	1	2	5	—	—	—	—	—	—	—	65	17	C.
	—	—	—	25	9	—	3	3	—	8	2	—	—	—	—	—	—	—	—	—	—	36	14	Not out
Allen	32	10	1	18	11	—	—	—	—	10	2	—	—	—	—	—	—	—	—	—	—	31	13	C.
	—	—	—	—	—	—	—	—	—	—	—	—	—	—	—	—	—	—	—	—	—	—	—	—
Paynter	—	—	—	84	31	—	34	17	—	40	10	1	6	—	—	17	11	—	5	4	—	218	83	C.
	—	—	—	3	4	—	1	6	—	7	4	—	—	—	—	—	—	—	—	—	—	11	14	Not out
Mitchell	—	—	—	4	—	1	—	—	—	—	—	—	—	—	—	—	—	—	—	—	—	4	—	L.B.W.
	—	—	—	—	—	—	—	—	—	—	—	—	—	—	—	—	—	—	—	—	—	—	—	—
Larwood	8	7	—	4	5	—	6	—	1	9	11	—	—	—	—	—	—	—	—	—	—	27	23	B.
	—	—	—	—	—	—	—	—	—	—	—	—	—	—	—	—	—	—	—	—	—	—	—	—
Verity	26	5	—	58	5	—	12	3	—	35	8	—	—	—	—	19	2	—	7	—	—	157	23	Not out
	—	—	—	—	—	—	—	—	—	—	—	—	—	—	—	—	—	—	—	—	—	—	—	—
1st Inngs. Total	202	—	1	409	—	4	139	—	2	258	—	3	60	19	—	42	17	—	12	4	—	—	—	—
” 2nd	42	—	1	180	—	1	48	—	—	210	—	2	—	—	—	—	—	—	—	—	—	—	—	—
G. Total	244	83	2	589	190	5	187	65	2	468	111	5	60	19	—	42	17	—	12	4	—	1602	489	—

ENGLAND 5TH TEST MATCH

Batsmen	Alexander			McCabe			O'Reilly			Ironmonger			Lee			Darling			Bradman			Totals		
	B.	R.	W.	B.	R.	W.	B.	R.	W.	B.	R.	W.	B.	R.	W.	B.	R.	W.	B.	R.	W.	Balls	Runs	How Out
Sutcliffe	35	28	–	13	5	–	21	6	1	45	14	–	23	3	–	–	–	–	–	–	–	137	56	C.
Jardine	21	11	–	5	1	–	24	6	1	–	–	–	–	–	–	–	–	–	–	–	–	50	18	C.
	24	11	–	–	–	–	18	8	–	15	5	1	–	–	–	–	–	–	–	–	–	57	24	C.
Hammond	35	18	–	30	13	–	63	33	–	44	14	–	33	23	1	–	–	–	–	–	–	205	101	L.B.W.
	6	5	–	22	6	–	16	18	–	59	12	–	26	27	–	11	7	–	–	–	–	140	75	Not out
Leyland	7	7	–	–	–	–	20	12	–	6	2	–	54	21	–	–	–	–	–	–	–	87	42	Run out
	–	–	–	–	–	–	–	–	–	16	0	1	–	–	–	–	–	–	–	–	–	16	0	B.
Ames	3	1	–	4	1	–	3	1	–	17	1	–	–	–	–	–	–	–	–	–	–	27	4	Run out
Paynter	2	–	–	–	–	–	8	2	–	–	–	–	13	5	1	6	2	–	–	–	–	29	9	B.
Allen	23	15	–	5	1	–	8	8	–	13	–	–	52	22	1	–	–	–	3	2	–	104	48	C.
Larwood	48	37	–	6	3	–	58	17	–	21	19	–	15	22	1	–	–	–	–	–	–	148	98	C.
Wyatt	18	6	–	9	3	–	53	18	1	34	8	–	43	13	–	36	1	–	3	2	–	196	51	C.
	36	9	–	8	4	–	56	6	–	66	17	–	48	25	–	1	–	–	–	–	–	215	61	Not out
Verity	10	3	1	–	–	–	4	1	–	–	–	–	–	–	–	–	–	–	–	–	–	14	4	C.
Voce	8	3	–	–	–	–	12	–	–	6	3	–	9	1	–	–	–	–	–	–	–	35	7	Not out
1st Inngs. Total	210	–	1	72	–	–	274	–	3	186	–	–	242	–	4	42	–	–	6	4	–	–	–	–
2nd "	66	–	–	30	–	–	90	–	–	156	–	2	74	–	–	12	–	–	–	–	–	–	–	–
G. Total	276	154	1	102	37	–	364	136	3	342	95	2	316	162	4	54	10	–	6	4	–	1460	598	–

SUMMARY OF ALL THE TEST MATCHES COMBINED

Bowlers	Sutcliffe			Wyatt			Hammond			Pataudi			Leyland			Jardine			Verity		
	B.	R.	W.	B.	R.	W.	B.	R.	W.	B.	R.	W.	B.	R.	W.	B.	R.	W.	B.	R.	W.
Wall	222	109	4	90	52	–	110	53	2	75	21	–	94	27	2	162	43	2	82	24	2
Nagel	74	36	–	27	8	–	39	24	1	96	35	1	–	–	–	18	7	–	–	–	1
O'Reilly	392	117	4	313	99	4	317	125	1	133	21	1	270	109	4	203	52	2	157	28	1
Grimmett	223	57	–	73	41	2	105	53	–	132	29	–	75	40	–	67	18	–	59	15	–
McCabe	57	32	–	69	18	–	120	145	1	22	10	–	81	35	–	84	17	1	28	9	–
Kippax	4	3	–	–	–	–	–	–	–	8	–	–	–	–	–	–	–	–	–	–	–
Ironmonger	140	50	–	194	49	1	251	56	1	28	6	1	203	67	2	190	33	4	95	30	–
Lee	23	3	–	91	38	–	59	50	1	–	–	–	54	21	–	–	–	–	–	–	–
Alexander	35	28	–	54	15	–	41	23	–	–	–	–	7	7	–	45	22	–	10	3	1
Bromley	15	3	–	10	4	–	10	2	–	–	–	–	–	–	–	11	5	–	–	–	–
Bradman	3	2	–	3	2	–	4	2	1	–	–	–	–	–	–	6	2	–	26	5	–
Darling	–	–	–	37	1	–	11	7	–	–	–	–	–	–	–	–	–	–	7	–	–
G. Total	1188	440	8	961	327	7	1067	440	8	494	122	3	784	306	8	786	199	9	464	114	4

SUMMARY OF ALL THE TEST MATCHES COMBINED

Bowlers	Allen			Ames			Larwood			Voce			Bowes			Paynter			Mitchell		
	B.	R.	W.	B.	R.	W.	B.	R.	W.	B.	R.	W.	B.	R.	W.	B.	R.	W.	B.	R.	W.
Wall	50	16	1	58	19	1	9	7	–	25	12	1	–	–	–	85	23	1	–	–	–
Nagel	10	–	–	–	–	–	–	–	–	–	–	–	–	–	–	–	–	–	–	–	–
O'Reilly	121	48	2	117	34	3	87	36	2	32	4	2	2	1	–	178	52	–	4	–	1
Grimmett	38	15	2	38	13	–	–	–	–	3	–	1	8	3	–	61	39	–	–	–	–
McCabe	20	12	–	15	5	–	12	3	1	–	–	–	–	–	–	53	29	–	–	–	–
Kippax	–	–	–	124	18	2	–	–	–	–	–	–	–	–	–	–	–	–	–	–	–
Ironmonger	110	33	1	–	–	–	45	40	2	17	9	–	1	–	–	63	19	1	–	–	–
Lee	52	22	1	–	–	–	15	22	1	9	1	–	–	–	–	13	5	1	–	–	–
Alexander	23	15	–	3	1	–	48	37	–	8	3	–	–	–	–	2	–	–	–	–	–
Bromley	–	–	–	2	5	–	–	–	–	–	–	–	–	–	–	6	–	–	–	–	–
Bradman	3	2	–	10	18	–	–	–	–	–	–	–	–	–	–	17	11	–	–	–	–
Darling	–	–	–	–	–	–	–	–	–	–	–	–	–	–	–	11	6	–	–	–	–
G. Total	427	163	7	367	113	6	216	145	6	94	29	4	11	4	–	489	184	3	4	–	1

AUSTRALIA 1ST TEST MATCH

Batsmen	Larwood B.	R.	W.	Voce B.	R.	W.	Hammond B.	R.	W.	Allen B.	R.	W.	Verity B.	R.	W.	Totals Balls	Runs	How Out
Woodfull	19	1	1	13	3	1	–	–	–	2	2	–	–	–	–	34	7	C.
	19	–	1	–	–	–	–	–	–	–	–	–	–	–	–	19	–	B.
Ponsford	17	8	1	23	8	–	14	6	–	14	6	–	11	4	–	79	32	C.
	–	–	–	9	2	1	–	–	–	–	–	–	–	–	–	9	2	B.
Richardson	37	25	–	8	2	1	7	3	–	30	16	–	26	3	–	108	49	C.
	–	–	–	–	–	–	1	–	1	–	–	–	–	–	–	1	–	C.
Kippax	16	5	1	11	3	–	–	–	–	–	–	–	–	–	–	27	8	L.B.W.
	17	5	1	2	2	–	16	12	–	–	–	–	–	–	–	35	19	B.
McCabe	49	40	–	79	65	–	45	20	–	33	39	–	27	23	–	233	187	Not out
	8	3	–	23	19	–	18	4	1	19	6	–	–	–	–	68	32	L.B.W.
Fingleton	15	3	1	37	19	–	10	3	–	8	–	–	7	1	–	77	26	B.
	29	5	1	29	14	–	37	20	–	19	1	–	6	–	–	120	40	C.
Oldfield	2	–	1	2	4	–	–	–	–	–	–	–	–	–	–	4	4	C.
	15	9	–	5	2	1	6	2	–	4	2	–	7	4	–	37	19	C.
Grimmett	1	–	1	–	–	–	–	–	–	–	–	–	–	–	–	1	–	C.
	9	6	–	14	1	1	13	–	–	6	–	–	17	14	–	59	21	B.
Nagel	–	–	–	4	4	–	–	–	–	4	–	–	–	–	–	8	4	Not out
O'Reilly	4	–	1	3	–	–	–	–	–	–	–	–	–	–	–	9	7	B.
	–	–	–	–	–	–	–	–	–	5	6	–	1	1	–	18	4	B.
Wall	13	4	–	1	–	–	4	–	1	–	–	–	–	–	–	29	20	C.
	8	3	–	9	16	1	5	1	–	7	–	–	–	–	–	–	–	C.
1st Innings Total	188	–	5	183	–	4	86	–	1	91	–	–	78	–	–	–	–	–
2nd „	108	–	5	107	–	2	90	–	2	56	–	1	24	–	–	–	–	–
G. Total	296	124	10	290	164	6	176	71	3	147	78	1	102	50	–	1011	487	

AUSTRALIA 2ND TEST MATCH

Batsmen	Larwood			Voce			Allen			Hammond			Bowes			Totals		
	B.	R.	W.	B.	R.	W.	B.	R.	W.	B.	R.	W.	B.	R.	W.	Balls	Runs	How Out
Woodfull	4	1	—	20	2	—	5	1	1	4	6	—	—	—	—	33	10	B.
	22	6	1	6	2	—	13	7	—	14	3	—	16	8	—	71	26	C.
Fingleton	63	19	—	43	18	—	48	18	1	28	8	—	45	20	—	227	83	B.
	4	1	—	—	—	—	4	—	1	—	—	—	1	—	—	9	1	C.
O'Brien	6	4	—	10	2	—	17	1	—	2	—	—	12	3	—	47	10	Run out
	3	3	1	—	—	—	9	5	—	—	—	—	1	3	—	13	11	B.
Bradman	—	—	—	—	—	—	—	—	—	—	—	—	1	—	1	1	—	B.
	43	30	—	40	22	—	23	24	—	34	18	—	6	9	—	146	103	Not out
McCabe	11	7	—	9	5	1	12	5	—	8	2	—	18	13	—	58	32	C.
	1	—	—	—	—	—	4	—	1	—	—	—	—	—	—	5	—	B.
Oldfield	20	6	—	17	11	—	7	2	—	15	5	—	7	3	—	66	27	Not out
	—	—	—	14	6	1	—	—	—	1	—	—	—	—	—	15	6	B.
Richardson	8	2	—	12	8	1	12	13	—	3	—	—	31	11	—	66	34	C.
	12	7	—	12	17	—	19	8	—	5	—	1	—	—	—	48	32	L.B.W.
Grimmett	—	—	—	3	1	1	3	1	—	—	—	—	—	—	—	6	2	C.
	—	—	—	4	1	1	1	—	—	—	—	—	—	—	—	5	1	B.
Wall	—	—	—	3	1	—	—	—	—	—	—	—	—	—	—	3	1	Run out
	6	3	—	15	—	—	—	—	—	1	—	1	—	—	—	22	3	L.B.W.
O'Reilly	10	9	1	3	6	—	—	—	—	—	—	—	—	—	—	13	15	B.
	—	—	—	—	—	—	—	—	—	8	—	1	—	—	—	8	—	C.
Ironmonger	4	4	1	—	—	—	—	—	—	—	—	—	—	—	—	4	4	B.
	—	—	—	—	—	—	—	—	—	2	—	—	—	—	—	2	—	Run Out
1st Innings Total	126	—	2	120	—	3	104	—	2	60	—	—	114	—	1	—	—	—
2nd "	91	—	2	91	—	2	73	—	2	65	—	3	24	—	—	—	—	—
G. Total — — —	217	102	4	211	101	5	177	85	4	125	42	3	138	70	1	868	400	—

AUSTRALIA 3RD TEST MATCH

Batsmen	Larwood			Allen			Hammond			Voce			Verity			Totals		
	B.	R.	W.	B.	R.	W.	B.	R.	W.	B.	R.	W.	B.	R.	W.	Balls	Runs	How Out
Woodfull	16	8	–	16	7	1	7	4	–	18	3	–	8	–	–	65	22	B.
	57	31	–	46	21	–	19	11	–	18	3	–	68	7	–	208	73	Not out
Fingleton	6	–	–	2	–	1	–	–	–	–	–	–	–	–	–	8	–	C.
	8	–	1	6	–	–	–	–	–	–	–	–	–	–	–	14	–	B.
Bradman	5	–	–	12	–	1	14	2	–	6	4	–	–	–	–	17	8	C.
	18	18	1	15	11	–	5	15	–	4	5	–	18	18	–	71	66	C. & B.
McCabe	16	1	1	–	–	–	–	–	–	–	–	–	–	–	–	25	8	C.
	–	–	–	8	5	1	–	–	–	–	–	–	11	1	–	19	7	C.
Ponsford	44	23	–	62	26	–	35	10	–	28	7	1	44	19	–	213	85	C.
	10	–	1	1	–	–	–	–	–	–	–	–	–	–	–	11	3	C.
Grimmett	2	1	–	7	3	1	3	3	–	12	1	–	–	–	–	24	10	B.
	3	6	–	1	5	1	–	–	–	–	–	–	–	–	–	8	6	B.
Wall	1	3	–	9	2	–	9	1	1	–	–	–	4	–	–	19	6	B.
	–	–	–	4	–	1	–	–	–	–	–	–	–	–	–	4	–	B.
Richardson	19	9	1	18	13	–	24	5	–	–	–	–	20	–	–	81	28	B.
	11	12	–	24	8	–	21	1	–	–	–	–	20	1	1	76	21	C.
Oldfield	33	10	–	12	10	–	22	5	–	23	5	–	24	11	–	114	41	Rtd. hurt
	–	–	–	–	–	–	–	–	–	–	–	–	–	–	–	–	–	did not bat
O'Reilly	8	–	1	–	–	–	1	–	–	–	–	–	–	–	–	9	–	B.
	9	4	1	1	1	–	–	–	–	–	–	–	–	–	–	10	5	B.
Ironmonger	–	–	–	–	–	–	–	–	–	–	–	–	–	–	–	1	–	Not out
	–	–	–	1	–	1	–	–	–	–	–	–	–	–	–	–	–	B.
1st Innings Total	150		3	138		4	106		1	85		1	96		–	–	–	–
2nd ” ”	116		4	107		4	54		–	24		–	121		1	–	–	–
Grand Total	266	126	7	245	121	8	160	57	1	109	28	1	217	57	1	997	389	

AUSTRALIA 4TH TEST MATCH

Batsmen	Larwood B	R	W	Allen B	R	W	Hammond B	R	W	Mitchell B	R	W	Verity B	R	W	Totals Balls	Runs	How Out
Woodfull	57	17	–	39	14	–	31	10	–	36	10	1	69	16	–	232	67	B.
	33	4	–	10	3	–	21	4	–	17	6	1	24	2	–	105	19	C.
Richardson	33	21	–	25	24	–	43	12	1	21	19	–	24	7	–	146	83	Stumped
	15	12	–	21	11	–	13	6	–	–	–	–	15	3	1	64	32	C.
Bradman	25	13	1	39	24	–	30	25	–	10	6	–	34	8	–	138	76	B.
	14	15	1	–	–	–	2	–	–	–	–	–	15	8	–	31	24	C.
Darling	3	5	–	5	7	1	9	4	–	–	–	–	4	1	–	21	17	C.
	18	11	–	31	13	–	5	3	–	2	–	1	26	12	–	80	39	Run out
Love	–	–	–	7	1	–	–	–	–	–	–	–	15	4	–	24	5	L.B.W.
	2	–	1	5	2	–	–	–	–	–	–	–	7	1	–	14	3	L.B.W.
Wall	8	3	–	–	–	–	5	2	–	12	1	–	–	–	–	25	6	Not out
	–	–	–	4	2	1	–	–	–	–	–	–	–	–	–	4	2	C.
McCabe	14	14	–	8	6	1	4	–	–	2	–	–	–	–	–	28	20	C.
	11	2	–	20	11	–	19	4	–	10	5	–	15	5	1	75	22	B.
Ponsford	14	6	1	9	4	–	2	3	–	3	4	–	12	2	–	40	19	B.
	–	–	–	1	–	1	–	–	–	3	3	–	–	–	–	4	–	C.
Bromley	23	16	1	12	3	–	7	3	–	–	–	–	5	1	–	52	26	C.
	10	1	–	8	2	1	–	–	–	5	3	–	12	4	–	30	7	C.
O'Reilly	6	1	1	–	–	–	–	–	–	–	–	–	–	–	–	11	6	C.
	4	4	1	–	–	–	–	–	–	5	6	–	–	–	–	4	4	B.
Ironmonger	6	6	0	–	–	–	7	2	1	–	–	–	–	–	–	13	8	Stumped
	–	–	–	2	–	–	–	–	–	–	–	–	–	–	–	2	–	Not out
1st Inngs. Total	189	–	4	144	–	2	138	–	2	96	–	2	163	–	–	–	–	–
2nd "	107	–	3	102	–	3	60	–	–	30	–	1	114	–	2	–	–	–
G. Total	296	150	7	246	127	5	198	79	2	126	60	3	277	69	–	1143	486	–

AUSTRALIA 5TH TEST MATCH

Batsmen	Larwood B.	Larwood R.	Larwood W.	Voce B.	Voce R.	Voce W.	Allen B.	Allen R.	Allen W.	Hammond B.	Hammond R.	Hammond W.	Verity B.	Verity R.	Verity W.	Wyatt B.	Wyatt R.	Wyatt W.	Balls	Runs	How Out
Woodfull	18	3	1	32	4	—	4	5	—	5	2	—	—	—	—	—	—	—	59	14	B.
	33	16	—	32	16	—	25	19	—	12	3	—	66	13	1	—	—	—	168	67	B.
O'Brien	25	22	—	26	20	1	11	6	—	10	8	—	16	5	—	—	—	—	88	61	C.
	—	—	—	2	2	1	9	1	—	—	—	—	9	2	—	—	—	—	20	5	C.
Richardson	5	—	1	—	—	—	—	—	—	—	—	—	—	—	—	—	—	—	5	—	B.
	2	—	1	—	—	—	—	—	—	—	—	—	—	—	—	—	—	—	2	—	C.
Bradman	15	11	1	10	8	—	24	24	—	7	5	—	—	—	—	—	—	—	56	48	B.
	31	28	—	8	8	—	18	18	—	6	7	—	6	10	1	—	—	—	69	71	B.
McCabe	33	6	—	34	25	—	38	37	1	10	5	—	10	—	—	4	—	—	129	73	C.
	—	—	—	6	4	1	—	—	—	—	—	—	—	—	—	—	—	—	6	4	C.
Darling	32	18	—	34	13	—	37	27	—	10	9	—	11	6	1	5	12	—	129	85	B.
	—	—	—	5	2	—	—	—	—	—	—	—	8	5	1	—	—	—	13	7	C.
Lee	13	9	—	4	6	—	5	—	—	—	—	—	22	27	1	—	—	—	44	42	C.
	—	—	—	—	—	—	14	15	1	—	—	—	7	—	—	—	—	—	21	15	B.
O'Reilly	8	3	—	—	—	—	14	11	1	—	—	—	5	5	—	—	—	—	27	19	B.
	—	—	—	—	—	—	1	1	—	—	—	—	2	—	1	—	—	—	3	1	B.
Ironmonger	2	—	1	—	—	—	1	1	—	—	—	—	1	—	—	—	—	—	4	1	B.
	—	—	—	—	—	—	—	—	—	—	—	—	3	—	—	—	—	—	3	—	Not out
Oldfield	33	15	—	5	4	—	10	11	—	6	3	—	39	19	—	3	—	—	96	52	Run out
	—	—	—	7	4	—	6	—	—	—	—	—	12	1	1	—	—	—	25	5	C.
Alexander	10	11	—	—	—	—	6	6	—	—	—	—	1	—	—	—	—	—	17	17	Not out
	—	—	—	—	—	—	—	—	—	—	—	—	1	—	1	—	—	—	1	—	L.B.W.
1st Inngs. Total	194	—	4	145	—	1	151	—	2	48	—	—	104	—	2	12	—	—	—	—	—
2nd „	66	—	1	60	—	2	73	—	1	18	—	—	114	—	6	—	—	—	—	—	—
G. Total — —	260	142	5	205	114	3	224	182	3	66	42	—	218	95	8	12	12	—	985	587	—

SUMMARY OF TEST MATCHES

Bowlers	Woodfull			Ponsford			Richardson			Kippax			McCabe			Fingleton			Oldfield			Grimmett			O'Reilly			Wall		
	B.	R.	W.	B.	R.	W.	B.	R.	W.	B.	R.	W.	B.	R.	W.	B.	R.	W.	B.	R.	W.	B.	R.	W.	B.	R.	W.	B.	R.	W.
Larwood	278	88	3	85	37	3	142	88	3	33	10	2	143	73	1	125	28	3	100	32	2	26	21	1	49	20	5	36	6	–
Voce	139	33	1	60	17	2	32	27	2	13	5	–	155	123	2	109	51	–	77	34	1	33	4	3	10	10	2	28	17	–
Hammond	113	43	–	51	19	–	117	27	3	16	12	–	109	37	1	75	31	3	44	13	–	9	5	–	9	–	1	24	4	3
Allen	160	79	3	87	39	1	149	93	1	–	–	–	142	110	3	87	19	3	35	23	–	16	8	2	21	19	1	24	4	3
Verity	235	38	–	67	25	–	105	14	1	–	–	–	63	24	2	13	1	–	75	31	1	11	4	–	8	6	1	–	–	–
Bowes	16	8	–	–	–	–	31	11	–	–	–	–	18	13	–	46	20	–	7	3	–	–	–	–	–	–	–	–	–	–
Mitchell	53	16	2	6	4	–	21	19	–	–	–	–	12	5	–	–	–	–	–	–	–	–	–	–	5	6	–	12	1	–
Wyatt	–	–	–	–	–	–	–	–	–	–	–	–	4	–	–	–	–	–	3	–	–	–	–	–	–	–	–	–	–	–
Total	994	305	9	356	141	6	597	279	10	62	27	2	646	385	9	455	150	6	341	136	4	95	42	6	102	61	10	124	42	6

Bowlers	Nagel			Love			Darling			O'Brien			Bromley			Ironmonger			Bradman			Alexander			Lee		
	B.	R.	W.	B.	R.	W.	B.	R.	W.	B.	R.	W.	B.	R.	W.	B.	R.	W.	B.	R.	W.	B.	R.	W.	B.	R.	W.
Larwood	10	6	1	2	–	1	53	34	–	34	29	1	33	17	1	12	10	2	151	115	4	10	11	–	13	9	–
Voce	14	1	–	–	–	–	39	15	–	38	22	2	–	–	–	–	–	–	64	42	–	–	–	–	4	6	–
Hammond	13	–	–	–	–	–	24	16	–	12	8	–	7	3	–	9	2	1	93	71	–	–	–	–	–	–	–
Allen	6	–	–	12	3	–	73	47	1	46	13	–	20	5	1	4	1	1	131	109	2	7	6	–	19	15	1
Verity	17	14	–	22	5	–	49	24	2	25	9	–	17	5	–	4	–	–	73	44	2	1	–	1	29	27	1
Bowes	–	–	–	–	–	–	–	–	–	13	6	–	–	–	–	–	–	–	7	9	1	–	–	–	–	–	–
Mitchell	–	–	–	2	–	1	–	–	–	–	–	–	5	3	–	–	–	–	10	6	–	–	–	–	–	–	–
Wyatt	–	–	–	–	–	–	5	12	–	–	–	–	–	–	–	–	–	–	–	–	–	–	–	–	–	–	–
Total	60	21	1	38	8	2	243	148	3	168	87	3	82	33	2	29	13	4	529	396	7	18	17	1	65	57	2

RESULTS OF MATCHES IN AUSTRALIA 1932–1933

Opponents	Town	Toss Results	Results
West Australia	Perth	England	Drawn
Australian XI	Perth	England	Drawn
South Australia	Adelaide	England	Eng. Won by Innings and 128
Victoria	Melbourne	Victoria	" Won by Innings and 83
Australian XI	Melbourne	England	Drawn
N. S. Wales	Sydney	N. S. Wales	" Won by Innings and 44
1st Test	Sydney	Australia	" Won by 10 wkts.
Country Dist.	Wagga	England	Drawn
Tasmania	Launceston	England	" Won by Innings and 126
Tasmania	Hobart	Tasmania	Drawn
2nd Test	Melbourne	Australia	" Lost by 111
Country Dist.	Bendigo	Bendigo	Drawn
3rd Test	Adelaide	England	" Won by 338
Country Dist.	Ballarat	England	Drawn
N. S. Wales	Sydney	N. S. Wales	" Won by 4 wkts.
Country Dist.	Toowoomba	England	Drawn
Queensland	Brisbane	Queensland	" Won by Innings and 61
4th Test	Brisbane	Australia	" Won by 6 wkts.
Country Dist.	Newcastle	Newcastle	Drawn
5th Test	Sydney	Australia	" Won by 8 wkts.
Victoria	Melbourne	England	Drawn (scores level at close with Victoria 7 wickets standing)
South Australia	Adelaide	England	Drawn

Total: Played 22, Won 10, Lost 1, Drawn 11

All 3 matches played in New Zealand against Wellington at Wellington, New Zealand at Christchurch and New Zealand at Auckland – were drawn.

TEST MATCH AVERAGES

Australia Batting (Tests)

Batsmen	Inngs.	Not Out	Highest Score	Runs	Average
Bradman	8	1	103*	396	56.5
McCabe	10	1	187*	385	42.7
Darling	4	–	85	148	37
Woodfull	10	1	73*	305	33.8
Lee	2	–	42	57	28.5
Richardson	10	–	83	279	27.9
Oldfield	7	2	52	136	27.2
Fingleton	6	–	83	150	25
Ponsford	6	–	85	141	23.5
O'Brien	4	–	61	87	21.7
Nagel	2	1	21*	21	21
Alexander	2	1	17*	17	17
Bromley	2	–	26	33	16.5
Kippax	2	–	19	27	13.5
Grimmett	6	–	19	42	7
O'Reilly	10	–	19	61	6.1
Wall	8	1	20	42	6
Love	2	–	5	8	4
Ironmonger	8	2	8	13	2.17

Bowling

Batsmen	Overs	M.	Runs	Wkts.	Average
Wall	170.1	33	409	16	25.5
O'Reilly	383.4	143	724	27	26.81
Ironmonger	245.1	96	405	15	27
Lee	52.4	14	163	4	40.75
Bradman	12	1	44	1	44
Nagel	43.4	9	110	2	55
Grimmett	147	41	326	5	65.20
McCabe	92.5	17	215	3	71.6
Alexander	46	3	154	1	154.0
Kippax	2	1	3	–	–
Darling	11	5	14	–	–
Bromley	10	4	19	–	–

* denotes not out.
Tests: 6 ball overs; other matches 8 ball overs.

England Batting (Tests)

Batsmen	Inngs.	Not Out	Highest Score	Runs	Average
Paynter	5	2	83	184	61.33
Sutcliffe	9	1	194	440	55
Hammond	9	1	112	440	55
Wyatt	9	2	78	327	46.71
Pataudi	3	–	102	122	40.66
Leyland	9	–	86	306	34
Verity	5	1	45	114	28.50
Larwood	7	1	98	145	24.16
Allen	7	0	48	163	23.28
Jardine	9	0	56	199	22.11
Ames	8	1	69	113	16.14
Voce	6	2	8	29	7.25
Bowes	2	2	4*	4	–
Mitchell	1	–	–	–	–

Bowling

Batsmen	Overs	M.	Runs	Wkts.	Average
Larwood	220.2	42	644	33	19.5
Mitchell	21	5	60	3	20
Verity	135	54	271	11	24.6
Voce	133.3	24	407	15	27.13
Allen	171	29	593	21	28.2
Hammond	120.5	27	291	9	32.3
Bowes	23	2	70	1	70
Wyatt	2	–	12	–	–

BOWLING

First Class Matches with Tests Included

	Overs	M.	Runs	Wkts.	Average
Paynter	32.2	7	71	5	14.2
Verity	325.2	119	698	44	15.8
Larwood	275.7	45	817	49	16.6
Sutcliffe	3	–	18	–	18
Mitchell	126.6	15	492	25	19.6
Allen	251.5	41	899	39	23.05
Brown	105.6	15	427	18	23.7
Tate	96.7	16	309	12	25.7
Voce	255.1	33	866	32	27.06
Bowes	209	22	838	29	28.8
Hammond	204	38	578	20	28.9
Jardine	13	3	42	–	42
Ames	16	1	51	1	51
Leyland	12.5	1	55	1	55
Wyatt	18	2	74	1	74

All Matches

	Overs	M.	Runs	Wkts.	Average
Larwood	295.5	49	889	64	13.8
Paynter	32.2	7	71	5	14.2
Verity	352.7	125	778	47	16.5
Mitchell	234.1	25	889	52	17.09
Sutcliffe	4	–	21	–	21
Allen	259.5	41	932	39	23.8
Brown	154.6	22	623	25	24.9
Tate	175.3	27	535	21	25.4
Bowes	265	25	1029	37	27.8
Hammond	208	38	589	20	29.4
Voce	275.1	35	981	33	29.7
Leyland	17.2	1	77	2	38.5
Jardine	13	3	42	–	42
Ames	16	1	51	1	51
Wyatt	18	2	74	1	74
Pataudi	1	–	12	1	12

BATTING

First Class, Including Tests

	Inngs.	*Not Out*	*Highest Score*	*Runs*	*Average*
Sutcliffe	19	1	194	1318	73.2
Hammond	18	1	203	948	55.7
Pataudi	13	–	166	623	47.9
Paynter	16	3	102	538	41.3
Leyland	21	1	152*	880	44
Tate	8	4	94*	157	39.2
Wyatt	25	2	78	883	38.3
Jardine	19	2	108*	628	36.9
Ames	21	1	107	604	30.2
Allen	16	–	66	397	24.8
Verity	17	3	54*	300	21.4
Larwood	13	2	93	258	23.4
Brown	12	1	29	186	16.9
Voce	15	6	46	143	15.8
Duckworth	9	3	27*	89	14.8
Bowes	10	5	20	38	7.6
Mitchell	8	1	10	28	4

All Matches of Tour in Australia

	Inngs.	*Not Out*	*Runs*	*Average*	*Century*
Sutcliffe	23	1	1452	66.0	5
Hammond	21	2	1142	60.1	4
Pataudi	17	1	853	53.3	4
Paynter	20	3	644	37.8	1
Leyland	24	1	976	42.4	2
Tate	13	6	233	33.2	–
Wyatt	27	2	917	36.6	–
Jardine	23	3	746	37.3	1
Ames	23	2	816	38.8	2
Allen	19	–	418	22.0	–
Verity	20	3	328	19.2	–
Larwood	15	2	298	22.9	–
Brown	17	1	316	19.7	–
Voce	17	6	179	16.2	–
Duckworth	13	3	126	12.6	–
Bowes	14	1	89	6.6	–
Mitchell	13	6	44	6.3	–

SCORES AND TIMES IN TEST MATCHES

England

Test	Scores	Byes	Leg Byes	Wides	No Balls	Time (Mins.)	Wkts. Fell
			Included in Scores				
1	524	7	17	–	6	609	10
	1 for 0						
2	169	1	2	–	2	251	20
	139	–	4	–	1	173	
3	341	1	7	–	7	437	20
	412	17	11	–	4	560	
4	356	6	12	–	3	599	14
	162 for 4	2	4	–	2	247	
5	454	7	7	–	2	500	12
	168 for 2	6	1	–	1	195	
Total	2726	47	65	–	28	3571	76

Average: 1 run per 1.3 minutes.
Average runs per wicket fallen 35.87.

Australia

Test	Scores	Byes	Leg Byes	Wides	No Balls	Time (Mins.)	Wkts. Fell
1	360	12	4	–	4	356	20
	164	12	2	1	2	214	
2	228	5	1	2	2	320	20
	191	3	1	4	1	216	
3	222	2	11	–	1	322	18
	193	4	2	1	5	235	
4	340	5	1	–	1	411	20
	175	13	9	–	1	244	
5	435	13	9	1	–	410	20
	182	4	–	–	3	198	
Total	2490	73	40	9	20	2926	98

Average: 1 run per 1.17 minutes.
Average runs per wicket fallen 25.41.

CENTURIES SCORED FOR ENGLAND IN AUSTRALIA

Sutcliffe	169	*v.* Australian XI, Perth.
	154	*v.* South Australia, Adelaide.
	132	*v.* New South Wales, Sydney.
	194	*v.* Australian 1st Test, Sydney.
	101	*v.* Tasmania.
Pataudi	166	*v.* West Australia
	129	*v.* Australian XI, Perth.
	102	*v.* Australia, 1st Test, Sydney.
	109	*v.* Tasmania.
Hammond	203	*v.* Victoria
	112	*v.* Australia, 1st
	101	*v.* Australia, 5th Test.
	101	*v.* Toowoomba, Queensland.
Jardine	108	*v.* South Australia.
Leyland	127 }	*v.* South Australia (Separate Matches).
	152	
	not out	
Ames	107	*v.* Tasmania.
	121	*v.* Toowoomba, Queensland.
Paynter	102	*v.* Tasmania.

CENTURIES AGAINST ENGLAND

McCabe	187 not out	1st Test.
Bradman	103 not out	2nd Test.
Richardson	134	For South Australia.
Fingleton	119 not out	For New South Wales.
Darling	103	For Victoria
Chipperfield	152	For Newscastle in Minor Match.
Little	117	For Newcastle in Minor Match.

CATCHES TAKEN BY ENGLAND

	In all Matches	*Tests Only*
Verity	19	3
Jardine	16	9
Allen	14	7
Hammond	14	6
Mitchell	11	1
Wyatt	9	2
Brown	8	–
Voce	7	3
Pataudi	6	–
Ames	6*	–
Sutcliffe	5	1
Paynter	5	–
Leyland	4	2
Larwood	3	2
Tate	3	–
Bowes	1	–
Total	131	36

* Taken by Ames when not wicket-keeping. When wicket-keeping Ames caught 11 and stumped 8 in all matches, his test figures being 8 and 2. Duckworth caught 15 and stumped 14 in all matches.

3 MATCHES IN NEW ZEALAND

Batting

Name	Wellington		Christchurch		Auckland		Totals				
	Runs	Time	Runs	Time	Runs	Time	Runs	Inns.	Not Out	Time	Average
Hammond	58	118	227	301	336	318	621	3	1	737	310.5
Ames	3	5	103	144	26	45	132	3	–	194	44
Voce	–	–	66	57	16	15	82	2	–	72	41
Wyatt	–	–	20	41	60	125	80	2	–	166	40
Brown	28	23	74	83	13	17	115	3	–	123	38.3
Jardine	25	47	45	75	–	–	70	2	–	122	35
Paynter	52	83	–	5	36	109	88	3	–	197	29.3
Tate	19	26	10*	10	–	–	29	1	1	36	29
Duckworth	13*	26	–	–	6*	30	19	–	2	56	19
Allen	–	–	–	–	12	29	12	1	–	29	12
Bowes	11*	21	–	–	–	–	11	–	1	21	11
Sutcliffe	3	4	–	–	24	55	27	3	–	59	9
Verity	–	4	–	–	–	–	–	1	–	4	–
Mitchell	–	–	–	–	–	–	–	–	–	–	–

Bowling in New Zealand

Name	Overs	M	Runs	Wkts.	Average
Bowes	32	7	62	7	8.8
Voce	32.3	6	62	5	12.4
Tate	53	22	70	3	23.3
Allen	32.1	9	66	2	33
Brown	21	10	66	1	66
Mitchell	24	3	66	1	66
Verity	36	9	111	1	111
Hammond	7	–	19	–	–

MATCH BY MATCH

Scores of all the matches of the tour, except the Test Matches, which are given separately, are as follow:

Versus West Australia

(*At Perth, October* 21–24. *Match drawn*)

ENGLAND

First Innings

Sutcliffe, st Lovelock, b Martin	54
Leyland, c O'Shaughnessy, b Inverarity	15
Pataudi, c Jarvis, b Martin	166
Wyatt, lbw, b Martin	22
Jardine, b Halcombe	38
Ammes, b Halcombe	0
Brown, c Calder, b Curtin	2
Larwood, not out	28
Verity, lbw, b Halcombe	1
Mitchell, not out	3
Extras	5
Total (for 8 wkts.)	334

Bowling Analysis – First Innings

	O.	M.	R.	W.
Halcombe	17	2	48	3
O'Shaughnessy	13	1	50	0
Inverarity	14	2	43	1
Curtin	11	1	40	1
Martin	16	1	115	3
Bryant	4	0	13	0
Drew	3	1	20	0

ENGLAND

Second Innings

Wyatt, b Halcombe	14
Leyland, c Hill-Smith, b Martin	69
Ames, b O'Shaughnessy	19
Brown, c Jarvis, b Martin	28
Verity, st Lovelock, b Martin	17
Jardine, not out	2
Extras	3
Total (for 5 wkts.)	152

Bowling Analysis – Second Innings

	O.	M.	R.	W.
Halcombe	9	0	38	1
O'Shaughnessy	5	1	31	1
Drew	3	0	7	0
Inverarity	4	1˘	18	0
Martin	7.6	0	50	3
Bryant	3	1	5	0

WESTERN AUSTRALIA

Hill-Smith, c Wyatt, b Brown	26
Curtin, b Larwood	0
Drew, c Wyatt, b Brown	17
Calder, b Brown	9
Jarvis, b Larwood	3
Bryant, b Verity	35
Inverarity, c and b Verity	15
Lovelock, not out	14
Martin, b Mitchell	2
O'Shaughnessy, run out	0
Halcombe, c Brown, b Mitchell	1
Extras	13
Total	135

Bowling Analysis – First Innings

	O.	M.	R.	W.
Larwood	6	0	17	2
Bowes	12	1	33	0
Mitchell	6	1	19	0
Brown	10	2	29	3
Verity	9	2	20	2
Wyatt	2	1	4	0

VERSUS COMBINED AUSTRALIAN XI

(At Perth, October 27–29. Match drawn)

ENGLAND

Sutcliffe, c sub, b Evans	169
Leyland, lbw, b McCabe	2
Pataudi, c Evans b Halcombe	129
Hammond, b Bryant	77
Ames, b McCabe	23
Jardine, c McCabe, b Bradman	98
Allen, lbw b Bradman	16
Paynter, not out	32
Verity, not out	14
Extras	23
Total (7 wkts. dec.)	583

Bowling Analysis

	O.	M.	R.	W.
Halcombe	29	3	81	1
McCabe	36	7	87	2
Evans	34	10	89	1
Martin	16	0	126	0
Bradman	19	1	106	2
Richardson	3	0	13	0
Bryant	16	1	58	1

COMBINED AUSTRALIAN XI

First Innings

Richardson, c Sutcliffe, b Verity	27
Fingleton, c Duckworth, b Verity	29
Bradman, c Hammond, b Verity	3
Lonergan, c Duckworth, b Verity	10
McCabe, b Paynter	43
Hill-Smith, c Jardine, b Verity	17
Bryant, c Mitchell, b Verity	0
Lovelock, c Hammond, b Mitchell	11
Evans, c Allen, b Verity	0
Martin, st Duckworth, b Mitchell	1
Halcombe, not out	1
Extras	17
Total	**159**

Bowling Analysis

	O.	M.	R.	W.
Allen	4	0	24	0
Hammond	9	1	29	0
Verity	18	7	37	7
Mitchell	13	2	37	2
Leyland	2	0	15	0
Paynter	2	0	0	1

Second Innings

Richardson, b Allen	0
Fingleton, not out	53
Bradman, c Pataudi, b Allen	10
Lonergan, b Paynter	23
Hill-Smith, Duckworth, b Ames	32
Bryant, not out	12
Extras	9
Total (4 wkts.)	**139**

Bowling Analysis

	O.	M.	R.	W.
Paynter	12	1	31	1
Hammond	3	1	7	0
Verity	1	0	2	0
Leyland	8	1	23	0
Allen	7	2	16	2
Ames	6	0	25	1
Sutcliffe	3	0	18	0
Jardine	2	1	8	0

VERSUS SOUTH AUSTRALIA

(At Adelaide, Nov. 4–8. England won by an innings and 128 runs)

ENGLAND

Leyland, c Nitschke, b Grimmett	127
Sutcliffe, c Nitschke, b Grimmett	154
Pataudi, run out	0
Hammond, st Walker, b Grimmett	27
Ames, c and b Jamieson	10
Jardine, not out	108
Verity, lbw, b Tobin	15
Wyatt, lbw, b Grimmett	61
Larwood, c Whitington, b Waite	81
Brown, c Nitschke, b Waite	27
Bowes, not out	3
Extras	21
Total (9 wkts. dec.)	634

Bowling Analysis

	O.	M.	R.	W.
Tobin	28	5	119	1
Jamieson	33	3	113	1
Grimmett	40	5	176	4
Lee	15	3	46	0
Waite	18	0	108	2
Whitington	2	0	20	0
Richardson	3	0	31	0

SOUTH AUSTRALIA

First Innings

Richardson, c Leyland, b Wyatt	134
Nitschke, b Verity	69
Lonergan, lbw, b Brown	3
Catchlove, st Ames, b Verity	17
Whitington, lbw, b Brown	5
Jamieson, c Hammond, b Verity	1
Tobin, b Bowes	10
Waite, c Verity, b Bowes	3
Lee, not out	22
Grimmett, c Ames, b Brown	17
Walker, b Brown	1
Extras	8
Total	290

Bowling Analysis

	O.	M.	R.	W.
Larwood	5	0	35	0
Bowes	13	1	82	2
Brown	21.1	5	81	4
Verity	26	10	45	3
Hammond	7	1	24	0
Wyatt	2	0	15	1

Second Innings

Richardson, lbw, b Verity	25
Nitschke, lbw, b Brown	28
Lonergan, c Brown, b Verity	20
Catchlove, c Pataudi, b Verity	65
Lee, lbw, b Brown	29
Whitington, run out	0
Jamieson, c and b Verity	7
Tobin, c Hammond, b Verity	19
Waite, b Bowes	1
Grimmett, b Bowes	2
Walker, not out	0
Extras	20
Total	216

Bowling Analysis

	O.	*M.*	*R.*	*W.*
Bowes	19	3	57	2
Wyatt	6	1	14	0
Verity	24.6	13	42	5
Brown	18	2	66	2
Hammond	6	1	17	0

Versus Victoria

(At Melbourne, Nov. 11–15. England won by an innings and 83 runs)

VICTORIA

First Innings

Woodfull, c Hammond, b Allen	5
O'Brien, c Verity, b Allen	45
Rigg, b Allen	1
Darling, lbw, b Voce	45
Oakley, not out	83
Thomas, c Duckworth, b Allen	1
Barnett, c Duckworth, b Voce	16
Nagel, b Voce	4
Fleetwood-Smith, b Verity	0
Alexander, b Voce	3
Ironmonger, run out	1
Extras	27
Total	231

Bowling Analysis

	O.	M.	R.	W.
llen	12	0	45	4
Voce	13.6	0	55	4
Verity	15	3	52	1
Hammond	6	0	25	0
Mitchell	7	2	20	0
Wyatt	2	0	7	0

Second Innings

Woodfull, b Verity	25
O'Brien, lbw, b Verity	4
Rigg, b Mitchell	7
Oakley, b Hammond	21
Thomas, c Duckworth, b Hammond	6
Darling, c Duckworth, b Allen	6
Barnett, b Allen	4
Nagel, run out	2
Fleetwood-Smith, run out	1
Ironmonger, not out	7
Alexander, b Allen	0
Extras	11
Total	94

Bowling Analysis

	O.	M.	R.	W.
Allen	5.5	1	21	3
Voce	11	0	28	0
Verity	6	2	10	2
Mitchell	4	0	16	1
Hammond	5	2	8	2

ENGLAND

Wyatt, c Barnett, b Ironmonger	74
Allen, lbw, b Nagel	15
Pataudi, lbw, b Ironmonger	6
Duckworth, lbw, b Fleetwood-Smith	15
Hammond, b Ironmonger	203
Jardine, lbw, b Darling	19
Ames, c Rigg, b Alexander	15
Paynter, c Barnett, b Fleetwood-Smith	37
Verity, run out	3
Voce, not out	3
Extras	18
Total (9 wkts. dec.)	408

Bowling Analysis

	O.	M.	R.	W.
Alexander	20	0	80	1
Nagel	19	2	86	1
Ironmonger	38	19	62	3
Fleetwood-Smith	25	3	124	2
Darling	7	0	38	1

VERSUS AN AUSTRALIAN XI

(At Melbourne, Nov. 18–22. Match drawn)

ENGLAND

First Innings

Wyatt, lbw, b Oxenham	29
Sutcliffe, c Bradman, b Ironmonger	87
Pataudi, b Nash	23
Leyland, c Darling, b Ironmonger	38
Allen, c Barnet, b Nash	48
Paynter, c Barnett, b Oxenham	6
Larwood, c Darling, b Oxenham	2
Brown, b Oxenham	27
Voce, lbw, b Oxenham	0
Duckworth, c Rigg, b Nash	3
Bowes, not out	2
Extras	17
Total	**282**

Bowling Analysis

	O.	M.	R.	W.
Nash	11.5	0	39	3
Nagel	20	6	37	0
Ironmonger	27	8	90	2
Lee	10	1	35	0
Oxenham	24	8	53	5
Darling	2	0	11	0

Second Innings

Sutcliffe, b Nagel	10
Wyatt, c Barnett, b Nagel	3
Leyland, b Nagel	6
Pataudi, c O'Brien, b Nagel	5
Allen, lbw, b Nagel	6
Paynter, b Nagel	12
Larwood, c O'Brien, b Nagel	0
Brown, b Oxenham	10
Voce, not out	0
Duckworth, lbw, b Nagel	4
Bowes, b Oxenham	0
Extras	4
Total	60

Bowling Analysis

	O.	M.	R.	W.
Nash	4	0	18	0
Nagel	10	3	32	8
Ironmonger	2	1	2	0
Oxenham	4.2	2	4	2

AUSTRALIAN XI

First Innings

Woodfull, lbw, b Bowes	18
O'Brien, b Larwood	46
Bradman, lbw, b Larwood	36
Rigg, c Brown, b Bowes	13
Darling, b Bowes	4
Oxenham, c Larwood, b Voce	12
Nash, b Larwood	0
Lee, c Paynter, b Brown	28
Barnett, b Voce	20
Nagel, lbw, b Larwood	15
Ironmonger, not out	5
Extras	21
Total	218

Second Innings

Woodfull, c Duckworth, b Larwood	0
O'Brien, not out	5
Bradman, b Larwood	13
Rigg, not out	0
Extras	1
Total (for 2 wkts.)	19

Bowling Analysis

	O.	M.	R.	W.
Larwood	3.7	1	5	2
Allen	3	1	13	0

VERSUS NEW SOUTH WALES

(At Sydney, Nov. 25–29. England won by an innings and 44 runs)

NEW SOUTH WALES

First Innings

Bill, c Jardine, b Tate	22
Fingleton, not out	119
Bradman, lbw, b Tate	18
Kippax, c Voce, b Tate	3
McCabe, c Allen, b Tate	67
Hird, c Ames, b Allen	9
Cummins, lbw, b Voce	0
Oldfield, c Sutcliffe, b Allen	5
O'Reilly, b Allen	0
Theak, b Allen	9
Howell, b Allen	7
Extras	14
Total	273

Bowling Analysis

	O.	M.	R.	W.
Allen	16.2	0	69	5
Voce	19	3	53	1
Tate	17	2	53	4
Brown	5	0	28	0
Hammond	5	0	26	0
Verity	6	1	30	0

Second Innings

Fingleton, b Brown	18
Bill, b Voce	1
McCabe, c Brown, b Voce	29
Kippax, c Sutcliffe, b Voce	24
Hird, c Tate, b Voce	15
Bradman, b Voce	23
Cummins, c Jardine, b Brown	71
O'Reilly, b Allen	11
Theak, b Allen	4
Howell, not out	0
Oldfield (absent ill)	0
Extras	17
Total	**213**

Bowling Analysis

	O.	M.	R.	W.
Voce	15	1	85	5
Tate	6	1	21	0
Allen	10	1	52	2
Brown	5.5	0	19	2
Verity	4	1	7	0
Hammond	4	0	12	0

ENGLAND

Sutcliffe, b Hind	182
Wyatt, lbw, b O'Reilly	72
Hammond, c Bradman, b O'Reilly	20
Pataudi, st sub., b Hird	61
Brown, st sub, b Hird	6
Ames, c Fingleton, b O'Reilly	90
Jardine, c sub, b Hird	4
Allen, lbw, b Hird	15
Voce, b Hird	46
Verity, lbw, b O'Reilly	2
Tate, not out	2
Extras	30
Total	**530**

Bowling Analysis

	O.	M.	R.	W.
Theak	18	1	76	0
McCabe	19	4	53	0
O'Reilly	45.5	16	86	4
Howell	22	4	59	0
Hird	30	1	135	6
Cummins	9	0	57	0
Kippax	3	0	10	0
Bradman	11	3	24	0

VERSUS SOUTHERN DISTRICT OF NEW SOUTH WALES

(At Wagga Wagga, December 10 *and* 12. *Match drawn)*

Southern Districts 1st innings – 226. (Sly not out 67; Mitchell 7 for 77.) Second innings – 68 for 7 (Mitchell 5 for 26). England 313. (Ames 91, Tate not out 52, Brown 51.)

VERSUS TASMANIA

(At Launceston, December 16–19. *England won by an innings and* 126 *runs)*

TASMANIA

First Innings

Badcock, b Mitchell	57
Burrows, st Ames, b Mitchell	41
Green, run out	8
Martin, lbw, b Mitchell	19
Putman, not out	56
Morrisby, b Bowes	4
Gourlay, st Ames, b Mitchell	1
Parry, st Ames, b Mitchell	0
James, c Paynter, b Mitchell	16
Walsh, run out	5
Rushforth (absent hurt)	0
Extras	22
Total	229

Bowling Analysis

	O.	M.	R.	W.
Voce	4	0	12	0
Bowes	16	2	70	1
Brown	10	2	45	0
Tate	4	1	10	0
Mitchell	17	0	70	6

Second Innings

Badcock, not out	43
Burrows, c Wyatt, b Tate	1
Green, b Mitchell	21
Martin, lbw, b Brown	13
Putman, b Mitchell	5
Morrisby, c and b Brown	20
Gourlay, st Ames, b Brown	0
Parry, c Voce, b Mitchell	24
James, c Brown, b Mitchell	10
Walsh, c Wyatt, b Mitchell	0
Rushford, absent	
Extras	10
Total	147

Bowling Analysis

	O.	M.	R.	W.
Voce	4	0	10	0
Bowes	6	1	15	0
Brown	11	3	28	3
Tate	7	2	10	1
Mitchell	13.6	0	74	5

ENGLAND

Wyatt, lbw, b Putman	33
Sutcliffe, c James, b Putman	101
Nawab of Pataudi, b James	109
Ames, c Green, b James	107
Paynter, c Green, b James	102
Brown, b Putman	1
Larwood, c Green, b Putman	1
Voce, c and b James	20
Tate, not out	10
Bowes, b James	3
Mitchell, st Parry, b James	0
Extras	15
Total	502

Bowling Analysis

	O.	M.	R.	W.
Burrows	12	1	48	0
Walsh	20	1	69	0
James	31	2	96	6
Putman	24	0	156	4
Gourlay	21	1	102	0
Martin	1	–	16	–

VERSUS TASMANIA

(At Hobart, December 23–26. Match drawn)

TASMANIA

First Innings

Atkinson, c Ames, b Allen	0
Badcock, c Ames, b Verity	4
Green, c Jardine, b Paynter	18
Burrows, b Paynter	38
Putman, c and b Paynter	20
Morrisby, not out	10
Broomby, not out	10
Extras	3
Total (5 wkts. dec.)	103

Bowling Analysis

	O.	*M.*	*R.*	*W.*
Allen	5	3	7	1
Bowes	5	2	6	0
Verity	1	1	0	1
Jardine	10	2	21	0
Paynter	20	6	40	3
Ames	10	1	26	0

Second Innings

Atkinson, b Bowes	4
Badcock, c Allen, b Bowes	0
Green, c Verity, b Bowes	7
Burrows, not out	33
Putman, c Allen, b Bowes	29
Morrisby, not out	10
Extras	6
Total (for 4 wkts.)	89

Bowling Analysis

	O.	M.	R.	W.
Bowes	8	1	18	4
Allen	5	0	17	0
Mitchell	5	1	8	0
Brown	2	0	24	0
Wyatt	1	0	6	0
Verity	4	1	6	0
Leyland	1	0	4	0

ENGLAND

First Innings

Wyatt, c Green, b Burrows	51
Leyland, c Morrisby, b Walsh	65
Jardine, lbw, b James	13
Allen, c and b Putman	20
Brown, c and b Putman	35
Paynter, st Parry, b Putman	5
Ames, c Gourlay, b James	52
Verity, not out	54
Duckworth, not out	27
Extras	8
Total (7 wkts. dec.)	330

Bowling Analysis

	O.	M.	R.	W.
Gourlay	6	0	26	0
Walsh	16	1	60	1
Burrows	8	0	57	1
James	20	2	82	2
Atkinson	6	0	25	0
Putman	15	1	72	3

VERSUS COMBINED COUNTRY XIII OF VICTORIA

(At Bendigo, January 7–9. Match drawn)

Victorians' 1st innings – 215. (Porter 55; Larwood 4 for 29). Second innings – 75 (Larwood 3 for 15). England – 286 (Sutcliffe 91).

VERSUS COMBINED COUNTRY XIII OF VICTORIA

(At Ballarat, January 21–23. Match drawn)

England – 255 (Nawab of Pataudi 84, Leyland 62). Victorians – 84 for 8 wickets (Gray 22; Mitchell 4 for 31, Tate 3 for 22).

VERSUS NEW SOUTH WALES

(At Sydney, January 26–28. England won by four wickets)

NEW SOUTH WALES

First Innings

Fingleton, b Mitchell	19
Brown, c Ames, b Bowes	69
Bradman, b Mitchell	1
Kippax, c Mitchell, b Bowes	3
Cummins, b Mitchell	0
Rowe, c Mitchell, b Verity	70
Love, c Ames, b Hammond	4
Hill, c Verity, b Hammond	0
Howell, c Brown, b Verity	0
Chilvers, lbw, b Hammond	4
Stewart, not out	0
Extras	10
Total	180

Bowling Analysis

	O.	M.	R.	W.
Bowes	15	2	48	2
Tate	10	1	42	0
Verity	5	1	9	2
Mitchell	10	1	32	3
Hammond	8.5	1	22	3
Brown	3	0	17	0

Second Innings

Fingleton, lbw, b Tate	7
Brown, c Duckworth, b Hammond	25
Bradman, c Ames, b Hammond	71
Kippax, c Verity, b Hammond	1
Cummins, c Verity, b Hammond	3
Rowe, c Bowes, b Hammond	11
Love, b Verity	2
Hill, c Mitchell, b Hammond	0
Chilvers, run out	0
Howell, b Verity	6
Stewart, not out	0
Extras	2
Total	128

Bowling Analysis

	O.	M.	R.	W.
Bowes	7	1	19	0
Tate	4	0	10	1
Verity	9.1	3	26	2
Mitchell	5	0	28	0
Hammond	13	1	43	6

ENGLAND

First Innings

Wyatt, lbw, b Hill	63
Pataudi, c Chilvers, b Howell	2
Hammond, c Rowe, b Howell	7
Verity, c Stewart, b Chilvers	33
Ames, b Chilvers	6
Leyland, c Rowe, b Chilvers	29
Brown, c Stewart, b Hill	29
Tate, c Fingleton, b Hill	15
Duckworth, not out	6
Bowes, st Love, b Chilvers	0
Mitchell, lbw, b Chilvers	0
Extras	9
Total	199

Bowling Analysis

	O.	*M.*	*R.*	*W.*
Stewart	6	0	38	0
Howell	13	2	40	2
Hill	19	6	39	3
Chilvers	17.3	2	73	5

Second Innings

Pataudi, b Hill	0
Wyatt, run out	3
Leyland, c Stewart, b Chilvers	33
Hammond, st Love, b Chilvers	24
Ames, st Fingleton, b Chilvers	3
Verity, c Chilvers, b Howell	1
Brown, not out	12
Tate, not out	26
Extras	8
Total (for 6 wkts.)	110

Bowling Analysis

	O.	M.	R.	W.
Howell	12	2	33	1
Hill	10	0	40	1
Chilvers	7.4	0	29	3

VERSUS QUEENSLAND COUNTRY XII

(At Toowoomba, February 1–2. Match drawn)

England 1st innings – 376. (Ames 121 not out; Hammond 101. 2nd innings – 376. (Ames 121 not out; Hammond 101. 2nd innings – 187 for 3 wkts. (Jardine, not out, 77.) Queensland – 210. (Brittle, not out, 65; Larwood 8 for 28.)

VERSUS QUEENSLAND

(At Brisbane, February 4–7. England won by an innings and 61 runs.)

QUEENSLAND

First Innings

Levy, c Allen, b Larwood	0
Cook, c and b Verity	53
Andrews, c Allen, b Larwood	45
Gough, b Verity	11
Litster, b Bowes	67
Bensted, b Bowes	1
Oxenham, b Allen	8
Waterman, run out	0
Gamble, b Bowes	1
Gilbert, st Ames, b Leyland	6
Govan, not out	5
Extras	4
Total	201

Bowling Analysis

	O.	M.	R.	W.
Larwood	9	1	24	2
Allen	11	3	37	1
Bowes	15	1	43	3
Verity	28	12	49	2
Hammond	6	3	15	0
Wyatt	3	0	16	0
Leyland	1.5	0	13	1

Second Innings

Gough, c Allen, b Larwood	0
Cook, c Jardine, b Larwood	11
Andrews, c Jardine, b Larwood	5
Levy, c Ames, b Larwood	6
Litster, c Hammond, b Verity	5
Bensted, lbw, b Verity	9
Oxenham, lbw, b Verity	17
Waterman, c Paynter, b Verity	0
Gamble, c Verity, b Larwood	14
Gilbert, b Larwood	1
Govan, not out	10
Extras	3
Total	81

Bowling Analysis

	O.	M.	R.	W.
Larwood	8	1	38	6
Hammond	2	0	5	0
Bowes	3	0	10	0
Allen	2	0	5	0
Verity	6.3	1	20	4

ENGLAND

First Innings

Jardine, b Oxenham	34
Verity, b Oxenham	21
Sutcliffe, lbw, b Oxenham	35
Leyland, b Gilbert	2
Wyatt, c Levy, b Govan	40
Hammond, c Levy, b Litster	27
Paynter, lbw, b Gilbert	19
Allen, c Gough, b Govan	66
Ames, st Waterman, b Oxenham	80
Larwood, c Litster, b Govan	1
Bowes, not out	2
Extras	16
Total	343

Bowling Analysis

	O.	*M.*	*R.*	*W.*
Gilbert	25	3	93	2
Gamble	18	3	58	0
Oxenham	33.6	11	70	4
Govan	6	0	59	3
Litster	4	0	10	1
Bensted	4	1	19	0
Andrews	2	0	18	0

VERSUS NORTHERN DISTRICTS OF NEW SOUTH WALES

(At Newcastle, February 18–21. *Match drawn)*

Northern Districts, 1st innings – 322. (Chipperfield, 152; Bowes 3 for 64.) 2nd innings – 236. (Little, 117; Mitchell 4 for 62.) England – 254. (Nawab of Pataudi, not out, 94; Wright, 6 for 79.)

VERSUS VICTORIA

(At Melbourne, March 3–7. Match drawn)

ENGLAND

First Innings

Sutcliffe, b Plant	75
Wyatt, c O'Brien, b Ebeling	8
Hammond, c Plant, b Fleetwood-Smith	59
Paynter, c Ironmonger, b Plant	30
Allen, c Oakley, b Ironmonger	0
Brown, st Barnett, b Ironmonger	4
Tate, not out	94
Voce, b Ebeling	7
Duckworth, c Ebeling, b Darling	15
Mitchell, c Oakley, b Ironmonger	6
Bowes, run out	20
Extras	3
Total	321

Bowling Analysis

	O.	M.	R.	W.
Alexander	13	0	49	0
Ebeling	17	3	56	2
Ironmonger	19	2	82	3
Fleetwood-Smith	7	0	67	1
Plant	8	1	55	2
Darling	2	0	4	1
Bromley	1.3	0	5	0

Second Innings

Sutcliffe, b Ebeling	11
Wyatt, c and b Fleetwood-Smith	29
Hammond, c O'Brien, b Ironmonger	64
Paynter, b Ironmonger	2
Allen, lbw, b Fleetwood-Smith	48
Brown, lbw, b Ironmonger	5
Tate, c Bromley, b Ironmonger	6
Voce, not out	2
Duckworth, c Ebeling, b Fleetwood-Smith	2
Mitchell, c Rigg, b Ironmonger	5
Extras	9

Total (9 wkts. dec.)	183

Bowling Analysis

	O.	M.	R.	W.
Alexander	12	3	33	0
Ebeling	13	4	44	1
Ironmonger	18.1	7	31	5
Fleetwood-Smith	17	1	66	3

VICTORIA

First Innings

O'Brien, lbw, b Voce	20
Rigg, c Verity (sub), b Bowes	21
Darling, c Duckworth, b Bowes	103
Bromley, c Hammond, b Brown	19
Oakley, c Wyatt, b Bowes	50
Plant, lbw, b Tate	1
Barnett, st Duckworth, b Mitchell	17
Ebeling, not out	68
Fleetwood-Smith, st Duckworth, b Brown	8
Alexander, lbw, b Brown	0
Ironmonger, b Voce	6
Extras	14

Total	327

Bowling Analysis

	O.	M.	R.	W.
Bowes	19	2	93	3
Voce	14.3	1	62	2
Tate	13	4	31	1
Hammond	2	0	14	0
Mitchell	8	1	50	1
Brown	12	1	63	3

Second Innings

O'Brien, c Duckworth, b Bowes	7
Rigg, c Mitchell, b Bowes	88
Darling, c Hammond, b Tate	19
Bromley, not out	56
Extras	7
Total (3 wkts.)	177

Bowling Analysis

	O.	M.	R.	W.
Bowes	8	1	56	2
Voce	3	0	22	0
Tate	6	0	35	1
Hammond	7	0	40	0
Mitchell	2	0	15	0
Brown	1	0	2	0

It is interesting to note that the aggregates were equal when Rigg was caught out off the last ball of the match.

Versus South Australia

(At Adelaide, March 10–14. Match drawn)

ENGLAND

First Innings

Paynter, c Ryan, Grimmett	62
Verity, c Ryan, b Williams	12
Wyatt, c Williams, b Grimmett	43
Leyland, c Nitschke, b Lee	36
Jardine, c Walker, b Tobin	48
Ames, c Lonergan, b Tobin	63
Tate, b Tobin	0
Voce, c Walker, b Williams	3
Duckworth, not out	13
Bowes, run out	4
Mitchell, c Shepherd, b Grimmett	10
Extras	4
Total	298

Bowling Analysis

	O.	M.	R.	W.
Tobin	15	1	65	3
Williams	20	3	46	2
Grimmett	25.1	2	124	3
Ryan	10	4	16	0
Lee	24	7	43	1

Second Innings

Paynter, c Lonergan, b Lee	47
Duckworth, run out	4
Wyatt, c Richardson, b Williams	11
Leyland, not out	152
Jardine, c Walker, b Tobin	65
Ames, c Ryan, b Williams	23
Tate, b Williams	4
Verity, b Lee	13
Mitchell, b Lee	4
Voce, not out	33
Extras	15
Total (8 wkts. dec.)	371

Bowling Analysis

	O.	M.	R.	W.
Tobin	11	0	65	1
Williams	21	2	107	3
Grimmett	23	3	85	0
Lee	15	3	65	3
Ryan	6	1	34	0

SOUTH AUSTRALIA

First Innings

Richardson, c Verity, b Bowes	0
Nitschke, c Paynter, b Voce	38
Lonergan, b Bowes	13
Shepherd, b Voce	17
Tobin, b Verity	18
Ryan, c Tate, b Bowes	61
Palmer, c Wyatt, b Tate	15
Lee, b Tate	8
Grimmett, c Mitchell, b Verity	7
Williams, not out	9
Walker, c Duckworth, b Tate	0
Extras	5
Total	191

Bowling Analysis

	O.	M.	R.	W.
Bowes	10	0	60	3
Tate	11.7	3	36	3
Voce	9	0	33	2
Verity	15	5	28	2
Mitchell	4	0	29	0

Second Innings

Richardson, b Voce	20
Nitschke, lbw, b Mitchell	87
Lonergan, c Verity, b Bowes	36
Shepherd, b Bowes	6
Ryan, c Voce, b Bowes	25
Tobin, not out	52
Palmer, b Tate	22
Lee, c Verity, b Bowes	5
Williams, c Voce, b Mitchell	23
Grimmett, not out	15
Extras	22
Total (8 wkts.)	313

Bowling Analysis

	O.	M.	R.	W.
Bowes	15	0	95	4
Tate	18	2	61	1
Voce	13	2	44	1
Verity	12	2	44	0
Mitchell	11	2	34	2
Jardine	1	0	13	0

VERSUS WELLINGTON, NEW ZEALAND

(At Wellington, March 21–24. Match drawn)

ENGLAND

Sutcliffe, b Parsloe	3
Paynter, c and b Freeman	52
Hammond, c and b Freeman	58
Ames, c James, b Freeman	3
Jardine, st Tindell, b Blundell	25
Tate, c Freeman, b Blundell	19
Brown, b Newman	28
Verity, lbw, b Blundell	0
Duckworth, not out	13
Bowes, not out	11
Extras	11
Total (8 wkts. dec.)	223

Mitchell did not bat.

Bowling Analysis

	O.	M.	R.	W.
Parsloe	11	1	37	1
Blundell	19	2	55	3
Newman	15	4	49	1
Freeman	15	0	71	3

WELLINGTON

Dempster, lbw, b Tate	47
Foley, c Voce, b Bowes	39
O'Brien, not out	26
Tindell, not out	12
Extras	17
Total (2 wkts.)	141

Bowling Analysis

	O.	M.	R.	W.
Bowes	11	2	24	1
Verity	10	1	47	0
Tate	13	5	23	1
Brown	6	2	13	0
Mitchell	6	2	17	0

VERSUS NEW ZEALAND

(At Christchurch, March 24–27. Match drawn)

ENGLAND

Sutcliffe, c James, b Badcock	0
Paynter, b Smith	0
Hammond, b Badcock	227
Wyatt, run out	20
Jardine, c James, b Badcock	45
Ames, b Vivian	103
Brown, c Kerr, b Page	74
Voce, c Dempster, b Page	66
Tate, not out	10
Extras	15
Total (8 wkts. dec.)	560

Allen and Verity did not bat.

Bowling Analysis

	O.	M.	R.	W.
Badcock	54	11	142	3
Smith	20	0	113	1
Newman	25	5	91	0
Freeman	20	2	78	0
Vivian	19	1	72	1
Weir	7	0	28	0
Page	2.3	0	21	2

NEW ZEALAND

First Innings

Dempster, c Wyatt, b Allen	8
Whitelaw, c Brown, b Verity	30
Weir, c Hammond, b Voce	66
Kerr, c Hammond, b Brown	59
Page, c Voce, b Allen	22
James, lbw, b Tate	2
Smith, b Tate	4
Newman, b Voce	5
Freeman, b Voce	1
Badcock, not out	10
Extras	16
Total	**223**

Vivian was absent injured.

Bowling Analysis

	O.	M.	R.	W.
Tate	37	16	42	2
Voce	17.1	3	27	3
Allen	20	5	46	2
Brown	19	10	34	1
Verity	23	7	58	1

Second Innings

Dempster, not out	14
Whitelaw, not out	17
Extras	4
Total (no wkt.)	**35**

Bowling Analysis

	O.	M.	R.	W.
Voce	4	0	13	0
Tate	3	1	5	0
Hammond	2	0	2	0
Allen	4.1	1	5	0
Verity	3	1	6	0

Versus New Zealand

(At Auckland, March 31–April 3. Match drawn)

NEW ZEALAND

First Innings

Whitelaw, b Bowes	12
Mills, b Bowes	0
Weir, b Bowes	0
Dempster, not out	83
Kerr, lbw, b Voce	10
Page, st Duckworth, b Mitchell	20
Badcock, b Bowes	1
James, b Bowes	0
Dunning, b Bowes	12
Newman, b Voce	5
Freeman, run out	1
Extras	14
Total	158

Bowling Analysis

	O.	M.	R.	W.
Allen	5	2	11	0
Bowes	19	5	34	6
Mitchell	18	1	49	1
Voce	9.5	3	20	2
Brown	2	0	19	0
Hammond	3	0	11	0

Second Innings

Whitelaw, not out	5
Mills, not out	11
Total (no wkt.)	16

Bowling Analysis

	O.	M.	R.	W.
Allen	3	1	4	0
Bowes	2	0	4	0
Hammond	2	0	6	0
Voce	1.3	0	2	0

ENGLAND

Sutcliffe, c Weir, b Freeman	24
Wyatt, b Dunning	60
Hammond, not out	336
Paynter, b Dunning	36
Ames, b Badcock	26
Allen, b Badcock	12
Brown, c Page, b Weir	13
Voce, b Weir	16
Duckworth, not out	6
Extras	19
Total (7 wkts. dec.)	**548**

Bowes and Mitchell did not bat.

Bowling Analysis

	O.	M.	R.	W.
Badcock	59	16	126	2
Dunning	43	5	156	2
Freeman	20	1	91	1
Newman	17	2	87	0
Page	6	2	30	0
Weir	11	2	39	2

MEMOIR

BY THE REV. FIANACH LAWRY (née Jardine)

After the 1932–3 Ashes, my father played only five more Test Matches, in which he averaged nearly 74 with the bat. Perhaps fittingly, he scored his only Test century against the West Indians (who were bowling Bodyline at him) in the summer of 1933. He never played against the Australians again. When Bradman's side came to England in 1934, he saved the selectors the embarrassment of making a decision by announcing that he had no intention of playing in the series, choosing instead to cover it for the Evening Standard. He had captained England in fifteen Tests, losing only once, with nine wins and five draws. His first-class career also came to an end after 1933–4 tour of India.

My parents married in September 1934. After a honeymoon spent big game hunting in Africa, they settled in a flat in Airlie Gardens in Kensington, where I was born in July 1935, and my sister Mel in November of the following year. Soon afterwards, we all moved to a beautiful house near Reading called The Crofts, surrounded by 35 acres of land. My mother ran the property as a smallholding business, growing peaches, nectarines, tomatoes and many other vegetables commercially, while father worked for a mining company.

Once as a toddler I wandered off down the lane, and was discovered by a local Bobby on his bicycle. When he asked me who I was and where I came from I could only answer (so I am told) that I was "Daddy's daughter" and wave vaguely back down the road. On my return, Father rigorously drilled me into saying my name over and over again. In retrospect, I suppose this experience gave me some insight into his style of captaincy!

During the Second World War, my father served in the Berkshire

Yeomanry. He returned safely from Dunkirk, and was involved in trying to reassemble the other troops who had been lucky enough to get home. For a while, we all stayed in rented lodgings with him in Harpenden. All too soon, though, he was posted to the hill towns of Simla and Quetta in his beloved India, where he had grown up. When my youngest sister Iona was born he sent a telegram home to my mother saying: "Have shot a tiger skin to wrap the baby bunting in . . ."

The strain of being alone at The Crofts with two small children and a business to run had been too much for my mother, and she sold the property, buying in its place a Manor house in the depths of Somerset. Life was not easy for Father when he came back to England in 1945. His job, which he had been promised would be kept open for him on his return, no longer existed, and there were huge medical bills to pay, my mother having been ill in his absence. He did finally find work in the City as Company Secretary for Wiggins Teape, the paper merchants, but for the rest of his life – though he scrupulously concealed it from us – he was anxious about his ability to provide for his family. Another small source of income was a sheep-farming business which he owned in New South Wales, which was eventually bought by the Scottish Australian Company.

Although Father had a deeply affectionate nature, he did not find it easy to communicate with teenage children. I was perhaps the closest to him: as the eldest of the four, I had had the chance to get to know him before the war, and was the only one who dared, on occasion, to stand up to him. I remember asking him, aged 21, how one "spotted a homosexual". He said, "Er, Um, Agh . . . come back to me in six weeks, and I will tell you . . ." In other words he hadn't a clue! He could be harsh in his judgements when others did not live up to the high standards he set for himself: he could never, for example, forgive the French for what he saw as a premature surrender to Hitler's armies.

In the mid-fifties my parents began to think about retiring to some land Father had bought on the outskirts of Salisbury, the capital of what was then Southern Rhodesia. In the last winter of his life, Father took my sister Mel to Africa as a 21st birthday present.

While he was there he caught tick fever, and seemed unable to shake it off. The doctors recommended that he take the boat home to give him more time to recover. It didn't work, and in London he was diagnosed with lung cancer. The following summer he died in a hospital in Switzerland. He was cremated there, and his ashes sent back to England.

Mama would have liked to have his ashes scattered in the Garden of Remembrance at Lord's, but the M.C.C. refused on the grounds that this was only for members who had died in one of the two World Wars. In the end, we decided on the summit of Crosscraig in Perthshire instead. It was a beautiful tranquil place, where he had, over many years, enjoyed stalking. I remember that the sun suddenly emerged from behind the clouds as we scattered the ashes and said the Lord's Prayer.

Father was an intensely shy and private person, and never complained about his treatment by the cricketing world, although he did say on more than one occasion that Bodyline bowling, and the field set for it, had all been agreed with the M.C.C. before the tour commenced.

Index

OBITUARY

MR. D. R. JARDINE
A Great Captain of England

Mr. D. R. Jardine died in Switzerland on Wednesday. He was 57. He became ill last year while visiting Southern Rhodesia, and never completely regained his health.

Douglas Jardine was an instance of heredity in cricket skill, for his father, M. R. Jardine, was four seasons, from 1889 to 1892, in the Oxford XI. In his last year, when Oxford under the captaincy of Lionel Palairet won the University match by five wickets, M. R. Jardine batted brilliantly, scoring 140 and 39. After leaving Oxford he entered the Indian Civil Service and was lost to English cricket. His son, Douglas, who was destined to become one of the most famous players of a later generation, was born at Bombay on October 33, 1900.

Douglas went to Winchester, and finished his school career about the time that the first European war came to an end. He was a member of the school XI for three seasons, and was captain of it during his last summer. He did well in some of the one-day wartime matches, which were arranged against various other schools, for in 1919, his last year at Winchester, he made 25 and 89 against Eton and 135 not out against Harrow.

He went up to New College, Oxford, and in accordance with expectation got his Blue as a freshman. He was thought by some good judges to be the best batsman on the university side, for he was constantly making runs. At Lord's he did nothing noteworthy against Cambridge in a game which was ruined by bad weather. In 1922, his third year, an accident to his knee obliged him to stand down in the inter-University match, but he rejoined the side in 1923 and made 39 against Cambridge.

After leaving Oxford he played little first-class cricket for some time, but as the years went on his appearances became more frequent, chiefly for Surrey, who welcomed his assistance. His batting gained in power and freedom, so that he came to be regarded as one of the best amateurs of the day. His qualities as a leader were also recognized: he was appointed captain of the Surrey team and filled the same office at other principal matches.

In the winter of 1928–29 he paid his first visit to Australia, as a member of the side captained by Mr. A. P. F. Chapman. The last two English tours in Australia had ended in the loss by England of nine Test matches out of ten, and the conspicuous success of Chapman's XI came as a welcome change to this depressing record, for they won four out of their five Tests. The third match proved the most remarkable victory of the series. England were left with 332 runs to win, a task formidable enough in itself, but rendered more difficult by the damaged condition of the wicket. However, Hobbs and Sutcliffe, our famous opening pair, faced the position with vigour, and brought up the hundred before they were parted At the suggestion of Hobbs, Jardine was sent in first wicket down, and supported Sutcliffe so effectively that the game was to all intents and purposes won before another wicket fell. Our margin was reduced by some careless play at the finish to three wickets.

Four years later Jardine was invited by M.C.C. to undertake the leadership of the English team that visited Australia in the winter of 1932–33. The trip from the point of view of winning matches was again a great success, for four out of the rubber of five Tests went in England's favour, but unfortunately this satisfactory result was to some extent obscured by the amount of controversy whch was created.

The subject of dispute was what was termed "leg theory" bowling. For many years it had been the occasional practice of various bowlers to pack the on-side with fieldsmen, and to bowl at the batsman's legs, or outside them. Nobody had ever dreamed of objecting, or of saying anything about it, except that it was rather a dull form of attack. But on this tour England had a fast bowler, Larwood, of Nottinghamshire, who was in a class by himself, being much faster than anyone else and more accurate. When his field was set for leg theory the Australian bastsmen were far from endorsing the dullness of the attack. It was the pace at which it was bowled that made the difference.

The sensation caused in Australia was considerable. The batsmen ducked their heads, or retreated to short leg, so that all might see the severity of the ordeal they were undergoing. The crowd kept up a chorus of insulting cries; the Press concocted stories of differences of opinion among the English players as to Larwood's bowling; somebody invented the epithet "Body Line" to emphasize the physical menace of the method employed. This confusion was followed by an exchange of cable messages between the Australian cricket authorities and M.C.C. The latter body met the complaint with the cold reply that if the Board of Control so desired they would consent with reluctance to the abandonment of the rest of the tour. This suggestion was promptly declined.

These difficulties connected with his tour in Australia have been treated at some length, because they form an important part of Jardine's cricket career. Supported as he was by the complete loyalty of his own men, and fortified, it must be owned, by the approval of many critics not only in England but also in Australia, he stuck to his guns with a tenacity which nothing could disturb. Tall and fiery in appearance, austere and aloof in expression, he became the centre of cricket's fiercest controversy; and on his return to England he published a book of his experiences.

Jardine played subsequently in only four more Test matches, two of them as captain against West Indies and two in India, where he took an M.C.C. side in the winter of 1933. In the second of the two matches against West Indies Constantine and Martindale gave him, as it were, a taste of his own medicine by making him the main target of a body-attack. Jardine's reply was his first century in Test cricket, and in the words of Wisden for 1934 he played this form of bowling "probably better than any other man in the world was capable of doing." But by 1934 his playing days were virtually over. An occasional broadcast and some part-time journalism continued to keep his name before the public, and he always took a lively interest in Surrey and Oxford cricket, being President of the Oxford University Cricket Club from 1955 to 1957.

Jardine qualified as a solicitor in 1926. He was chairman of the N.S.W. Land Agency, Ltd., and a director of the Scottish Australian Company, Ltd. In the war of 1939–45 he served with The Royal Berkshire Regiment in France, Belgium, and India. In 1934 he married Irene Margaret, daughter of Sir Henry Peat, by whom he had a son and three daughters.